GALATA, PERA,
A BIOGRA

D0901627

Brendan Freely was born in New J̶⎯⎯⎯, ⎯⎯⎯⎯, ⎯⎯⎯ ⎯⎯ 1966
was moved to Istanbul, where he spent his childhood and
adolescence. He studied at Rockwell College in Ireland and
at Yale University. Later, he traveled and performed a variety
of odd jobs, including a stint with a circus in California, after
which he worked as a social-worker in Boston for some years.
In 1995 he returned to Istanbul, where he earns his living as
a freelance literary translator.

John Freely was born in New York in 1926. He joined the U.S.
navy at the age of seventeen and served in commando unit in
the Pacific, Burma and China for the last two years of World
War II. After the war, he graduated from Iona College and
received his PhD degree in physics from New York University.
In 1960 he moved to Istanbul, where he taught physics,
astronomy and the history of science at Robert College, which
later became Boğaziçi University. His first book, *Strolling
Through Istanbul*, co-authored with Hilary Sumner-Boyd, was
published in 1972. He has written over fifty books, many
of them about Turkey. Among his books published by YKY
are: *A History of Robert College, the American College for Girls
and Boğaziçi University* (2000) and the 5 volume *Türkiye
Uygarlıklar Rehberi [Guide to the Civilizations of Turkey]* (2002).

BRENDAN FREELY
JOHN FREELY

Galata, Pera, Beyoğlu:
A Biography

YAPI KREDİ YAYINLARI

Yapı Kredi Yayınları - 4562
Literature - 1294

Galata, Pera, Beyoğlu: A Biography / Brendan Freely - John Freely

Editor: **Nazlı Güher Beydeş**
Proofreading: **Darmin Hadzibegoviç**

Cover design: **Nahide Dikel**
Page layout: **Mehmet Ulusel**
Graphic design: **İlknur Efe**

Print: Acar Basım ve Cilt San. Tic. A.Ş.
Beysan Sanayi Sitesi, Birlik Caddesi, No: 26, Acar Binası
34524, Haramidere - Beylikdüzü / İstanbul
Tel: (0 212) 422 18 34 Faks: (0 212) 422 18 04
www.acarbasim.com
Certificate Number: 11957

1st print: İstanbul, February 2016
ISBN 978-975-08-3589-6

Yapı Kredi Kültür Sanat Yayıncılık Ticaret ve Sanayi A.Ş.
İstiklal Caddesi No: 142 Odakule İş Merkezi Kat: 3 Beyoğlu 34430 İstanbul
Phone: (0 212) 252 47 00 (pbx) Faks: (0 212) 293 07 23
http://www.ykykultur.com.tr
e-mail: ykykultur@ykykultur.com.tr
Internet sales address: http://alisveris.yapikredi.com.tr

Yapı Kredi Cultural Activities, Art and Publishing is a member of
PEN International Publishers Circle.

Table of Contents

Preface

Books about Istanbul invariably focus on the historic peninsula known to ancients as Byzantium and the Greeks as Constantinople, capital of the Byzantine Empire until its conquest by the Turks in 1453. But the present book concentrates on Beyoğlu, the district on the north side of the Golden Horn across from the Constantinopolitan peninsula. Beyoğlu today includes Galata, the old port quarter of Istanbul at the confluence of the Golden Horn and the Bosphorus, which is just as old as Constantinople and was once a district of the Byzantine capital. During the last two centuries of the Byzantine era, Galata was controlled by the Genoese, and even after the Turkish conquest it continued to be the Latin quarter of Istanbul, its inhabitants including Italians, French and Maltese as well as Turks, Greeks, Armenians, Jews and Levantine Europeans. The district on the hills above Galata, formerly known as Pera, was where the first European embassies and churches were built along Grand Rue de Pera, now Istiklal Caddesi, the main avenue of Beyoğlu. Thus Beyoğlu, though now predominately Turkish in its population, has churches of many different faiths, including Greek Orthodox, Greek Catholic, Armenian Gregorian, Armenian Catholic, Syrian Orthodox, Chaldean Catholic, Russian Orthodox, Roman Catholic and Anglican, as well as a dissident sect known as Turkish Orthodox, along with synagogues of Sephardic, Ashkenazi and Karaite Jews, together with Ottoman Turkish mosques, *medreses*, and an ancient lodge of the Mevlevi, the famous whirling dervishes. Its historic monuments include several medieval Genoese churches, the oldest of which is now a mosque, as well *hamams* and fountains.

Galata was notorious for its bawdy night life, in the days when it was a port and sailors from around the Mediterranean thronged its taverns and bordellos. The night life has now moved up the hill to the part of Beyoğlu once known as Pera, which in late Ottoman times was the only district of Istanbul that had restaurants, cafés, cinemas and an opera house. During the past decade this part of

Beyoğlu has become one of the hottest spots in the world, with many hundreds of places to eat, drink and hear music, as well as two museums of modern art, scores of art galleries, several cultural centers, and an opera house. And yet there are byways of Beyoğlu that are still reminiscent of old quarters of Genoese Galata and Levantine Pera, in vine-shrouded squares and cobbled alleyways with names like the Street of the Lion's Bed [Aslan Yatağı], the Street of the Chicken that Cannot Fly [Tavuk Uçmaz], and the Street of the Bird of Night [Gecekuşu]. This book will take the reader down all of these streets and more, both by day and by night, evoking the life of the Latin quarter of Istanbul, past and present, which in this fascinating part of the city are intimately entwined.

The book begins with a general historical introduction, followed by a series of interconnected walking tours through the various parts of Beyoğlu, including the old Genoese quarter of Galata and the more modern downtown area known in times past as Pera. Beyoğlu's historic monument includes Muslim, Christian and Jewish places of worship as well as secular buildings of the Genoese, Ottoman and early Republican eras. These walks are interspersed with vignettes evoking the way of life of Istanbul's Latin quarter, past and present, day and night, introducing some of the writers, artists and eccentrics who made this a bohemian quarter rivaling the left bank of Paris in the twenties, setting the stage for the extraordinary resurgence of night life in Beyoğlu in recent years.

Since its earliest days, Pera has had a character and identity quite distinct from the city across the Golden Horn. In Roman times it was associated with Honorius, Emperor of the West rather than with Arcadius, Emperor of the East. The Byzantine despised the Catholic Periots as *frangofouromeni*, or wearers of Western clothes, and the Ottoman despised them as infidels. For centuries it was governed as a separate city, and for centuries after that it was inhabited largely by Europeans (and local Christians under the protection of foreign embassies) who were not subject to Ottoman law, each embassy having its own court, its own postal service and sometimes even its own jail. Pera's ties were to Europe, and those who lived there did their best to make it resemble a European city.

Despite the suspicion and disdain with which the people of Constantinople and Istanbul regarded Pera, it also offered them a window to the West. In Pera they could encounter the latest trends in European fashion, art, literature, music, technology and political philosophy, as well as a wide range of entertainment, from the refined to the debauched, that was not available and often forbidden in their part of the city.

After the Turkish Republic was established, Pera lost its privileged status and saw frequent and deliberate assaults on its character and identity. The embassies moved to Ankara, Turkish replaced French as the language of commerce, the names of streets, businesses and institutions were changed and most of the Christian and Jewish population either left voluntarily, were deported or were intimidated into leaving.

In spite of this, Pera, now Beyoğlu, managed to retain much of its character and identity. In recent years it has experienced a boom, becoming once again a center of fashion, art, literature and music, as well as a wide range of entertainment, and has perhaps as large a foreign population as it ever had.

This book follows the development and social history of the district street by street from the earliest settlements on the Golden Horn to the most recent settlements beyond and around Taksim, examining not just the buildings and those who built them, but those who lived in them as well, from murderers, gangsters and prostitutes to bankers, diplomats and socialites.

CHAPTER 1
Galata – Pera - Beyoğlu

A description of Constantinople written ca. 447, *Notitia urbis Constantinopolitanae*, records that the city was divided into fourteen regions, the same as in Old Rome. Thirteen of these regions were within the Theodosian walls, while one was across the Golden Horn in Sycae, the present Galata, corresponding to the region across the Tiber in Rome known today as Trastevere.

According to *Notitia*, the Regio Sycaena, as it was called, had 431 houses, along with a church, a forum, public baths, a theater, and a harbor, all surrounded by a defense wall. In 528 the Emperor Justinian restored the theater and the church and renamed the region Justinianae, a name which was soon forgotten after the emperor's death in 565. The Emperor Tiberius II (r. 578-82) built a fortress on the shore in Sycae, from which a chain could be stretched across the Golden Horn to close the port in the event that an enemy fleet approached the city. The substructure of this fortress, which came to be known as the Castle of Galata, can still be seen in Yeraltı Camii, the Underground Mosque, across from the passenger terminal of the Turkish Maritime Lines.

The name Sycae continued to be in use until, in the ninth century, the name Galata began to supplant it, at first for a small district only, then for the whole region. The derivation of the name Galata is unknown, though that of the other toponym, Pera, is quite straightforward. In Greek *pera* means 'the other side', at first in the general sense of 'across the Golden Horn', later restricted to medieval Galata, and still later to the heights above. During the past century these old Greek names have been supplanted by Turkish ones, so that the whole district north of the Golden Horn is now called Beyoğlu, including the downtown area once known as Pera, while the maritime area at the confluence of the Golden Horn and the Bosphorus is now Karaköy. Nevertheless the name Galata is still used in referring to the quarter along the shore between the Galata and Atatürk bridges, the two spans that cross the Golden Horn to the old city.

Constantinople was captured in April 1204 by the Latins of the Fourth Crusade and the Venetian navy, who established the so-called Kingdom of Roumania from the fragment of the Byzantine Empire they had conquered. Greeks who had fled Constantinople established small empires in exile with their capitals at Nicaea in northwestern Anatolia and at Trebizond in Pontus. The emperor Michael VIII Palaeologus, who usurped the throne at Nicaea in 1259, recaptured Constantinople from the Latins in August 15, 1261, restoring the Byzantine Empire in its ancient capital.

The Genoese had established an alliance with the Byzantines of Nicaea in the spring of 1261, when they signed the Treaty of Nymphaion, in which Galata 'was given over to the glorious community of Genoa on the order of the great and holy Emperor.' The Genoese governed Galata as a semi-independent colony, with its own *podesta*, or governor, appointed annually by the Genoese Senate. The *podesta* and his council met in a building called the Podestat, popularly called Palazzo del Commune. Although the Genoese were expressly forbidden to fortify Galata, they began to do so early in the following century and went on expanding its area and fortifications until the mid-fifteenth century.

The first fortified area, walled in as early as 1304, was a long and narrow rectangle along the Golden Horn between the two present bridges. Then, in order to defend themselves more adequately on the heights above the Golden Horn, the Genoese added a triangular wedge above the rectangular area, erecting at its apex a powerful fortress known as the Tower of Christ, which came to be known as the Galata Tower, completed in 1348. Subsequently, in 1352 and 1387-97, they fortified two areas to the northwest of the tower, and finally in 1446 they walled in the eastern slope of the hill leading down to the Bosphorus. The final defense system thus consisted of five walled enclosures, with the outer wall bordered by a deep moat. Only three of these enceintes can be seen in the earliest extant map of the city —the view by Buondelmonti in 1422— whereas all five are apparent in the Vavasore engraving of 1530. Both of these views show the Galata Tower dominating the defense system from the

The Galata Tower.

highest point in the circuit, with the outer wall extending from the tower down to the Golden Horn on one side and to the Bosphorus on the other. Sections of the Genoese walls with a few towers and one postern are still in existence and will be seen on the itineraries in Galata.

During the latter Byzantine period Genoese Galata became one of the principal ports in the Levant, handling three times as much trade as Greek Constantinople. The importance of the Genoese port is noted by the Muslim traveler İbn-i Battûta, who visited Galata in

1334; he says that its population was predominately Latin, though there were Greeks living there as well:

> Galata is reserved for the Frankish [European] Christians who dwell there. They are of different kinds, including the Genoese, Venetians, Romans [Byzantines, i. e., Greeks] and Franks; they are subject to the king of Constantinople. They are all men of commerce and their harbor is one of the largest in the world; I saw there about a hundred galleys and other large ships, and the small ships were too many to be counted. The bazaars in this part of the town are good but filthy, and a small and very dirty river runs through them. The churches too are very filthy and mean.

Another very interesting description is that of Ruy Gonzalez de Clavijo, Spanish ambassador to the court of Tamerlane, who visited Galata at the beginning of the fifteenth century. Clavijo refers to the town as Pera, noting that the Greeks called it Galata.

> The city of Pera is a small township, but very populous. It is surrounded by a strong wall and has excellent houses, all well-built. It is occupied by the Genoese, and is of the lordship of Genoa, being inhabited by Greeks as well as Genoese. The houses of the town stand on the seashore and lie so close to the sea that between its waters and the town there is barely the width of a carrack's deck... The wall here runs along the strand for some length, but then mounts up the shore of the hill, to where on the summit stands a very tall tower [the Galata Tower]... The Genoese call their town 'Pera', but the Greeks name it 'Galata'.

During the final Turkish siege of Constantinople in 1453 by Sultan Mehmed II, known to the Turks as Fatih, the Genoese in Galata were officially neutral, though many of them fought in the defense of the city under Giovanni Giustiniani Longo. The Genoese in Galata surrendered to Fatih without a struggle two days before his conquest of Constantinople on May 29, 1453. Fatih forced the Genoese to pull down sections of their fortifications, sparing the Galata Tower, which he garrisoned with a detachment of janissaries. Galata lost its independence, but as long as the Genoese obeyed the Ottoman law and paid their taxes Fatih allowed them some local autonomy, as well as the right to worship as they pleased and to retain their Roman Catholic churches. According to the Turkish historian Halil İnalcık, Fatih's imperial decree of June 1, 1453 stated the conditions under which the Genoese of Galata would be governed in his reign:

> ...their money, provisions, property, storehouses, vineyards, mills, shops and boats, in short all their possessions, as well as their wives, sons, daughters and slaves of both sexes, be left in their hands as before and that nothing be done contrary to their livelihood, as in other parts of their dominions, and travel by land and by sea in freedom without any hindrance or molestation by anyone and be exempt from extraordinary impositions; that I impose upon them the Islamic poll-tax [*haraç*] which they pay each year as other non-Muslims do, and in return I will give my attention (and protection) as I do in other parts of my dominion; that they keep their churches and perform their customary rights in them with the exception of ringing their church bells and rattles; that I do not take from them their present churches and turn them into mosques, but they also do not attempt to build new churches; that the Genoese come and go by land and sea for trade; pay the customs deeds as required under the established rule and be free from molestation by anyone.

Fatih appointed an official known as a *voivode* to govern Galata. Beside the *voivode*, who was changed each year in March, legal management was carried out by a *kadi*, who was paid 500 gold pieces annually. There was also a military governor, who commanded the garrison that occupied the Galata Tower and the little citadel within its barbican.

Nevertheless, Galata had for a time some limited degree of autonomy over its internal affairs. The Catholic churches of Galata as well as their religious and fraternal organizations remained under the control of a Christian body known as the Magnifica Communita di Pera until 1682. Otherwise all the non-Muslims of Galata were under the jurisdiction of various *millets*, or 'nations', established by Fatih, the Greeks and Armenians headed by their patriarchs and the Jews by the chief rabbi.

Although Galata was for centuries governed by the Genoese, it was never an exclusively Italian town. There was a substantial Greek population before the conquest, and in the century afterwards it was repopulated by Turks, Greeks, and Armenians from the provinces. A document of 1477 records that in Galata, besides 260 shops,

15

there were the following numbers of houses owned by the various ethnic groups: 535 Muslims, 592 Greeks, 62 Armenians, and 332 Europeans, the latter predominately Italian. Then in the last decade of the fifteenth century large numbers of Moors and Sephardic Jews were welcomed to the Ottoman Empire by Bayezid II, Fatih's son and successor, after they were evicted from Spain in 1492 by King Ferdinand and Queen Isabella.

By the seventeenth century some of the European powers had built palatial embassies in Pera on the heights above Galata. Each embassy formed a separate 'nation' which had under its protection various churches in both Pera and Galata. The various ethnic and religious groups tended to live in their own quarters, each practicing certain trades or commercial activities, as the Turkish architectural historian Doğan Kuban points out in his magisterial work, *Istanbul, an Urban History.*

Kuban writes that the Greeks were the most numerous ethnic group in Ottoman Galata and lived in several quarters, where they were further divided into rich and poor. The rich Greeks were merchants and the others tended to be artisans, tailors, weavers, bakers, porters, tavern-keepers, or owners of *bozahanes*, places selling *boza*, a drink made from millet. Armenians, many of whom were from Kaffa in Crimea, had much the same trades as Greeks and often lived in the same quarters. The Orthodox Jews for the most part dwelt in two different quarters, while the schismatic Karaite Jews dwelt farther up the Golden Horn in the village of Hasköy, where they were resettled in the mid-seventeenth century after being evicted from Eminönü in the old city to make way for Yeni Cami, the New Mosque of Valide Sultan, erected by Turhan Hatice, mother of Mehmed IV. Many of the Jews of Galata became prosperous merchants, and a number of them were physicians, some of whom served the sultan in Topkapı Sarayı [Topkapı Palace].

Kuban notes that in 1455 there were only twenty Turks living in Galata, their chief being the *subaşı*, the commanding officer of the garrison, who had two houses. According to Kuban: 'Turks living in Galata had either Greek or Armenian wives... One could find a Muslim child living with his Christian mother. Hacı Mehmed from Ankara had a Christian wife and owned a bath in the Jewish quarter. His wife owned a house in another quarter.'

The Turkish quarter was known as Hacı Hamza, as Kuban notes, referring to a deed of foundation dated 1472. He observes that Muslim merchants of Galata were involved in trade between the Ottoman Empire and Italy, and that the Turkish inhabitants included sea captains, painters and scribes. He also refers to the register of *vakıfs*, or deeds of foundation, in Haghia Sophia, dating to 1519, to show that many of the Muslims in Galata at that time were converts to Islam.

The most complete description of early Ottoman Galata is that of Petrus Gyllius, who made a detailed study of the topography and Byzantine antiquities of Istanbul in the years 1544-50. His description refers to the regions as they are defined in *Notitia*, which he calls *Ancient Description of the City*. The last part of his section on Galata seems to be a description of the highroad on the ridge above the old Genoese quarter that later came to be known as Grand Rue de Pera.

> The Sycaeane ward [region], which is commonly called Galata, or Pera, should be more properly called the Peraean Ward... The shore around the town is full of havens. Between the walls and the bay there is a stretch of shore where there is an abundance of taverns, shops and victual houses, besides several wharfs where they unload their shipping. It has six gates, at three of which they have stairs [landings] from which you sail over to Constantinople... Where Galata rises highest there stands a lofty tower [the Galata Tower]. Here there is an ascent of about three hundred paces, full of buildings, and around that is the ridge of the hill, which is level, about two hundred paces broad and two thousand paces long. Through its middle runs a broad way full of houses, gardens and vineyards. This is the most pleasant part of town.

Besides the various ethnic and religious groups in Galata there was a floating population of seamen, itinerant traders and merchant adventurers who came sailing into the port from all over the Mediterranean and around the Black Sea. Evliyâ Çelebi, the seventeenth-century Turkish chronicler, gives a vivid description of the rich ethnic mixture in Galata in his *Seyahatnâme*, or *Narrative of Travels*, written ca. 1660:

> In Galata there are eighteen wards inhabited by Muslims, seventy by Greeks, three by Franks, one by Jews and two by Armenians.

17

In the citadel there are no infidels at all, indeed there are none till you come to the Mosque of the Arabs... From the sea shore up to the Galata Tower there are houses of the Genoese, all built of stone, and the streets regularly laid out... the most frequented are the great road by the sea shore, that of the Mosque of the Arabs, and that of the Galata Tower. The different wards of the town are patrolled day and night by watchmen to prevent disorders of the population, who are of a rebellious disposition, on account of which they have from time to time been chastised by the sword. The inhabitants are either sailors, merchants or craftsmen such as joiners and caulkers. They dress for the most part in Algerine fashion, for a great number of them are Arabs or Moors. The Greeks keep the taverns; most of the Armenians are merchants or money-changers; the Jews are the go-betweens in amorous intrigues and their youths are the worst of all the devotees of debauchery.

The port quarter in Galata was noted for the number and liveliness of its taverns, of which Evliyâ gives a particularly colorful description, reassuring his readers that he frequented these disreputable places only as an observer and not as a habitué:

In Galata there are two hundred taverns and wine-shops where the infidels divert themselves with music and drinking. The taverns are celebrated for the wines of Ancona, Saragossa, Mudanya, Smyrna and Tenedos. The word *günaha* [temptation] is most particularly to be applied to the taverns of Galata because there all kinds of dancing boys, mimics and fools, flock together and delight themselves day and night. When I passed through this district I saw many bare-headed and barefooted lying drunk on the streets; some confessed aloud the state they were in by singing such couplets as these:

'I drank the ruby wine, how drunk, how drunk am I!
A prisoner of the locks. How mad, how mad am I!'

Another sang,

'My foot goes to the tavern, nowhere else.
My hand grasps tight the cup and nothing else.

Cut short your sermon, for no ears have I,
But for the bottle's murmur, nothing else.'

God is my witness that not a drop did I drink at the invitation of these drunkards, but mingling amongst them I could not but become aware of their condition.

Beginning in the mid-nineteenth century Galata was gradually renovated in an attempt to make it a more Western town. Signs with street names were put up in 1854-5 and the streets were illuminated by gas lamps in 1857. The municipal organization was established in 1855 its aim being to renovate and modernize the city, with municipal services for police, post, fire, communications and sewage. That year Altıncı Daire-i Belediye [Sixth Municipal Division], which comprised Galata and Beyoğlu (Galata later became part of greater Beyoğlu) was established by Server Efendi (later pasha), whose first project was the demolition of the Genoese defense walls. Tramways were introduced in 1869, with one line crossing Galata Köprüsü [Galata Bridge] and proceeding along the shore of the Bosphorus as far as Ortaköy. Then in 1876 the underground funicular known as Tünel was opened, carrying passengers from Karaköy to the lower end of Grand Rue de Pera and sparing them the long climb uphill on the ancient step street known as Yüksek Kaldırım.

Hotels and boarding houses in the European style were first opened in the second quarter of the nineteenth century; they were listed in *Murray's Guide* of 1845. All of these were in Pera, as noted

Altıncı Daire-i Belediye [Sixth Municipal Division].

19

Beyoğlu exit of Tünel.

in the 1893 edition of *Murray's Guide*: 'All the hotels frequented by European travelers are in Pera and most of them are on Grand Rue.' The guide writes of Galata that its 'innumerable alleys, passages and lanes... in dirt and wretchedness surpass the worst parts of Stamboul [the Old City]. It goes on to write of the districts along the waterfront in Galata: 'Here, in the adjoining side-streets, are warehouses, small shops, cafés, and filthy lodging houses, in which one of the most depraved populations of Europe find a home.'

The first bridge across the Golden Horn opened in 1836 between Azapkapı in Galata and Unkapanı in the old city, on the site of the present Atatürk Köprüsü. The present Galata Köprüsü between Karaköy in Galata and Eminönü in Istanbul is the fifth bridge to have been built between these two points; the first one, a floating wooden structure, was erected in 1845 and the first metal span opened in 1878.

Galata Köprüsü has always been the best place to view the passing parade of Istanbul life, but the clothing reforms of the early Turkish Republic has eliminated the colorful clothing and national costumes that one would have seen there in Ottoman times, as Edmondo de Amicis describes it in his *Constantinople* (1896):

Standing there you can see all of Constantinople pass in an hour...
advancing among a mixed crowd of Greeks, Turks and Armenians
may be seen a gigantic eunuch on horseback, shouting 'Vardah!'
(Make way!), and closely following him a Turkish carriage
decorated with flowers and birds filled with the ladies of a harem...
A Mussulman woman on foot, a veiled female slave, a Greek with
her long flowing hair surmounted by a little red cap, a Maltese
hidden in her black faletta, a Jewess in the ancient costume of
her nation, a Negress in a many-tinted Cairo shawl, an Armenian
from Trebizond, all veiled in black – a funereal apparition; these
and many more follow in line as though it were a procession
gotten up to display the dress of the various nations of the world...
No two persons are dressed alike. Some heads are enveloped in
shawls, other covered with rags, decked out like savages – shirts
and undervests striped or particolored like a harlequin's dress;
belts bristling with weapon, some of them reaching from the waist
to the armpits; Mameluke trousers, knee breaches, tunics, togas,

Galata Köprüsü [Galata Bridge].

21

Galata Köprüsü [Galata Bridge].

long cloaks which sweep the ground, capes trimmed with ermine, waistcoats encrusted with gold, short sleeves and balloon-shaped trousers, monastic garb and theater costumes; men dressed like women, women who seem to be men, and peasants with the air of princes.

Galata and Pera today —subsumed within modern Beyoğlu— have changed beyond recognition from the town of Genoese and Ottoman times, although the labyrinthine street patterns remain to remind us of its medieval origins. The population now is predominately Turkish, with much diminished percentages of Greeks, Armenians, Jews and Levantines, along with the rare family of Genoese origins, for the Magnificent Community of Pera has now all but vanished. But monuments of the Genoese era remain, as do those of the Byzantine and Ottoman periods, and we will see these juxtaposed in our strolls through greater Beyoğlu, which in its exuberant night life has revived the spirit of Istanbul's old Latin quarter.

CHAPTER 2
Along The Golden Horn

The area through which our first stroll takes us is by far the oldest of the district. Very little is known about the pre-Doric settlements that existed here, but legend tells us that Megarians Hipposthenes and Auletes (whose burial sites were identified by Dionysus of Byzantium as late as AD 196) settled here at about the same time as Byzas established his city.

Though officially the thirteenth district of Byzantium, Sycae [Galata] was seen as a suburb, and historians showed little interest in it. One of the few details that emerges about the inhabitants is that many of them supported the Blue faction during the Nika riots, and that a group of young Blues rowed across the Golden Horn to set fire to warehouses on the other side (that this was one of very few commercial properties deliberately attacked during the riots suggests that there may have been another motive). Sycae seems to have been completely depopulated during an outbreak of the plague in the 6th century. Procopius tells us that men were sent to climb the towers of the fortifications of Sycae, tear off the roofs, fill the towers with dead bodies and then replace the roofs. He adds that 'as a result of this an evil stench pervaded the city, further distressing the inhabitants.'

The Emperor Justinian rebuilt the district and designated it as a separate city called Justinianopolis. The area remained densely populated from the reign of Constantine to that of Theodosius. At the beginning of the tenth century, Italian city-states were given the right to establish trading posts along this shore, and first the Amalfians, then the Pisan and the Venetian and later the Genoese began to settle here. In 1261, after the Treaty of Nymphaion, Galata 'was given over to the glorious community of Genoa on order of the Great and Holy Emperor,' becoming a center of trade with the colonies on the Black Sea.

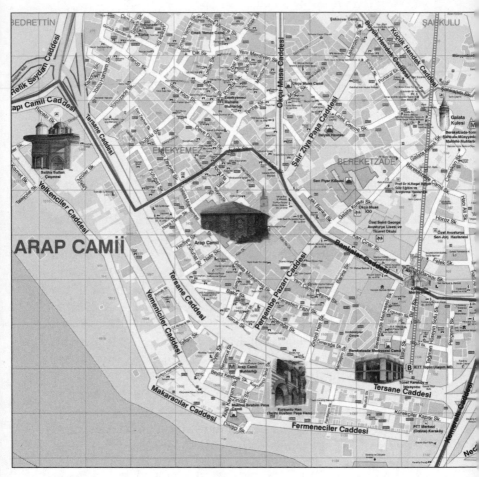

© Beyoğlu Belediyesi Emlak ve İstimlak Müdürlüğü

Until the Turkish conquest, Galata was governed by a *podestat* appointed each year from Genoa, after which it was governed by a *voivode* appointed by the sultan. The Genoese were allowed to form an institution known as the *magnifica communita di Pera* (headed by the *magnifico*, prior of the Brotherhood of St. Anne, aided by a superior and twelve counselors), which was responsible for little more than the upkeep of churches. A large part of this Genoese community came not from Genoa itself, but from the island of Chios, where the Genoese had intermarried widely with local Greeks, while others had come from Genoese colonies on the Black Sea.

By the beginning of the fifteenth century, the Genoese began moving their homes uphill, and it soon ceased to be a residential area. From then until the 1940s it remained an area of warehouses, inns for sailors and travelers and establishments for the supplying and repairing of ships. Indeed until the main port was moved to Kadıköy in 1945 the area was known as Kalafat Yeri, or the Caulking Yard. Many of the streets retain the names of the professions with which they were associated, such as Kürekçiler Kapısı Sokak, the Street of the Gate of the Oar-makers, Yelkenciler Sokak, the Street of the Sail-makers, etc. Some of the famous Jewish wine shops, run mostly by Jews from Çanakkale and Gallipoli who imported wine from the islands of Limnos and Imbros, remained in operation until the first decades of the twentieth century.

In the late 1940s the area was taken over by wholesale dealers in plumbing and mechanical supplies, and remains dominated by them today. Part of the area was destroyed during the widening of Tersane Caddesi [Tersane Avenue] in 1958, and in 1984, Mayor Bedrettin Dalan demolished a large swath along the shore to create a park. For decades this park, a neglected, muddy strip, was used only by drunks and stray dogs. However, when the Karaköy Fish Market was moved here in the first years of this century, a few informal fish restaurants began to operate in the park. Over the years these have expanded and become quite popular, bringing new life to the area, especially on summer evenings. For some years now, an ambitious project known as Galataport has envisioned demolishing the area altogether and turning it into a zone of parking lots, shopping malls and hotels.

Karaköy Meydanı [Karaköy Square], where we begin our stroll,

Karaköy Meydanı [Karaköy Square].

has for centuries retained its identity as a center for the selling
and exchanging of, and speculation in, imported goods. Nicholaos
Papadopoulos, in his *Encyclopedia of Commerce*, which was commissioned by the Greek merchants of Istanbul and published in Greek
in Venice in 1817, describes the area as it was at the beginning of
the nineteenth century:

> The merchants in Galata who trade with Russia are in the Havyar
> Han. Because space in the Han is limited, they have built a
> number of large stone warehouses nearby. The Frankish customs
> house near the Havyar Han is full of goods that have been brought
> to Galata by sea from Europe and Russia. The carpenters from
> the Aegean islands who have their workshops nearby make very

fine furniture in the European style, as well as mirrors and icons, from walnut and elm wood. Barrel making is also an important industry in Galata. Many merchant ships procure their barrels here, and they are used for wine, olives and olive oil. The iron workers of Galata make ship anchors as well as iron gates, doors and shutters.

The wealth of Russia flows into Galata. Wheat, butter, leather, Crimean wool, iron, hemp, silver thread, caviar and sable fur are the principal products. From Austria, by way of Trieste or the Danube, come Bohemian glass, Saxony porcelain, ready-made clothes, gold cord and mirrors. From Italy come Florentine thread and paper, from France, Marseille cloth, from England clocks and fine clothing, from Holland precious stones, from Egypt rice, cotton thread, Arabic coffee and incense, and from the Aegean islands wine, *rakı*, olives, olive oil, wheat, salt, cotton, lemons and woven fabric.

By the middle of the nineteenth century Havyar Han was being used as a general auction house, and also accommodated money-changers and currency traders, whose speculation in the first Ottoman bank-notes, which were handwritten and bore no serial numbers, and were therefore easy to counterfeit, created havoc in the Ottoman economy. During the Crimean War, an informal stock market began meeting in Havyar Han, trading mostly in securities and consolidated bonds. There were no controls over who could be a broker and no restrictions on fraudulent practices. Fortunes were made in market manipulations and what the Ottomans called 'air games' [*hava oyunları*], but public confidence suffered.

Skarlatos D. Byzantinos describes Havyar Han as it was in the 1860s:

> Today the Havyar Han, as well as being, as its name suggests, the center of the Caviar trade, and in spite of the newly built stock exchange across the street, is still the heart of the stock market. This is where the most valuable bonds are traded, and where the fates of the largest commercial houses are decided. This is where the value of money is assessed, and where the financial strength of the Ottoman Empire is shaped... On entering the Havyar Han for the first time, one might not realize that one is in the presence of the God of Commerce. But as soon as one looks more closely at this crowd of brokers and money-changers, the seriousness of the situation

becomes apparent. These men are constantly rushing about and whispering into each other's ears. The excitement here is like the excitement at the gambling table. Except that at the gambling table one sits down, whereas here one is in constant motion.

In 1864 the first association of legitimate stockbrokers was formed to limit buying and selling to known traders of repute. In 1866 an official stock exchange, Dersaadet Tahvilat Borsası [Istanbul Bond Exchange], modeled after the exchanges of Europe, was founded and moved to a new building across the street that was known variously as Borsa Han, Komisyon Han and Konsolide Han (and which Edwin Grosvenor later described as a 'pandemonium of clutching fingers and ravenous eyes'). An Exchange Committee of 20 members was formed, all of whom were Greeks. The Ministry of Finance was empowered to supervise, and appointed a chairman to ensure trading conformed to the newly established regulations. Trading was limited to the exchange floor, and fines and expulsions were stipulated for rule breakers. Trading was transacted through open auction in a large hall among traders [*mubayaacı*], brokers [*dellal*]and middlemen [*simsar*].

I. N. Karavias, writing in 1933, tells us that,

> The stock exchange was in the building where the shoe-makers and the Tokatlı restaurant are now, right across from the Havyar Han. It was a three-storey building. Inside the large hall there were iron stairs and galleries. Trading in currency and securities was conducted there. Consolidated bonds were also traded there, which is why it was called the Konsolide Han. This was the heart not only of the markets of Galata, but of the markets of all Istanbul. It was also undoubtedly the noisiest place in Istanbul. Passersby were disoriented by this cacophony, and visitors to the city were often convinced that something alarming was going on inside.
>
> In the evening, when the *han* closed, the commotion would come to a sudden end. Because most of the brokers and money-changers had their safes in the building, it was guarded by a large crew of watchmen. The area next to the stock exchange and in front of the Havyar Han was taken up by the money-changers' counters. Most of the money-changers were wealthy men. The poor of the city and indeed even of the hinterlands sold their gold to the money-changers when they were strapped for cash. The money-changers also gave loans in exchange for gold and

jewelry. On each of the counters there would be a red, wooden box filled with the currencies of various nations.

The present shape of Karaköy Meydanı dates from after the urban renewal project that was completed in 1958. Previously the square was much smaller, indeed barely a square at all. To the left after crossing the bridge was the squat, neoclassical Aziziye Police Station, which was built in the late nineteenth century to replace a previous police station that was housed in a surviving tower of the Genoese fortifications. Behind and beyond the police station were the *hans* of what was known as Fermeneciler Çarşısı [Vest-makers' Market], occupied by the makers and wholesale merchants of ladies' apparel. The only survivor of these *hans* is Selanik Han, now occupied by shops selling electronic goods. To the right of the bridge, beyond the building (still standing) that once housed the Austrian Bank, was Merzifonlu Camii, which was restored by Raimondo D'Aronco after it was damaged in the earthquake of 1894. Just beyond were the famous Havyar Han and Konsolide Han. Also demolished were Stein department store and a branch of French Bon Marche stores and a street called Domuzhane Sokak that was lined with pork butchers. Çerkezo, the only of these pork butchers to survive, moved to nearby Yüksek Kaldırım, where it continued to operate until the mid 1990s. Domuzhane Sokak was also home to a number of restaurants that catered mostly to businessmen and bankers.

We begin our stroll by walking up the Golden Horn on Tersane Caddesi, which extends between Galata Köprüsü Atatürk Köprüsü.

Most of the area along the Golden Horn between the two bridges was walled in by the Genoese in 1303, the part closest to Atatürk Köprüsü being part of the enceinte built in 1387-97. The Genoese sea-walls in this quarter were demolished after the Turkish conquest, but two short stretches of the land walls have survived and can still be seen near Atatürk Köprüsü.

The handsome neo-classical building on the corner is Oyak Sigorta Binası. This was originally Nordstern Han, a commercial structure built in 1930, most of its original occupants, both European and Turkish, being involved in import and export business at the port of Galata.

About 150 meters from Karaköy Meydanı we turn left into Kardeşim Sokak. We then turn right at the next corner into an alleyway that leads into a handsome but dilapidated old commercial building, Rüstem Paşa Hanı.

The *han* was built by the great Ottoman architect Sinan for the Grand Vizier Rüstem Pasha shortly before 1550. The date of construction is fixed by Petrus Gyllius, who says that while he was in the city, 1544-50, the Latin church of St. Michael was demolished to make way for the *han*, an inner city caravanserai. Gyllius notes that near the *han* there was a forum, which Honorius, Emperor of the West (r. 395-403) is believed to have built in Sycae along with a theater. Gyllius, in describing the topography of Sycae, implies that the forum had disappeared during his time in the city.

> We can only guess so far from the rules of usage of architecture that the Theater and Forum of Honorius stood at the bottom of the hill [of Galata], as I observed on my travels through Greece. When I first came to Constantinople there was standing a forum on level ground near the haven [the port of Galata] where a caravanserai is now being built in the ruins of a church dedicated to St. Michael. This forum was well supplied by an ancient subterranean aqueduct. In short, there is nothing to be seen of old Sycae at present.

A Corinthian capital from the church can be seen to the left of the entryway to the building.

Rüstem Pasha, the founder of the *han*, was twice grand vizier under Süleyman the Magnificent, and husband of the Sultan's only daughter, Mihrimah Sultan, by his favorite wife Roxelana. Rüstem, an odious character, was known in his time as *Kehle-i İkbal*, 'the Louse of Fortune', a nickname that he acquired when he married Mihrimah. It seems that one of the many enemies of Rüstem, who at the time of his engagement to Mihrimah, was governor of Diyarbakır, tried to prevent him from marrying the princess by spreading the rumor that he had leprosy. But when the Sultan's doctors examined Rüstem they discovered that he was infested with lice; consequently they concluded that he was not leprous, for accepted Ottoman medical belief had it that lice never inhabit lepers. Rüstem was thus given a clean bill of health and allowed to marry Mihrimah, whereupon Süleyman appointed him second vizier. Five years later he was appointed grand vizier, beginning the first of his two terms in that office under Süleyman, during which time he became the wealthiest and most powerful of the Sultan's subjects. Thus it was that Rüstem Pasha came to be called *Kehle-i İkbal*, from the old Turkish proverb that 'When a man has his luck in place, even a louse can bring him fortune.'

We now make our way back to the main avenue and continue on in the same direction. After the first side street we come to an ancient and imposing building with nine domes. This is Galata Bedesteni, a covered market built by Fatih soon after the conquest. Whereas in Ottoman times a *bedesten* like this would have been used to store and sell only the most precious goods, today Galata Bedesteni is used by dealers in heavy industrial machines. The building is still in excellent condition.

Just beyond the *bedesten* we turn left on Arap Kayyum Sokak. This leads to Eski Yağ İskelesi, one of the ancient landing-places on the Golden Horn. Small boats ferry passengers across the Golden Horn from here to Yemiş İskelesi in Eminönü in the old city. According to Petrus Gyllius, this ferry service has been operating since the earliest days of the city, and the older of the two authors has been using it for half a century. Eski Yağ İskelesi is outside the course of the Genoese sea-walls, and the landing stage here would have been approached through a gateway known in Turkish as Kürkçü Kapısı, the Gate of the Furriers, which would have been end of Arap Kayyum Sokak.

The oldest of the few buildings that still stand along the shore just above Eski Yağ İskelesi is Yelkenciler Hanı, the Han of the Sail-Makers. The *han* dates to the seventeenth century and is the oldest commercial building still standing along the Galata shore of the Golden Horn. It looks to be in very poor condition; nevertheless it is still very much in use.

Up until the 1960s one of the old buildings next to Yelkenciler Hanı still housed a Jewish wine-shop where passengers being ferried to and from Eski Yağ İskelesi could drop in for a drink. There were several Jewish wine-shops in Galata in the time of Evliyâ Çelebi, and he tells us that they were the last to pass in the fabulous procession of the guilds that took place in 1638, during the reign of Murad IV:

In Istanbul there are one thousand places of misrule [wine houses] kept by Greeks, Armenians and Jews. In the procession wine is not produced openly, and the tavern-keepers pass all in disguise and clad in armor. The boys of the taverns, all shameless drunkards, and all the partisans of wine pass singing songs, tumbling down and rising again. The last to pass were the Jewish tavern-keepers of Galata, all masked and wearing the most precious dresses bedecked with jewels, carrying in their hands crystalline and porcelain cups, out of which they pour sherbet instead of wine for the spectators.

Eremya Çelebi Komucuyan also tells us about the 'Jewish houses and rooms' in this area. 'These houses are on the shore and there are shops under them. They cook fish for the guests and serve pickles, dried sturgeon and codfish. There are Jewish butchers as well as small taverns where *rakı* is sold.'

Fariba Zarinebaf tells us that in the 18th century there were 'regular' as well as 'illegal' taverns here. The 'regular' taverns, identified by symbols such as a dagger rather than by signs, were known for their clean kitchens and excellent food. These taverns usually consisted of large rooms with high ceilings supported by pillars, and it was customary for there to be a barrel of salted fish next to the central pillar. Glasses and bowls were polished with clean cloths, floors were swept and tables were wiped regularly and the waiters always wore clean clothes. The tables all had candles in ceramic holders, around which the *meze* were arranged, and large wooden salt-shakers that symbolized abundance. The *meze* placed on the table when the customers arrived were free; customers only paid for their drinks and any extra *meze* they ordered. The customers were largely artisans and foremen from the shipyards and the armory, though some taverns catered mostly to janissaries. Boatmen, *hamals*, bath attendants and 'rowdy rogues' were discouraged.

The 'illegal' taverns, or *koltuk meyhane*, were often in the back rooms of grocers and greengrocers and were frequented by civil servants and clerks who did not bring alcohol to their homes. There were also peddlers known as 'roaming taverns' who sold wine or rakı. Most of these were Armenian. They carried sheepskin bladders around their waists, concealed by a robe, and metal cups in their pockets, and were adept at serving their customers surreptitiously.

They were identifiable by the napkins they wore on their shoulders. Most of the time they offered a grape or a small piece of fruit to go with the drink.

Returning to Tersane Caddesi, we continue walking in the same direction. As we do so we pass our left a short stretch of ancient wall with a series of arches, part of the fortifications of Genoese Galata that was revealed when the surrounding houses were demolished in the late 1970s. This was part of the sea-wall of the enceinte erected by the Genoese in 1387-97, extending to just beyond the present Atatürk Köprüsü.

At the end of the avenue we come to Azapkapı Sebili, one of the most beautiful Ottoman street-fountains in the city. This baroque structure was founded in 1732-3 by Saliha Valide Hatun, mother of Mahmud I.

We now walk over to the handsome mosque on the shore of the Golden Horn beside Atatürk Köprüsü. This is Azapkapı Camii, built by Sinan in 1577-78 for the Grand Vizier Sokollu Mehmed

Azapkapı Camii [Azapkapı Mosque].

Pasha, for whom the architect had six years earlier built another mosque on the First Hill below the Hippodrome.

Sokollu was perhaps the greatest of the long line of able grand viziers of the sixteenth century. He was the son of a Bosnian Orthodox priest and was born in the castle of Sokol, 'the falcon's nest', in Bosnia, from which he took his first name. He was taken up as a *devşirme*, the periodic levy of Christian youths who were inducted into the Ottoman army, and, after being converted to Islam, were trained in the Ottoman army. Sokollu Mehmed was one of the elite group who were educated in the famous Palace School at Topkapı Sarayı, which produced many of the grand viziers of the Ottoman Empire. After rising rapidly in the ranks of the army he became a pasha and was married to Esmahan Sultan, daughter of Selim II, son and successor of Süleyman the Magnificent. He was Süleyman's last grand vizier, and continued to hold the post throughout the reign of Selim II and on into the reign of Selim's son and successor, Murad III. His brilliant career finally ended in 1579, when he was murdered by a mad soldier in the *Divan*, or Imperial Council.

We now cross Tersane Caddesi, and on the far side we come to an old Turkish bath known as Yeşildirek Hamamı. This was built by Sinan for Sokollu Mehmed Pasha in 1577-8, part of the *külliye*, or mosque complex, of Azapkapı Camii. The *hamam* is no longer of any architectural interest, since it has been totally rebuilt in modern times. It has been recently restored and is once again in use. Next to the *hamam* on the right there is a classical *sebil*, also part of the *külliye* of Azapkapı Camii. The cul-de-sac just to the right of the *sebil* is Eflatun Çıkmazı, the Dead-End of Plato, a name whose origin is anyone's guess.

We turn in to the street just to the left of the *hamam*, Yolcuzade Sokak. This takes its name from Yolcuzade Mescidi, the little mosque up the street, founded in 1476 by one Hacı Ömer. On the right side of the street we see a stretch of the fortifications of Genoese Galata, part of the land wall that separated the enceinte built in 1303 from the one added in 1387-97.

At the end of the block we turn right on to Yanıkkapı Sokak, the Street of the Burnt Gate, which takes its name from the ancient portal we now see in front of us. This is the only surviving gateway of Genoese Galata, opening between the enceinte of 1387-97 and that of 1352. Above the archway of the gate there is a bronze tablet emblazoned with the cross of St. George, symbol of Genoa the Superb, between a pair of escutcheons bearing the heraldic arms of the noble houses of Doria and De Merude.

We continue on Yanıkkapı Sokak to the first intersection and turn right, after which we turn left on Galata Mahkemesi Sokak. We then come to a very unusual edifice ending in a tall square tower with a pyramidal roof; this is known in Turkish as Arap Camii [Mosque of the Arabs], one of the surviving Latin churches of Genoese Galata.

There are many baseless legends concerning the origin and history of the building, some of which are repeated in recent guidebooks. But the evidence indicates that it was constructed by the Dominicans during the years 1323-37 and dedicated to St. Dominic; it seems to have included a chapel of St. Paul, by whose name the church was popularly known. Early in the sixteenth century it was converted into a mosque, and given over to the colony of Moorish refugees who had settled in Galata; hence its Turkish name, Arap Camii. These Andalucian Arabs mostly engaged in the making and selling of candied fruit, *helva* and *şerbet*. Arap Ahmed Pasha, who took part in the conquest of Cyprus, was from this community. According to Dwight, by the beginning of the twentieth century this neighborhood was largely inhabited by Muslim Albanians, many of whom worked as bank guards in the nearby banks.

The building has been partially burned and restored several times; on one occasion it was considerably widened by moving the north wall several meters to the north. Nevertheless, it remains a rather typical medieval Latin church, originally Gothic: a long hall ending in three rectangular apses, and with a belfry (now the minaret) at the east end. The flat wooden roof and the rather pretty wooden galleries date from a restoration in 1913-19. At that time also the original floor was uncovered and large quantities of Genoese tombstones of the late Byzantine period came to light. Some of the tombstones bore the date 1347, the year when the Black Death struck Constantinople before ravaging Western Europe; these are now in İstanbul Arkeoloji Müzesi [the Istanbul Archaeological Museum]. Fragments of a fourteenth-century fresco were recently discovered in the central apse.

On the north side of the mosque there is a picturesque courtyard with a *şadırvan*, or ablution fountain, an octagonal marble structure standing on a three-stepped platform.

The first Masonic lodge in Istanbul is said to have been established near Arap Camii in 1721, though its exact location is not known. This may be the lodge associated with the story of the possibly fictitious Clotilde Bersone. The story goes that Clotilde, a beautiful seventeen year-old girl who was an honor student and could speak six languages, was sold to the Masonic lodge by her father in order to clear his gambling debt of 60,000 liras. Clotilde, full of hatred for everyone in the lodge, was determined to rise through the ranks and learn all their secrets and eventually reveal these secrets to the world in order to take revenge against those who had violated her womanhood and brought her innumerable miseries and horrors. She rose from the rank of Nymph of the Night to Nymph Initiated to Secrets, Illuminati, Sovereign Grand Master Nymph and then Bride of Lucifer or Queen of the Illuminati. She moved to Paris, where for a time she was the lover of James Garfield, who would later become president of the United States, and where she published a book titled *L'Elue du Dragon* [The Elect of the Dragon], in which she exposed the true nature of Freemasonry. Among the secrets she revealed was that Satan was the true ruler of France.

We continue along Galata Mahkemesi Sokak, where we have now passed from the enceinte of 1348 to the original walled enclosure.

At the next intersection, we turn left on Perşembe Pazarı Caddesi, the Avenue of the Thursday Market. This street is lined with picturesque old houses and *hans* which used to be identified as Byzantine or Genoese, although in fact they are typical Turkish buildings of the eighteenth century. The most handsome is the one near the next corner on the left, dated by an inscription to 1735-6.

Jean Sauvaget tells us that this was the commercial center of Genoese Galata, and was lined with small shops and taverns. He is also confident that this was the site of a weekly market since long before Ottoman times. A number of buildings on the street were demolished when it was widened in 1874. Dwight describes this market as it was at the beginning of the twentieth century:

'On Thursdays awnings shade the little streets around Arab Jami, and venders of dreadful Manchester prints, of astonishing footwear, of sweets, of perfumes, of variegated girdles, leave no more than a narrow lane for passersby, and there is infinite bargaining from sunrise to sunset.'

We now turn off Perşembe Pazarı Caddesi into Yeni Camii Çeşme Sokak, a short side street that leads to an intersection with Zincirli Han Sokak and its continuation, Banka Sokak. Here we see an old bath called Perşembe Pazar Hamamı, founded in 1767 by Kaymak Mustafa Pasha.

Yeni Camii Çeşme Sokak takes its name from Yeni Camii of Galata, an imperial Ottoman mosque that was demolished in 1936, except for its *medrese* and a *çeşme*, or fountain. The mosque grounds occupied the entire block between Zincirli Han Sokak, Banka Sokak, and the next street beyond, Bereketzade Medresesi Sokak.

Yeni Camii was built in 1697 by Sultan Mustafa II in honor of his mother the Valide Sultan Gülnuş Umettulah. The mosque was erected on the ruins of the Catholic church of St. Francis, which had been destroyed by fire in 1696. St. Francis was founded in 1227, during the Latin occupation of Constantinople. A traveler in the early Ottoman period reported that 'It equaled Haghia Sophia in height, grandeur, form and structure; it was ornamented both inside and out, with paintings and mosaics presenting evangelical truths.'

The *medrese* of Yeni Camii was erected in 1705 by the Vizier Mehmed Pasha, and the following year the fountain was built opposite. Both the *medrese* and the fountain can be seen by walking up Bereketzade Medresesi Sokak from the main avenue.

Walking back towards Karaköy along the main avenue we now pass the lower entrance to Tünel, the underground funicular railway, which in a minute and a half ascends to the heights of Pera. Tünel was built by French engineers in 1875 and was one of the first underground railways in the world. Locals at first objected to Tünel, but it soon gained acceptance, sparing residents of Pera the long walk up the hill from the port.

We now turn into Perçemli Sokak, a cul-de-sac. At the end of the street and on the right is Zulfaris Sinagogu [the Zulfaris Synagogue]. This is the oldest extant synagogue in Galata, founded in 1671 and rebuilt in 1890. Closed for many years, the synagogue was restored and then reopened in 1992 as a museum, with exhibits commemorating the five-hundredth anniversary of the welcoming of the dispersed Sephardic Jews from Spain in 1492 by Sultan Bayezid II, who resettled them in Istanbul and other places in the Ottoman Empire. The museum has photographs and memorabilia of the Jewish communities of Istanbul, including the ones in Galata, Hasköy on the north shore of the Golden Horn, and Balat in the old city. There is also an exhibit honoring the heroic Turkish consul who served in Barcelona during World War II, when he issued Turkish passports to hundreds of European Jews, saving them from being sent off to concentration camps.

We now return to Karaköy Meydanı, where we end our first stroll.

CHAPTER 3
Along The Bosphorus

We begin in Karaköy Meydanı, the great square at the northern end of Galata Köprüsü. The area along the shore beside the bridge is extremely lively and colorful, with ferries and motor launches criss-crossing the confluence of the Golden Horn and the Bosphorus, where their waters meet and flow together into the Sea of Marmara.

Until the end of the nineteenth century, the shore of what is now known as Karaköy was a narrow, sandy beach. Ships tied up to buoys and pontoons (owned by a company that charged substantial fees), and were unloaded onto *mavnas* (a Black Sea variation, with a broader, galleon-like hull, of a typical Mediterranean type of boat). The cargo was then unloaded onto roughly constructed wooden piers or onto larger *mavna* (*mavna bumbarta*) that served as warehouses and were more or less permanently anchored along the shore. Passengers were brought, either by *sandal* (a type of rowboat that held 10 to 15 people) or *kayık* (a long, narrow boat that held 3 to 4 people), to a customs pier across from what is known as Fransız Geçidi [Cité Française]. The *sandalcıs* were mostly Greeks from Kefalonia, Nisiros and the Marmara Islands, and the men who loaded and unloaded the *mavnas* were almost all Greeks from Kefalonia. The *kayıkçıs* were mostly Turkish.

During the Crimean War the British and the French experienced great frustration and delay in loading and unloading their supply ships, and at the peace talks of 1856 pressured the Ottoman government to construct proper docks. However, it was not until 1879 that the contract for the construction of these docks was given to two Frenchmen, Marius Michel (Compte de Pierredon, later known as Michel Pasha, a naval officer who had ended up in Constantinople after being shipwrecked in the eastern Mediterranean) and Bernard Camille Collas, both of whom had been building, inspecting and repairing lighthouses on the Black

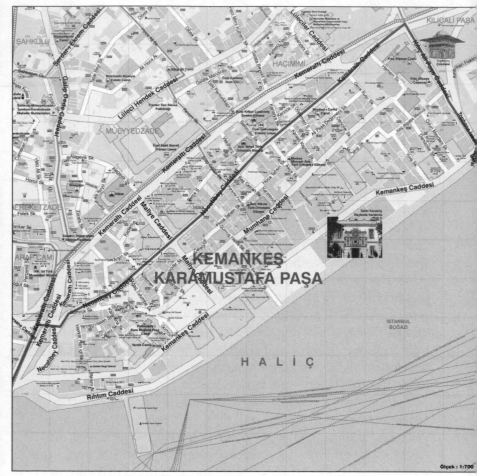

Sea and Aegean coasts. Their intention had been to construct a quay with landfill and wooden paling, but it soon became clear that because of the strong currents and the nature of the shore (in some places there were sheer drops to a depth of 35 meters and in others a dense clay that defied paling), this would be impossible. They also realized that they did not have nearly enough capital to build a stone quay, so in 1890 they asked for and were granted an extension, and set about trying to form a company to finance to project. Then, in 1891, Michel Pasha and Monsieur Collas turned over their contract to the newly formed and French owned *Dersaadet Rıhtım, Dok ve Antrepo Şirket-i Osmaniyesi* [Ottoman Pier, Warf and Warehousing Company of Constantinople], which had capital of 23 million gold franks, for shares worth 3 million gold franks. Michel Pasha remained as the director of the company, and Monsieur Collas used his share of the proceeds to buy the Jerusalem to Jaffa railroad. In exchange for building the docks, warehouses and administrative buildings, the company would be granted the right to charge docking and warehousing fees.

Construction of the 758-meter quay from Karaköy to Tophane began in April 1892, and proceeded slowly. Huge blocks of stone had to be quarried on Marmara islands and the Black Sea coast and transported by *mavna*, and as there was a shortage of skilled labor, foreign workers and foremen had to be brought in. Work was frequently interrupted by acts of sabotage, obstruction and violence carried out by *sandalcıs, kayıkçıs* and *mavnacıs* who feared that the new quay threatened their livelihood, and there were several outbreaks of cholera among the workers. Meanwhile, the port continued to operate, and progress was hampered by the constant loading and unloading of ships. The quay was nearly completed when the foundations were damaged by the earthquake of 1894 (which also killed a number of workers).

In September 1895, the *Memphis* of the Messageries Maritime Lines, became the first passenger ship to dock at the new quay. A group of angry *sandalcıs* and *kayıkçıs* tried to prevent the ship from docking, and succeeded for several hours, until soldiers arrived and fired shots into the air to disperse them. (Some years later, at the beginning of World War I, when the young Frenchmen of Beyoğlu were boarding the *Memphis* to return to France to enlist, a

Karaköy Rıhtım [Karaköy Quay].

large crowd came to see them off, and a popular singer of the time, Mademoiselle Henriette Le Blond, stood on top of a barrel and led a rousing rendition of the Marseillaise). Soon afterwards, sections of the quay collapsed, and work continued for another five years.

Meanwhile, a series of intrigues involving agents of the company, several pashas in the government and a group of Armenian businessmen, and accusations that the French company was unfairly preventing Turkish ships from docking, led Michel Pasha to decide to abandon his responsibilities and flee back to France (where he began building what was to be a modern tourist resort, though it remained unfinished after his wife was stabbed to death by a madman) and to the company being taken over by the Ottoman Bank.

It was also in 1895 that Istanbul's first automobile, which the press dubbed *Zat-ül Hareke*, was lowered onto these docks to great fanfare. Within minutes Istanbul experienced its first automobile accident when *Zat-ül Hareke* crashed into a tree behind Dolmabahçe Sarayı [Dolmabahçe Palace].

Over the years, these docks saw several great migrations. The ships carrying the Russians who fled the Bolshevik Revolution, and who were to have such an impact on the social life of Beyoğlu, docked here, and many of the refugees settled nearby before fanning out through the rest of the city. (After the fall of the Soviet Union, the ships involved in the 'blue jean trade' also docked here, and for some years the waterfront cafes and restaurants were once again filled with Russians.) In 1922-3, after the Turkish Republican forces had retaken the city from the Allied occupation forces, as many as 50,000 Istanbul Greeks, as well as thousands of Armenians, Jews and Levantines who had publicly supported the occupation, boarded ships here, fleeing in fear of retaliation. Many of the Russian refugees left with them, seeking better opportunities in Europe and America. Between 1948 and 1952, many of Istanbul's Jews embarked here for the newly established state of Israel, and in the 1960s, when the offices for the recruitment of *Gastarbeiter* were housed at Tophane end of the docks, the area was crowded with Turkish workers seeking to migrate to Germany.

Leonard of Chios tells us of events that took place here many years before the docks were built, in the hours after Constantinople fell to the Turks. Those Christians of Galata who had actively supported and assisted the Byzantines, by providing arms and supplies and in some cases fighting alongside them, began to flee in fear of retribution. 'Those of them who did not manage to board their ships before the Turkish vessels reached their side of the harbor were captured; mothers were taken and their children left, or the reverse, as the case might be; and many were overcome by the sea and drowned in it. Jewels were scattered about, and they preyed on one another without pity.'

In 1821, with the outbreak of the Greek War of Independence in the Peloponnese, there was another mass exodus of Greeks fearing retribution. Georgios Zafiris, whose family managed to escape to Odessa, tells us that 'the port was full of boats with their sails unfurled, all ready to sail. The throng of people was out of all proportion as the number of Greeks fleeing from the threat of slaughter swelled. The main problem, though, was that this mass of people was behaving confusedly, not knowing for which place to embark'.

Until the building of the docks and warehouses, many of the fabled taverns of Galata were situated along this shore. Evliyâ Çelebi writes that in his time there were two hundred taverns here, and names eight of them (Taşmerdiven [Stone Steps], Kefeli, Manyalı, Mihalaki, Kaşkaval, Sümbül, Constantine and Saranda). This also seems to have been the location of the famous Laverintos Tavern, which is said to have been in continuous operation from the beginning of the seventeenth century to the end of the nineteenth century. Some believe that the name Laverintos is connected to the folk legend about a labyrinth of tunnels beneath Galata. Another folk legend about the Laverintos holds that during the reign of Abdülhamid II, a gigantic white spider, thought to be three hundred years old, was found in a disused barrel in the basement.

Sermet Muhtar Alus, writing of the scene on the waterfront in the nineteenth century, tells us that:

> Before the quay was built, the road was lined with taverns. The basements were windowless, but the upper stories, of wood, and always painted in the blue and white of the Greek flag, had wide windows. When you passed you could see the large engravings on the walls. King George I of Greece and his wife Queen Olga, the heroes of the Greek Revolution, Ipsilantis, Miaoulis and Lord Byron and the Tsars Alexander I and Nicholas I. There would always be guitar and mandolin music, often somewhat out of tune. There would be shouts in Greek of *yassou* and *zito*, and the smell of alcohol wafted out into the street.

And according to Reşad Ekrem Koçu:

> In Galata, which until recently was inhabited mostly by Greeks and Franks, all of the taverns that had existed since the conquest of the city were run for centuries by Greek tavern-keepers famous for knowing how to keep drinkers happy. These taverns were frequented by seamen, foreign bachelors and all manner of thrill-seeking lowlife, and employed staff whose character did not dispose them to object to occasional sexual harassment.

Lord Byron himself made several visits to these taverns during his visit to Istanbul in 1811, as his travelling companion John Cam Hobhouse relates:

> Hearing music, we went into a room like a hall with a gallery all round it. This was a wine-house and here I saw a boy dancing in a style indescribably beastly, scarcely moving from one place, but making a thousand lascivious motions with his thighs, loins,

and belly. Small tables set out in various parts of the gallery. The boys were Greeks with very thick and long hair. An old wretch striking a guitar and singing kept close to the dancer, and at the most lecherous moments cried out, 'Ομορφα ομορφα!!' (Beautiful, beautiful!!)'... and a few days later, 'This day, went with Byron and a party to the wine houses of Galata. Took pipes, and saw two old and ugly boys, who wrung the sweat off their brows, dance as before, waving their long hair. Also they spread a mat and, putting on a kind of shawl, performed an Alexandrian woman's dance – much the same, except that they knelt, and, covering each other's heads, seemed as if kissing. One of Mr. Adair's Janissaries, who talks English and has been in England, was with us. I asked him if these boys would not be hanged in England. 'Oh yes, directly. De Turk take and byger dem d'ye see?' For this beastly sight we paid fifty-five *piastres*, five to the boys each, and five to all fiddlers and singers and performers &c., nor is this dear, I understand. Turk boys are not allowed to dance.

We have no record of Byron's own impressions.

The world of the Galata taverns on the waterfront and in the streets behind saw one of its last great flowerings during the Crimean War. The taverns filled with foreign soldiers and sailors, and with this boom came an increase in prostitution and criminal activity. The situation became so bad that after the war the Beyoğlu Municipality brought in 100 British policemen, who cleaned up the area and imposed order, to the detriment of other hitherto respectable neighborhoods of Beyoğlu, to which the prostitutes and criminals quickly relocated.

After the last decades of the nineteenth century, most taverns were located on or near Grand Rue de Galata, now Necatibey Caddesi. Two subcategories of tavern in this period were the *koltuk meyhane*, usually a small, narrow room where customers stood at a counter that ran along the walls, and the *çalgılı meyhane*, which was usually larger, with tables and chairs, and offered musical entertainment. Some of the best remembered taverns of this era was Seropi on Arkadi [now Serçe] Sokak, which is said to have been a favorite hangout of the *tulumbacıs* [fireman], (At that time Istanbul had no fire brigade, what it did have were *tulumbacıs*, who would run to the scene of a fire carrying water pumps. Each neighborhood had its own team of *tulumbacı*. The *tulumbacıs* of Galata were reputed to be expert at retrieving valuable objects from burning buildings. They were also reputed to run extensive extortion and protection rackets, and were often hired as 'bouncers' at the local taverns), and the nearby Küplü Meyhane, whose owner, a certain Papazoğlu, nicknamed Fazıl Baba [Father Virtuous], was much loved by the down-and-out of the neighborhood because he often allowed them to drink for free. Also often mentioned is a tavern on Leblebici Şaban Sokak that was operated by a certain Madame Bella, who though in her forties did not look a day over twenty-five, and who, though her beauty turned many heads, was known to be as tough as nails. According to one story her tavern was burned down by a *tulumbacı* after a complicated series of events involving one Stavros, a cunning and ambitious young man from Mytilene, and a local prostitute. According to another, after Stavros, who was besotted with Bella, murdered a customer of whom he had become jealous, the police closed down the tavern and deported Bella.

I. N. Karavias, in his book *Alotate kai Tora*, which was published in Greek in Istanbul in 1933, describes these taverns as they were in the early years of the Turkish Republic:

> There were many taverns in old Galata. It was customary for them not to open until evening. By law they were required to close at 1:30 am. There were stiff penalties for staying open later. However, either because of the tavern keepers' greed or because the customers simply wouldn't leave, they often did stay open

Tulumbacıs [firemen] running for the scene of a fire with water pumps.

46

past closing time. Large amounts of *duziko* (*rakı*) and *mastika* (*rakı* flavored with mastic) were drunk in these taverns. When closing time approached, the tavern-keepers would bring the last *mezes* and present the bill. The last *meze* usually consisted of *pastırma* or fried *kaşar* cheese. The last *mezes* were a polite way of reminding the customers that it was almost time to leave. The Foskolos beer hall in Galata was famous for its rich variety of *mezes*. The plates would cover the entire table, and would sometimes be stacked because there wasn't enough room.

The taverns were usually on the ground floor, and on the second floor or in the basement was often to be found a type of establishment known as the *baloz*. As opposed to the all-male taverns, the *baloz* employed women as *consommatrices*, that is, to act as companions to the male customers. The *baloz* also offered music and dancing. The best remembered of the *baloz* were Universal, owned by Yannis Vlahos, Anatoli, owned by Christos Petropoulos, Afrika, owned by Ioannis Kairis, and Antilop and Moskova.

According to Sermet Muhtar Alus:

> Most of the women who ran the *baloz* were wizened old prostitutes who were raised in the quagmires of prostitution and entered this line of work, under the protection and patronage of their former lovers, after their youth and beauty had vanished. The customers were foreign ship's captains, crew and stokers from places such as Moscow, France, Malta and Greece. From time to time, callow playboys would take to slumming among these drunken men and wretched prostitutes, and more often than not it would end disastrously for them. These places usually had a small dance floor and a seven or eight piece orchestra.

In about 1918, a type of establishment known as the *gazino* began to appear in Istanbul. Although the term is loose, and has had different meanings in different periods, it was generally a much classier type of establishment than the *meyhane*, had better food and drink, usually offered entertainment by well-known singers and musicians, and the customers sometimes included 'respectable' women (accompanied, of course). The first of these to appear in Galata was Arkadi Gazinosu, on Arkadi Sokak. It was at the Arkadi Gazinosu that the game of bingo [*tombala*] was first played in Istanbul, with lovely Russian hostesses [Harasho] drawing the tiles.

Another popular *gazino* in the area was Pirinçci, where musicians such as Hanende Karakaş, Tanburi Ovakım and Kanuni Şemsi used to perform.

In addition to the *meyhane* and *baloz* on Grand Rue de Galata, there were also several theaters. The best known of these were the Theatro Evropi, the Theatro Tou Laou (The Popular Theater, or Halk Tiyatrosu in Turkish, formerly known as the Theatro Afrikis and later renamed the Theatro Apollon) and the Theatro Amerikis, all of which were established in the middle of the nineteenth century, and where local Greek drama companies performed plays in Greek.

These theaters were also the heart of the world of the *kanto*, a musical form combining Western instruments with Eastern musical modes, that was popular from the time of Sultan Abdülaziz to the 1920s, when it was replaced by the tango, foxtrot and charleston. An orchestra made up of trumpets, trombones, violin, trap drums and cymbals would accompany a singer. According to Cem Ünlü, the general form for the singer was, 'First the introduction, then the lyrics, shake your shoulders to a violin solo, cock your head and shimmy in oriental dance style, leap around like a partridge, then slowly disappear behind the curtain'.

About an hour before the show, the orchestra would begin to play popular songs and marches in front of the theater, and when they played the Izmir March it meant that the show was about to begin. The show usually began with slapstick routines and broad comedy sketches performed by popular Greek comedians such as Pascal Andon, Georgie and Todori, who had such thick Greek accents and whose Turkish was so broken that the Turks in the audience had difficulty understanding them. Then, after an interval, the *kanto* would begin.

At the Theatro Amerikis it was usually Küçük Amelya (Little Amalia), who performed, often wearing a sailor outfit with a short skirt, and at the Theatro Evropi it was usually Peruz. Ahmet Rasim describes a performance by Peruz:

> Everyone thought Peruz was the most flirtatious, most skillful and most provocative. The seats closest to the stage were always crammed full... They said of Peruz that 'she is a trollop who has ensnared the heart of many a young man and has made herself

48

the enemy of many.' Her song would hardly be finished when flower bouquets and beribboned letters would come flying from the box seats, and it seemed as if the building might be shaken to the ground... The audience included artillerymen from the Tersane, female bath attendants wearing jodhpurs and hooded robes, male bath attendants, police spies, *mavnacıs*, sailors, and young men-about-town. Occasionally there were fights involving slaps, fists, razors, knives and even guns.

Peruz Terzakyan, a native of Sivas, began singing *kanto* in Istanbul in 1880 when she was almost fourteen and continued performing until 1912, usually writing and composing her own songs. In 1919 she played the lead role in a silent film called *Mr. Fahri in the Macaroni Pot* by İsmet Fahri Gülünç.

Also on and off the Grand Rue de Galata, particularly towards Tophane end, were the infamous 'hashish coffee houses,' which were frequently the target of indignant newspaper editorials until they were finally closed in 1917.

The world of the Galata taverns saw its last great boom during the Allied occupation of Istanbul from 1918 to 1923, when the taverns and *baloz* were filled with foreign soldiers and lovely Russian hostesses. Maria Yordanidou describes the scene in her book *Diakopes Sto Kavkaso* [*Vacation in the Caucasus*].

> When Anna returned to Istanbul from Russia in August 1920, she found it a completely different city. Karaköy square was full of British, French and Greek soldiers, Russian refugees, Jews, Levantines and the newly wealthy Istanbul Greeks. The *hamals* [porters] and cart-drivers were nowhere to be seen. French military trucks roared through the narrow streets of Galata sounding their deafening klaxons. British soldiers were breaking up a Karaköy *börek* shop because they didn't sell whisky. Laternas decorated with flowers and little paper Greek flags ground out the melodies of songs praising Venizelos [the Greek Prime Minister], whose picture adorned the walls of all the coffee houses.

The story goes that the labels on bottles of a locally produced whisky sold to British soldiers in Galata were misspelled to read 'Misky.'

Of the many colorful characters of this world, perhaps the best known was Bıçakçı Petri, or Petri the Knife, sometimes referred to as the Monster of Galata. Petri, a native of the Ionian island of

Lefkada, came to Galata in 1874, when he was 17 or 18, with the Kefalonian pirate Captain Lefteri. The night they arrived, he murdered Captain Lefteri for his money and valuables. (This was his second murder, he had already killed another Greek pirate captain during his travels). A few days later he murdered a local ruffian known as Kalopedi (from *Kalo Pedi*, Good Boy in Greek) in a waterfront tavern. For some years after this he worked as a stoker aboard an Austrian steamship, committing more murders in Trieste, Thessalonica, Constança and Beirut. When Petri returned to Galata in 1880 he was recognized by Lefteri's brother Lambo, who ambushed and killed him early one morning. Petri is thought to have committed at least seventeen murders, most of them with a knife to the heart. He always wore a type of backless, round-heeled, pointed-toed slipper, and he left a pair of these slippers at the scene of each murder.

Another well-known figure was Demirci Andon, or Andon the Safe-cracker. During the last years of the reign of Sultan Abdülhamid II, when he was still only 18 or 19, he became the best known safe-cracker of Galata, working, together with Jean the Frenchman and One-Armed Odyssea, in a gang led by Armenian Mike. Andon took over leadership of the gang after Mike was killed, but disappeared during the Allied occupation. There were also Burunsuz Eleni, or Noseless Eleni, a Galata brothel madam whose nose had been cut off by a jealous lover in her youth, and who was strangled to death in 1905 by a gardener who believed she was corrupting his son Pandeli, and Horoz Corci, or Georgie the Rooster, the son of a prominent Izmir family who was disinherited after a scandal and was reduced to selling dirty postcards and working as a pimp in Galata.

Yet another denizen of Galata in his youth was Sir Basil Zaharoff (originally Vassilis Zacharias), the notorious international arms trader and financier who became the chairman and director of Vickers-Armstrong munitions firm during World War I, and who is said to have fueled conflicts in order to sell weapons to both sides. As a boy, Basil worked as a 'guide' for tourists in Galata, helping them find forbidden pleasures beyond the bounds of normal prostitution. Later he became a *tulumbacı*, and also worked as a money-changer. There is an unverified accusation that he would pass counterfeit currency to tourists who would not notice until they were safely on a ship steaming away from the city.

The world of the Galata taverns went into decline during World War II, and had disappeared by the 1960s. In the 1970s there were still a handful of *koltuk meyhanes* in the streets off Necatibey Caddesi, some of which were rumored to sell wine laced with opium, but these too have since vanished, and the district is now occupied mostly by shops selling machine pumps and such.

After the building of the quay, the cafés and restaurants on the waterfront near Karaköy Meydanı were somewhat more respectable than the taverns of the Grand Rue de Galata, were places where Ottoman and Levantine businessmen felt comfortable drinking and chatting while waiting for the paddle-wheel ferry to Bakırköy. The writer Abdülhak Şinasi Hisar and the poet Ahmet Haşim were said to become so involved in their conversations here that they often missed their ferry. Today, these restaurants and cafés fill in the evening with office and shop workers meeting for tea or beer before catching the ferry to Kadıköy.

Until early in this century, the Karaköy Fish Market was located here, but the then mayor, Ali Müfit Gürtüna, decreed that it be moved to the other side of the square for fear that tourists might find it unsightly.

From the downstream side of Galata Köprüsü the shore road, Rıhtım Caddesi, leads past the large ferry-terminal and towards the docks along the lower Bosphorus.

The large and handsome building on the shore at the end of Rıhtım Caddesi is Çinili Rıhtım, built in the years 1912-14 as offices for those involved in the shipping industry. It is now the headquarters of the Turkish Maritime Lines, and its ground floor is the passenger terminal for cruise ships docking in Istanbul.

Above the passenger terminal is the famous Liman Lokantası, which first opened in 1947, and which from 1953 to 1968 was presided over by Silvian Fontana, who for years was Atatürk's chef. In 1968, Liman Lokantası was the scene of a sensational shootout. Gary Bouldin and Patricia Seeds of California aroused suspicion as they were driving through Beyoğlu (according to some accounts Interpol had alerted the Turkish police to their presence in the country) in a Volkswagen bug with Italian license plates, and were taken to an office of the Treasury Police in Çinili Rıhtım. When it was discovered that Mr. Bouldin was using a false passport, he drew two pistols, shot and killed a senior police officer, as well as two bystanders in the hallway, and escaped with Ms. Seeds to the restaurant, where a four hour gunfight ensued. Two FBI agents with sub-machine guns arrived, and Mr. Bouldin was eventually killed. Newspapers reported that there were 62 bullets in his body. An unfortunate waiter was also killed during the battle, and three more bystanders were wounded. Ms. Seeds survived, and was charged with involvement in a drug smuggling plot. The restaurant closed in the late 1970s, and reopened in 1997.

Turning left, we cross Kemankeş Caddesi to the beginning of Gümrük Sokak. There on the left we come to two contiguous mosques; the large one to the west is Kemankeş Mustafa Paşa Camii and the other is Yeraltı Camii.

The first of these mosques was built in 1624 by Kemankeş Kara Mustafa Pasha, grand vizier of Murad IV, who erected it on the site of the Latin church and hospital of St. Anthony, which had been demolished in 1606. Besides the mosque, the complex also included a *çeşme*, or fountain, which can be seen farther up Gümrük Sokak at the beginning of Galata Mumhanesi Caddesi. On the side street behind the mosque there is a handsome old *mektep*, or primary school. This is sometimes said to be part of the *külliye*, or complex, of Kemankeş Mustafa Paşa Camii, but it was actually founded in 1732 by İsmail Efendi, a high official in the Ottoman admiralty. The *mektep* is one of the finest extant examples of a one-room Ottoman schoolhouse.

Yeraltı Camii means 'the Underground Mosque,' so-called because the prayer room is below street level. The mosque is housed in the low, vaulted cellar or keep of a Byzantine tower or castle, which some scholars have identified with the ancient Castle of Galata, originally constructed by the emperor Tiberius II (r. 578-82). This was the place where one end of the famous chain that closed the mouth of the Golden Horn in times of siege was fastened; the other end was fixed somewhere along Sarayburnu, and the chain was kept afloat by buoys. When the Latin army of the Fourth Crusade first attacked Constantinople in April 1203 they captured the Castle of Galata, which allowed them to open the chain and sail into the Golden Horn. (Part of the chain is on exhibit in the Istanbul Through the Ages gallery at İstanbul Arkeoloji Müzesi.) The castle was connected by a curtain wall to the first enceinte of the walled town of Galata in 1348, then in 1446 the wall was extended along the lower Bosphorus to create the last walled extension of the Genoese town.

Descending into the mosque, you find yourself in a maze of dark, narrow passages between a forest of squat pillars supporting low vaults; six rows of nine each, or 54 in all. Toward the rear of the mosque are two large chambers separated from the rest of the interior by grills. These are the tombs of two sainted martyrs, Abu Sufyan and Amiri Wahibi, both of whom died in the first Arab siege of Constantinople in 674-8. The site of their graves was revealed in a dream to a Nakşibendi dervish one night in 1640. When Murad IV learned of this he had the graves opened and the saints reinterred in a shrine on the site; later, in 1757, the whole dungeon was converted into a mosque by Köse Mustafa Pasha, who was grand vizier under three sultans: Mahmud I, Osman III, and Mustafa III.

The sea-wall of the 1446 enceinte probably extended along a line between the present Galata Mumhanesi Caddesi and the parallel avenue just to its left. The first stretch of the latter avenue is Demir-ciler Sokak, which soon becomes Hoca Tahsin Sokak and then Ali Paşa Değirmeni Sokak. Some of the very short cross streets between the two avenues probably mark the sites of the gates through the sea-walls, which were demolished soon after the Turkish conquest.

The neighborhood just inside the sea-walls of the 1446 enceinte was inhabited almost entirely by Greeks up until late Ottoman times. This is evident from the fact that at least ten Greek Orthodox churches are known to have been in this quarter in the period 1453-1696. Nine of these ten churches are mentioned by Tryphon Karabeinikov, who in 1583 came to Istanbul as a representative of Czar Ivan IV, the Terrible.

Only three of the ten churches still exist (several having been destroyed during the widening of Kemeraltı Caddesi in the late 1950s), although none of them now belongs to the Greek Orthodox Church. These are the churches of Aziz Yahya [Haghios Ioannis Prodromos], Aya Nikola [Haghios Nikolaos], and Aziz Meryem

[Haghia Panaghia]. All three of these churches currently belong to the Turkish Orthodox Church, whose symbol is a cross with the Turkish star and crescent in the upper right-hand quadrant.

This sect was founded by one Pavlos Karahisaridis, who was born in the village of Akdağmadeni in the province of Yozgat in 1884 and took the name Efthemios when he was ordained as a Greek Orthodox priest by Metropolitan Nicholas of Kayseri in 1915 (later, after he was excommunicated by the Greek Orthodox Church, he changed his name to Zeki Erenerol). Karahisaridis was a member of a community of Turkish-speaking Greek Orthodox Christians from Anatolia, sometimes referred to as Karamanlı, who wrote Turkish using the Greek alphabet, and some of whom sided with Atatürk against the Greek army during the Turkish War of Liberation. Eftim, as Karahisaridis was now known, was, as leader of the General Congregation of the Anatolian Turkish Orthodox, among the religious leaders who recited prayers at the opening of the Turkish Parliament in Ankara on April 23, 1920, and for his subsequent efforts was praised by Atatürk for having 'rendered greater service to the nation than an entire army'. In 1922 he founded the Autocephalous Turkish Orthodox Church at the Zincirlidere Monastery in Kayseri, and gave himself the title of Patriarch Efthemios I. Henceforth he was known as Papa Eftim. At the time of the exchange of minority populations in 1923, the Turkish government moved Papa Eftim and some 250 of his followers from Anatolia to Galata and gave him title to the churches of Aziz Yahya and Aziz Meryem. The church of Aziz Yahya was returned to the Greek Orthodox Church in 1947, but this and the church of Aya Nikola were seized during the riots of September 1955. (Although Papa Eftim and his followers were exempted from the population exchange, three of his four sisters chose to go to Greece). The congregation was joined by a group of 80 young Christian Gagauz Turks from Romania, who were invited by the then Turkish ambassador to Bucharest, Hamdullah Suphi. From 1919 until his death, Papa Eftim engaged in a running battle with the Ecumenical Patriarchate, sometimes involving dissident elements of the Istanbul Greek community, the dispute in its early years reaching the League of Nations. After his death Eftim was succeeded by his eldest son, Dr. Turgut (Yorgo) Erenerol, who on his demise was succeeded by his brother Selçuk.

In 1966, 20 churches in the United States organized the Turkish Orthodox Church in America under Archbishop Civet Kristof, an African-American physician originally named Christopher M. Cragg. This organization disappeared in the early 1980s.

In 2008 Papa Eftim's grand daughter (and sister of Papa Eftim IV) Sevgi Erenerol was arrested for involvement with an alleged murky underground Turkish nationalist organization called Ergenekon. It was also alleged that the Patriarchate served as the headquarters for the organization. Sevgi Erenerol is known for her involvement in Turkish nationalist politics, and once ran for Parliament as a candidate for the Nationalist Movement Party (MHP).

Although the church is reputed to have amassed enormous wealth, the congregation dwindled steadily over the years, and according to most observers there are currently no members outside the Erenerol family. Since the 1960s the church of Aziz Yahya has been leased to and used by the Assyrian Church of the East.

According to the records of the Greek Orthodox Patriarchate and the Greek Embassy, the Greek community of Galata consisted of 1,200 families at the end of the nineteenth century, and was divided into four administrative sub-districts; Kale Kapısı, inhabited mostly by Greeks from the Morea and Kefalonia; Mumhane, by Karamanlı Greeks from Cappadocia, and the Beyazıd and Voyvoda districts by Greeks from the island of Chios. The 'Chiotis' constituted the majority in this community, and always maintained strong ties with Chios. The first migrants from Chios arrived shortly after the Turkish conquest to work in the *tersane* and on the ships that were built there, and their number was augmented by two large waves, the first following the Rape of Chios in 1822 and the second following the earthquake that devastated Chios in 1880. The Greek population of Galata was estimated at 4,200 at the time of the riots of September 1955, but scarcely exists today. During its heyday in the nineteenth century it boasted dozens of cultural, musical, dramatic, educational, and charitable societies, a hospital, a Red Cross clinic and two schools.

In the years following World War I, there was considerable tension in this community, as in Greece itself, between the Venizelists, who were strongly nationalist and republican and dreamed of a Greater

Greece, and the anti-Venizelist coalition, an unlikely coalition of monarchists, Marxists, progressive liberals, conservative democrats and 'free-thinking radicals', who favored withdrawal of the Greek army from Anatolia and negotiation with Ankara. While the majority of the Greeks of Istanbul supported Venizelos, there was a strong anti-Venizelist element, particularly in Galata, and particularly in the Karamanlı community. This anti-Venizelist sentiment gained strength after the collapse and retreat of the Greek army in Anatolia, when many local Greeks, recognizing the likelihood that they would soon once again be living under Turkish rule, felt it urgent to reach rapprochement with the new government in Ankara.

The rift between the controversial and staunchly Venizelist Patriarch Meletios IV and the Greek community of Galata deepened when one of their leaders, Damianos Damianidis, was removed from his position of church trustee on what they insisted were trumped-up charges of embezzlement. In May of 1923 they began holding secret meetings in the church of Aziz Meryem to plot the removal of Meletios, whose policies they felt would have disastrous consequences for them. After receiving the support of the director of the Galata School Board, they made contact, through a Turkish police chief by the name of Vehip Bey, with the government in Ankara and with Papa Eftim, and reached agreements with both.

On June 1st 1923, a large crowd of Galata Greeks, together with Papa Eftim and his supporters, marched on the patriarchate with the aim of seizing Meletios and handing him over to the Turkish police for deportation. The Turkish police guarding the patriarchate allowed the crowd to pass, but a detachment of French military police, one of the few Allied units still remaining in the city, arrived in time to disperse the crowd before they seized the patriarch. Three months later, Patriarch Meletios resigned and left his post, ostensibly for reasons of ill health. He was later appointed Bishop of Alexandria. In October of the same year, Papa Eftim led another crowd to the patriarchate, seeking to oust several bishops, but this time was turned back by the Turkish police.

The church of Aziz Yahya (St. John the Baptist) is just off Necatibey Caddesi, the next street beyond Hoca Tahsin Sokak, Vekilharç Sokak. The first reference to the church is by Tryphon

Karabeinikov in 1583. The church burned down in 1696 and was rebuilt three years later by wealthy merchants from Chios, after which it was known as 'St. John of the Chiots.' The church was again destroyed by fire in 1731, and rebuilt, only to be burned yet again in 1771. A rebuilding in 1774 resulted in the church that we see today. The elaborate iconostasis dates from this reconstruction, though a number of the icons date from earlier times, the most notable being the silver-plated icon of St. John the Baptist, a late-seventeenth-century work brought by the Chiots from a church on Antigone [Burgaz Adası], one of the Princes' Isles in the Sea of Marmara. The *ayazma*, or sacred well, in the narthex dates from 1867 and is dedicated to St. Anthony. In the forecourt of the church are the graves of a number of prominent Chiotis, the most notable being Konstantinos Argenti (1822-62) and several members of the famous Mavrokordatos family, the earliest monument that of Demetrios Louka Mavrokordatos (1796-1851).

The church of Aya Nikola [St. Nicholas] is at Hoca Tahsin Sokak and Galata Mumhanesi Caddesi. There is a tradition that this too was Byzantine in foundation, though the earliest reference to the church is in Tryphon's list of 1583. It was rebuilt after fires in 1660 and 1695, taking on its present for, after a complete rebuilding early in the nineteenth century. The silver-plated icon of St. Nicholas on the iconostasis was dedicated by the ship owners of Galata. One of the ornaments in the church is a gold-inlaid model of a galley under full sail, dedicated by the captains and sailors of Galata to their patron saint, Haghios Nikolaos.

The church of Aziz Meryem is at Ali Paşa Değirmeni Sokak. It is dedicated to the *Koimesis tis Theotokou*, the Dormition of the Virgin. The church is popularly known as Panaghia Kafatiane, our Lady of Kaffa, because it was founded by Greeks from Kaffa in the Crimea. According to tradition, the first church on this site dated from the Byzantine period, but was in ruins by the time of the Turkish conquest. A new church was built on the site in 1462 or 1475 by the Greek refugees from the Crimea. It too is mentioned in Tryphon's list of 1583. The present edifice dates from a rebuilding three years after a fire in 1731, and since 1924 it has been the patriarchal seat of the Turkish Orthodox Church. Its most treasured possession is an icon of the Hodegetria known as the Black Virgin, dating from the late Byzantine era, which was brought from Kaffa in 1475. On the wall next to the side door in the narthex there is a memorial plaque with the names of the furriers, timber merchants and goldsmiths who contributed to the restoration of the church after the fire of 1731. What remains of the foundations of the original Byzantine structure is accessible from the central aisle of the church.

There are also four Russian Orthodox chapels in this neighborhood, all of them on the top floor of buildings, noticeable by their tiny blue-domed cupolas on high drums. These chapels were founded by the czars in the nineteenth century for the use of Russian pilgrims to the Holy Land. The chapel of Aya Andrea [St. Andrew] is on Galata Mumhanesi Caddesi; Aya Pantaleymon [St. Panteleimon] is at Hoca Tahsin Sokak; Aya İlya [St. Prophet Elias] is on Hoca Tahsin Sokak; and Aya Triada [the Holy Trinity] is on Galata Mumhanesi Caddesi. The walls and ceiling of Aya Andrea are decorated with portraits of saints done in the late nineteenth century by Russian icon-painters from monasteries on Mt. Athos.

The oldest mosque in the neighborhood is Sultan II. Bayezid Mescidi, which is near the far end of Necatibey Caddesi. As its name suggests, this small mosque was founded during the reign of Bayezid II (r. 1481-1512), son and successor of Mehmed II, the Conqueror. The mosque was rebuilt in the nineteenth century and now has no architectural interest.

At their far end all of the avenues of this neighborhood converge at Tophane, where the land walls of Genoese Galata joined the sea-walls along the Bosphorus. Here we come to Kemeraltı Caddesi, the main highway from Galata Köprüsü.

Off to the right, on the near side of Necatibey Caddesi just beyond the multiple intersection, we see Kılıç Ali Paşa Camii, the most impressive mosque on the European shore of the Bosphorus. The mosque was built by Sinan in 1580 for Kılıç Ali Pasha, one of the great admirals in Ottoman history. Born in Calabria of Italian parents, he was captured in his youth by Algerian pirates and spent 14 years as a galley slave. After regaining his freedom he entered Süleyman's service as a buccaneer, becoming a Muslim and changing his name to Uluç Ali. He distinguished himself in several naval engagements, and as a reward for this he was made an admiral and was also given the post of Governor of Algiers. He was one of the few officers to serve with distinction at the disastrous Ottoman defeat at the battle of Lepanto in 1571. As a result of this Selim II appointed him *Kaptan Pasha*, the chief of command of the entire Ottoman navy, and renamed him Kılıç Ali, or Ali the Sword.

While serving as Governor of Algiers Kılıç Ali Pasha came into contact with Miguel Cervantes, who had been enslaved there after his capture at the battle of Lepanto. Five years after being brought to Algiers Cervantes managed to escape, but he was recaptured and brought before Kılıç Ali Pasha. Ali Pasha was apparently impressed with Cervantes, for he released him from captivity and gave him enough money to return to Spain. Cervantes paid tribute to the kindness of Ali Pasha in Chapter 32 of *Don Quixote*, where 'The captive relates his life and adventures'.

The climax of Ali Pasha's career came in 1573, when he recaptured Tunis from Don Juan of Austria. Seven years later he retired to Istanbul, when he decided to build his mosque complex. When Ali Pasha asked permission from Murad III to build his mosque, so the story goes, the Sultan sarcastically suggested that he construct it on the sea, since that was the Kaptan Pasha's domain. Ali Pasha proceeded to do just that, and commissioned Sinan to build him a mosque on land he had filled-in along the shore of the Bosphorus in Tophane.

Although Sinan had been deeply impressed and inspired by Haghia Sophia, he had always avoided any kind of direct imitation of that edifice. Now in his old age –he was nearly ninety when he built the mosque– he designed a near replica of the Great Church. It is one of his least successful buildings, perhaps because the greatly reduced proportions make the building seem heavy and squat.

Sinan's main departures from the plan of Haghia Sophia are these: the provision of only two columns instead of four between each of the piers to the north and south, and the suppression of the exedrae at the east and west ends. Both of these departures seem to have been dictated by the reduced scale; had the original disposition been retained the building would certainly have been even heavier and darker. Nevertheless, the absence of the exedrae deprives the mosque of what in Haghia Sophia is one of its main beauties. The *mihrab* is in a square projecting apse, where there are some Iznik tiles of the best period. At the west there is a kind of pseudo-narthex of five cross-vaulted bays separated from the prayer area by four rectangular pillars.

The *külliye* of Kılıç Ali Paşa Camii is extensive, including a *medrese*, a *hamam*, and the *türbe*, or tomb, of the founder, who died in 1587. (The nineteenth-century historian Joseph von Hammer thus describes Ali Pasha's death: 'Although ninety years of age, he had not been able to renounce the pleasures of the harem, and he died in the arms of a concubine.') The *türbe* is in the pretty graveyard behind the mosque; it is a plain but elegant octagonal building with alternately one or two windows in each façade, in two tiers. The *medrese*, opposite the southeast corner of the mosque, is almost square; like the mosque itself it is a little squat and shut in. This structure is probably not by Sinan, since it does not appear in *Tezkiretü'l Ebniye*, the list of his works; it is now used as a clinic.

Across the side street north of Kılıç Ali Paşa Camii is one of the most famous of the baroque street-fountains in the city, Tophane Çeşmesi. Built in 1732 by Mahmud I, it has marble walls completely covered with floral designs and arabesques carved in low relief,

Tophane Çeşmesi [Tophane Fountain].

which were originally painted and gilded. Its charming domed and widely overhanging roof was lacking for many years but has recently been restored.

Directly across the avenue from Kılıç Ali Paşa Camii is a little mosque known as Karabaş Mescidi. The mosque was founded in 1530 by Karabaş Mustafa Ağa, who served as Chief Black Eunuch during the reign of Süleyman the Magnificent.

The building was restored in 1962 and is once again in use.

Across the side street from Karabaş Mescidi is the building from which the whole district takes its name; this is Tophane, the Cannon House, which was once the principal military foundry in the Ottoman Empire.

The original Ottoman foundry was built on this site by Mehmed II soon after the conquest. It was extended and improved by Bayezid II, but then demolished by Süleyman the Magnificent, who replaced it with a larger and more modern establishment in preparation for his campaigns of conquest. Süleyman's foundry has long since disappeared; the present structure was built by Selim III in 1803, doubtless in connection with his own attempt to reform and modernise the Ottoman army.

The foundry is a large rectangular building of brick and stone, with eight great domes supported by three lofty piers. The building has been restored in recent years and is now open to the public as a museum and exhibition hall.

Beyond the foundry itself, along the height overlooking the street, we see a series of ruined substructures, walls and domes; these once formed part of the general complex of Tophane, which included extensive barracks for the artillerymen. Across the street there is a small kiosk in the *Empire* style that was also part of the Tophane complex; this was built by Abdülaziz as a pavilion from which he could review parades of his artillery troops. Evliyâ Çelebi describes the artillerymen who in his time were stationed in these barracks:

> The barracks of the artillerymen were, like the foundry, built by Mehmet II, Beyazıt II and Süleyman I.... Inside are rooms inhabited by colonels, captains, veterans, cooks and artillerymen; they dress like Janissaries in leather gowns and wear knives with silver chains. They are the bravest troops, and in twenty-two battles, wherein I

was present, I saw no braver, because, the enemy, pointing their guns on ours, swept away forty or fifty gunners at a discharge, they were as busy with their guns as ants.

Beyond the kiosk is Nusretiye Camii, the Mosque of Victory. This was built between 1822 and 1826 by Mahmud II; it was completed just after the Sultan's extermination of the janissaries in 1826, and its name commemorates that event. The architect was Kirkor Balyan, the founder of a family of Armenian architects who served the sultans through most of the nineteenth century and who built many of the mosques and palaces that you see today along the shores of the Bosphorus. Kirkor Balyan had studied in Paris and his mosque shows a curious blend of baroque and *Empire* motifs, highly un-Turkish, but not without charm. In building the mosque he abandoned the traditional arrangement of a monumental courtyard and substituted an elaborate series of palace-like apartments in two stories; these form the western façade of the building, a feature which became a characteristic of all the Balyan mosques.

The new museum of modern art, Istanbul Modern, is housed in a reconverted customs warehouse between Nusretiye Camii and the shore of the Bosphorus. The founders of the museum, which opened in 2005, say in their statement of purpose that 'as a living museum Istanbul Modern aims to set the art agenda in Turkey and

Nusretiye Camii [Nusretiye Mosque] and Tophane Müşirliği [Tophane Marshalcy]. The latter has not survived.

reach out to a broad range of the public through an educational, engaging, dynamic, and diverse environment, and to introduce Turkish artists to the international art world.'

The entrance ramp leads to the uppermost of the two floors, where the permanent collection is exhibited, while temporary exhibits are on the lower floor. The upper floor also has a museum shop, café, conference room and educational hall, while on the lower floor there is a cinema and auditorium, library, video room, and photographic gallery. The renowned Turkish artists represented in the permanent collection include Osman Hamdi Bey, Bedri Rahmi Eyüboğlu, Fahreinisa Zeid, Aliye Berger-Boronai, and the photographer Ara Güler.

Evliyâ Çelebi gives a description of Tophane and the adjacent districts farther up the hill as they were in his time, the mid-seventeenth century:

> The greatest number of inhabitants of Tophane are merchants, sailors and merchantmen, flocking together from the shores of the Black Sea ... and a great number of Georgians and Abaza. The Abaza, to keep their children from growing up like the boys of Constantinople, send those of one or two years with their nurse on board ship and brought up there until they are fifteen years old, when they are brought back to Constantinople.... In proportion to the size of Tophane it has but few fountains and marketplaces, but the houses are all provided with wells. The best houses are those of Cihangir and Ayas Pasha, they rise above one another and are surrounded by gardens; the roads are wide, and the mosques are near one another, for the people are pious. The great men wear splendid costumes, and the merchants dress according to their revenue. The women wear the cloak called ferajeh; with a turban on their head and a veil before their faces, and are thus well dressed; they also are very amiable.

We now make our way back along the inner side of the coastal highway to Galata. Just beyond the multiple intersection at Tophane we cross Lüleci Hendek Sokak. This takes its name from the deep moat that was dug outside the land walls of Genoese Galata. On the far side of the street we see a massive fragment of the medieval fortifications that still survives in the structure of the teahouse at the street corner. This was part of a tower that formed the junction between the walls running along the Bosphorus and those coming down from the heights above.

As we cross the next side street, we see on the opposite side of Kemeraltı Caddesi a church built of gleaming white stone. This is Ermeni Surp Krikor Lusavoriç Kilisesi [the Armenian Gregorian church of Surp Krikor Lusavoriç, St. Gregory the Illuminator], erected in 1960 after the previous church near the site had been demolished to widen the avenue. The original church was erected in 1431 on land purchased from the Genoese of Galata. The new church was designed by Bedros Zobyan as a replica of the famous church of St. Gregory at Echmiadzin in Armenia, a seventh-century structure which is one of the masterpieces of medieval Armenian architecture.

Two blocks farther along Kemeraltı Caddesi we come a church with a tall bell tower. This is Saint Benoît Latin Katolik Kilisesi [the Roman Catholic church of Saint Benoît, St. Benedict], founded by the Benedictines in 1427; later it became the royal chapel of the French ambassadors to the Ottoman Empire, several of whom are buried here. After being in the hands of the Jesuits for several centuries, it was given, on the temporary dissolution of that order in 1773, to the Lazarists, to whom it still belongs. In 1804 they established a school next to the church; this is still in operation and continues to be one of the best foreign lycées in the in the city. Of the original fifteenth-century church, only the tower remains, with the rest of the building dating from two later reconstructions: the nave and south aisle in 1732, and the north aisle in 1871.

The funerary inscriptions in the church include memorials to several French ambassadors, along with one to Count Ferenc Rakoczy (1676-1735), a Hungarian nobleman who tried to free Transylvania from Austrian rule. Rakoczy accepted an offer from Sultan Ahmed III (r. 1703-30) to raise an army in Turkey to fight against the Austrians. But the plan never materialized, and in 1735 Rakoczy died in exile at Rodosto [Tekirdağ] on the Sea of Marmara, after which his remains were brought here for burial.

Continuing along Kemeraltı Caddesi, on the next block we come to a large church with a belfry at its far end. This is Ermeni Surp Hisus Pırgiç Kilisesi [the Armenian Catholic church of Surp Hisus Pırgiç, Christ the Savior] built in 1834. It was the first church of the

Armenian Catholics in Istanbul; its most notable work of religious art is a sacred icon of the Virgin credited with stopping a plague.

We now retrace our steps to the previous corner, where we turn left on Alageyik Sokak, the side street that leads uphill between Surp Hisus Pırgiç and Saint Benoît. At the end of the block we come to the shell of an abandoned nineteenth-century synagogue. Just beyond the synagogue there was until recently an area occupied exclusively by brothels. The poet Murat Nemet Nejat, a Turkish Jew, has written a moving poem about Kuledibi, describing how those who worked in the brothels graciously offered glasses of water to the Jews who passed on their way from the synagogue after completing a day of fasting.

Alageyik Sokak veers to the left and intersects Zürafa Sokak. Looking to the left at the intersection, we see Aşkenaz Sinagogu [the Ashkenazi Synagogue]. This was founded in 1901 by Ashkenazi Jews from Russia who had moved to Istanbul, its inauguration ceremony presided over by the Austrian ambassador, Baron de Calice. The original synagogue was built of wood, subsequently replaced by the present stone and masonry structure, whose façade bears the inscription 'German-Israelite'.

Zürafa Sokak was for centuries the center of the world of the Galata brothels. There seem to have been brothels in this area since Galata became a major port, but in 1855, the newly formed Beyoğlu Municipal Council, as part of their general effort to establish order, made a decision to control prostitution and its associated ills by registering brothels and confining them to specific areas. The area set aside for brothels in Galata included Zürafa, Beyzade, Şerbethane, Karaoğlan, Badem, Şeftali, Oğlak and Bülbül streets, and both the brothels and their inmates were subject to regular inspection. In 1884, the police chief of Galata, Süleyman Efendi, further decreed that the windows of all brothels be covered with lattice screens, so that the honor of passersby would not be offended by the sight of prostitutes leaning out of windows. Unregistered brothels and casual prostitution continued to exist in the surrounding area, varying in its extent from one period to another according to prosperity, demographics and politics, and to the attitude and efficiency of the local police, until the 1990s.

Of the three official brothel districts of Beyoğlu, that of Galata seems to have been ranked in the middle in terms of its attractiveness to customers. It was considered less attractive than Abanoz Sokak, but not quite as bad as Ziba Sokak.

Describing this area at the end of the nineteenth century, Reşad Ekrem Koçu writes that most of the women who worked here had come here after having squandered their beauty and freshness in Beyoğlu, and that the customers were shiftless and grimy. He goes on to say that the best known brothels at this time were Pissy Despoina's house, Grey-eyed Eleni's house, Mama Margoro's house, Mama Froso's house, and Gypsy Despoina's house, and that the prostitutes had nicknames like Drunken Ağavni, Vasiliki the Dove, Rusty Eudoxia and Triandafila the Jaguar. Another infamous brothel owner of the time was Madame Eudoxia, whose career ended in 1899 when she was arrested for the murder of her lover Manoli.

According to the 1922 *Pathfinder Survey of Constantinople*, there were 77 registered brothels in Galata at this time. Of these, 28 were owned by Greeks, 6 by Armenians, 42 by Jews and 1 by a Hungarian. The nationalities of the 662 prostitutes working there were given as 335 Greeks (28 of whom were Greek citizens and 307 of whom were Ottoman subjects), 169 Russians, 68 Jews, 47 Armenians, 19 Austrians, 12 Romanians, 4 Italians, 2 Bulgarians, 2 Serbians, 1 American, 1 French, 1 German and 1 described as 'African.' It is noted that 'probably the number of Russians is greater than indicated.' The registered prostitutes were required to be over 18 (it is said that a number of underage girls were working in the unregistered brothels), and very few were over 25. The prices ranged from 15 kuruş in the cheaper establishments to 1 lira in the 'better' houses (as compared to 5 liras at the Yankee House on what is now Acara Sokak near Galatasaray). The prostitutes kept half of the fee and were given room and board.

Survey goes on to say: 'In Galata, the best houses are in Şerbethane Sokak. Those on the other streets might rightly be termed shacks. There is an out-of-bounds for British, French and Italian soldiers and sailors in this district. Even if the American sailors are allowed to visit here, they are seldom or never seen in this district.'

The brothels were required to close at 10 p.m., and were fined for staying open even a few minutes late. This was a source of complaint from the brothel owners, who claimed that business only started to pick up at that hour.

Describing the scene in those years, Özdemir Arkan writes of 'hundreds of naked women warming themselves around braziers, and bringing their customers to what were more like cages than rooms.'

Beyzade, Şerbethane and Şeftali streets were demolished during the widening of Karaköy Meydanı and Kemeraltı Caddesi in the years 1956-8. By the late 1960s, the majority of prostitutes working in this district were Turkish, and the average age was 35.

In the 1990s, most of these brothels were owned by the Armenian real-estate tycoon Matild Manukyan, who for five consecutive years was the single highest tax-payer in Turkey. In 1995 alone she paid $616,300 to the tax office, for which she was presented with an award. Manukyan was once arrested on suspicion of running unregistered brothels staffed by underage girls, but she was cleared of these charges. In 1995 she was shot in the leg in an attack she claimed was aimed at her bodyguard, who was not injured. After Matild Manukyan died in February 2001, her son closed down all of the brothels she had owned and refused to sell them.

Of the 18 brothels that remained open, six were owned by Yaşar Ceyhan Muniz, and 12 were owned by Neriman Akarsu, who went by the nickname Sümbül [Hyacinth], and who also had the distinction of being Turkey's highest tax-payer for several years in the 1980s. When she died in September 2006 at the age of 82, all of the brothels were closed so that those who worked in them could attend her funeral, at which a number of well-known personalities were also said to have been present.

There were 120 women working in these 18 brothels, and they entertained an estimated 5 to 7 thousand visitors a day. The brothels were closed on Sundays. On the May 15, 2009, the Greater Istanbul Assembly voted to close this last official brothel district of Beyoğlu, and it was finally closed on the May 20, 2010.

A short way farther along Alageyik Sokak we come to Yüksek Kaldırım, the High Cobbled Street, (known to the local Greeks as *Ta Skalakia* and to the Genoese as *Strada Selciata a picco*) which

Yüksek Kaldırım.

has been for many centuries the main street leading up from the Golden Horn past the Galata Tower to the heights of Pera.

This was originally a step street, leading uphill just outside the line of walls separating the enceinte of 1446 from those of 1303 and 1348. One of the gateways through the walls was known in Turkish as Horoz Kapı, the Gate of the Rooster, whose site is now Horoz Sokak, the very short side street on the other side of Yüksek Kaldırım just below Alageyik Sokak. Yüksek Kaldırım continued to be a step street until the late 1950s, when it was paved in the interests of the automobile, ending an age in the history of Galata.

In the last half of the 19th century Yüksek Kaldırım was home to furniture and clothing stores, several small and short-lived schools and to a number of hotels and boarding houses for seamen, traders and travelers of modest means. Much the street was destroyed by fire in 1897. Since the middle of the twentieth century it has been dominated by sign and plaque makers, with the appearance in more recent years of shops selling satellite antennae.

We now descend Yüksek Kaldırım to Karaköy Meydanı, where this stroll comes to an end.

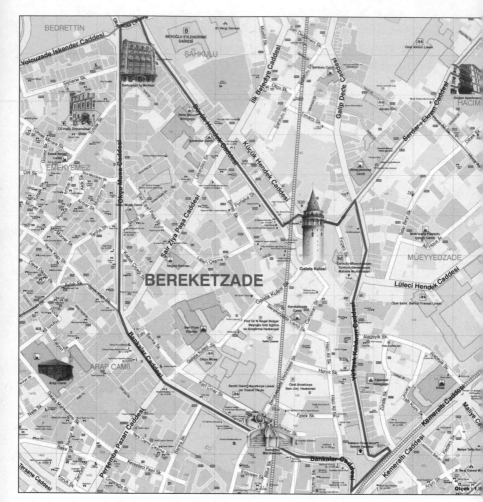

© *Beyoğlu Belediyesi Emlak ve İstimlak Müdürlüğü*

CHAPTER 4

From Karaköy To The Galata Tower

We begin this stroll where the last one ended, at the bottom of Yüksek Kaldırım, where it joins Kemeraltı Caddesi and Karaköy Caddesi at the inner end of Karaköy Meydanı. On the other side of Kemeraltı Caddesi we see the most prominent building at this end of the square. This is Karaköy Palas, a handsome commercial building designed by the Italian architect Giulio Mongheri and completed in 1920.

We now make our way around to the right to Bankalar Caddesi, originally known as Voyvoda Caddesi, the principal business street of Galata, whose course takes it just inside what was once the southern wall of the 1348 enceinte. According to Edhem Eldem, in his book about Bankalar-Voyvoda Caddesi, the avenue took its present name, which means 'Banks Street,' around 1910 from the large number of banks that flanked its course, though, as he points out: 'Of course there were never merely banks on Bank Street. There were also other major companies, including a large number of insurance companies. But "Insurance Street" would not have sounded as right as Banks Street, I suppose. Nor "Architects Street" or "Lawyers Street" for that matter.'

Yaşar Danacıoğlu, a former police chief who worked in the pickpocket squad from 1955 to 1961, says that the trams that used to run up Bankalar Caddesi were a prime target for pickpockets because many of the passengers were coming from banks and were loaded with cash. The pickpockets usually worked in pairs, one slipping his fingers into pockets and the other hiding him from view as he did so. The more daring pickpockets used razor blades to slit the inner pockets of jackets. They would hop off the tram and escape into the back streets up towards the Galata Tower. Then the first order of business was to take the cash and get rid of the wallet, because getting caught with a wallet meant certain conviction.

The most notorious and accomplished of these pickpockets were Şakir the Kurd and his son-in-law Ali Dalmış. Şakir used to tell the story of having stolen a particularly fat wallet only to find that it was filled with dog excrement. A note in the wallet read, 'Dear Pickpocket, the last time you stole my wallet you enjoyed spending (eating) my money. I hope you enjoy (eating) this even more.'

Bankalar Caddesi was also a favorite target for con-artists and safe-crackers. Danacıoğlu tells the story of a safe-cracker who was at work in one of the banks here on the day the Turkish Nationalist forces entered Istanbul. When he heard the troops marching up the avenue on their way to Taksim he leaned out the window to cheer them, and the bank guards noticed and apprehended him.

Our stroll up Bankalar Caddesi will be literally a review of the business enterprises of the late Ottoman Empire and the early Turkish Republic, much of which was concentrated on this avenue, the information based mostly on Edhem Eldem's study of the history of the individual buildings.

Minerva Han: This small but beautiful building, distinguished by the blue tiles on its rounded façade, was built in the years 1911-13 at the northwest corner of Yüksek Kaldırım and Bankalar Caddesi. It is believed to have been built by the Greek architect Basile Couremenos for the Bank of Athens, which occupied the building until the early 1920s. It was subsequently used in turn by Deutsche Orientbank, Yapı Kredi, Doğan Insurance Company, Aksigorta Insurance, and, most recently, Sabancı University.

İmar Bankası Binası: This building stands on an L-shaped plot which had its long side on Bankalar Caddesi and extended well up the stepped side street, Hacı Ali Sokak. Much of the site on Bankalar Caddesi was occupied by a ruined tower of the Genoese walls, which would have formed the southeastern corner of the enceinte of 1348. The tower was demolished in the 1880s when the tramway was laid down, revealing a cistern beneath it. Charles Goad's insurance map of 1905 shows that the side wall of the tower was still in place behind the present building, which was erected in the years 1890-5, and that a stretch of the Genoese wall itself ended along the rear of Macri Han, the contiguous building on Hacı Ali Sokak. The latter building, erected in the 1890s, is still standing and bears its original name. The present building on Bankalar

Caddesi takes its name from the İmar Bank, which has been in residence here for more than three decades. The previous owners included the Greek banker Stephanos Pezmazoglu, Banco di Roma, and the Chamber of Commerce of Constantinople.

Tütün Han: There were originally three buildings on this site in the 1870s all of them owned by Camondo Bank. The buildings were demolished in 1910 to make way for the present structure, inaugurated in 1911 as Union Han, taking its name from Union de Paris Insurance Company. The ground floor housed the offices of the Banco di Roma, followed by the National Bank of Turkey, and, in 1934 by the first Galata branch of Türkiye İş Bankası. Union Insurance Company itself moved into the building in the 1940s. The building took its present name in 1944 when it was acquired by the Tütün [Tobacco] Bank, and though it was subsequently bought by the Yaşar Bank and Batı Sigorta [Insurance] it is still called the Tütün Han.

Vakıflar Bankası Binası: This *han* was built in 1966 on the site of Kavafyan Han, one of the oldest buildings on the avenue, mentioned as early as 1868. Kavafyan Han housed a number of lawyers and commercial firms as well as Düyun-u Umumiye [the Stamp Bureau of the Ottoman Public Debt] and the German Post Office.

Ankara Han: Originally known as Lorando Han, this handsome building, distinguished by the four enormous columns of its neoclassical façade, was built in 1911-12. The building houses law firms, an insurance agency, and a transport company.

Jeneral Han: Built in 1904-5, it was originally known as Azaryan Han, after its original owner, Bedros Azaryan, president of the Istanbul Chamber of Commerce. The companies that have had their headquarters here include Bomonti-Nectar Brewery, Eskihisar Cement Factory, Banca Commercial Italiana, Banca di Roma, Steaua Romana, and, more recently Pamukbank [Cotton Bank] and Koçtuğ Shipping Company.

Bozkurt Han: It appears that this building, erected in the 1870s, originally belonged to Sultan Abdülaziz (r. 1861-76), and was known by his name up until 1903, when it came to be called Gümüşlü Han. It took its present name in 1930, when Bozkurt Insurance Company moved into the building from its original headquarters in Union Han across the avenue. Numerous lawyers, insurance companies and architects have had their offices here, along with larger corporations.

Sümerbank Binası: The building, dating from the 1880s, was originally used by Crédit Général Ottoman Bank until its liquidation in 1899, when it came to house Chemins de fer d'Anatolie [Anatolian Railways]. Beginning around 1910 the building was also used by Deutsche Bank. It took its present name in 1933 when it was acquired by Sümerbank, which continues to operate there today.

İş Bankası [İşbank] Binası: The building was erected by Osmanlı Sigorta Şirket-i Umumiyesi [the Ottoman General Insurance Company] in the years 1913-18. In 1953 it was acquired by İşbank, which is still in residence here.

Yeni Bahtiyar İş Merkezi: The original Bahtiyar Han is mentioned as early as 1874, when Camondo Han was housed here, remaining so long in residence that the building was also known as Camondo Han. The present building was erected no later than 1903-4, the only change since then being the addition of the upper two stories. Camondo Bank functioned here until the late 1920s. Other tenants included lawyers, insurance brokers, engineers and architects. The latter included Michel Nouridjian and his associate Edhem Bey, son of Osman Hamdi Bey, founder of the Imperial Museum, now known as İstanbul Arkeoloji Müzesi.

Assicurazioni Generali Han: This handsome neoclassical edifice was built in 1909 by Giulio Mongheri for the Assicurazioni Insurance Company. Other occupants of the building included the Bank of Salonika and the architect Giulio Mongheri himself.

Osmanlı Bankası [the Ottoman Bank] and Merkez Bankası Binaları: The Ottoman Bank was founded in 1856, but for the first quarter-century of its existence it was housed in Saint Pierre Han, which we will see later on this stroll. It remained there until the inauguration of its new building here in 1892.

In the early afternoon of August 26, 1896, twenty-six men and women of the Armenian Revolutionary Federation (Dashnak Party), armed with pistols, knives and bombs, seized the Ottoman Bank with the primary intention of bringing their grievances to the attention of the British and French governments (at that time most of the bank's employees were British and French). In the first stages of the seizure, the Albanian bank-guards engaged the

Dashnaks in a gun battle in which four of the Dashnaks were killed (including their leader Papken Siuni) and five were wounded (it is not known how many casualties there were among the bank guards.) Meanwhile, others of the Dashnaks began tossing bombs out of the upper windows, wounding several passersby and later killing and wounding a number of the soldiers who tried to storm the building.

The Dashnaks sent out one of the French employees with a message for the ambassadors of the Great Powers, who authorized the director of the bank, Sir Edgar Vincent (who had been in his office at the bank at the time of the seizure, but who managed to escape through a skylight) and the Chief Dragoman of the Russian Embassy, Maximov (who we will encounter again later in this book) to conduct negotiations. They first went to Yıldız Sarayı [Yıldız Palace] to speak to Sultan Abdülhamid II, who was about to give orders that the bank be bombarded. Upon being told that if he did so his palace would be shelled by Russian warships, he agreed to allow the Dashnaks safe passage out of the country. They then went to the bank to negotiate with the Dashnaks, and fourteen hours after the seizure began the Dashnaks were escorted to Sir Edgar's yacht, from which they were placed on a ship bound for Marseilles.

Edhem Eldem thus describes the subsequent history of the Ottoman Bank building:

> This building ... was used as the bank's head office until 1998. Today it is the bank's Karaköy office and hosts the Ottoman Bank Banking and Financial History Research and Documentary Center. The neighboring twin building of the Tobacco Regie Administration was the headquarters of the Regie until June of 1925, when all Regie property, including its head office, was seized by the government of the Republic of Turkey. The building was then transferred to the newly established State Tobacco Monopolies. It was purchased for the sum of 400,000 Turkish liras from the State Monopolies by the Central Bank of the Republic of Turkey in 1934, and has served as the Istanbul branch of the Central Bank ever since.

The building was recently restored by Mimarlar Tasarım, under the supervision of architect Han Tümertekin, and now houses SALT Galata, which includes exhibition space, an auditorium, open archives, a restaurant, a bookstore and the Ottoman Bank Museum Permanent Collection, with displays of historical share issues, banknotes and bonds issued during the years when the Ottoman Bank was most active.

Has Han: This handsome neoclassical building is one of the few structures along the avenue that has not changed in appearance since it was first erected, probably in the 1870s. During the years 1901-5 it served as the Ottoman Post Office.

Just beyond the Has Han we see the so-called Kamondo Merdivenleri [Kamondo Steps]. This is a remarkable double stairway whose curving steps intersect twice on their sinuous way down from the street above, Kart Çınar Sokak, to Bankalar Caddesi. The architect is unknown, but it is believed that the stairway was built in the 1880s by the Camondo family.

Demirbank Binası: This distinguished neo-classical edifice, which stands to the left of Kamondo Merdivenleri, was built in the 1880s by the French architect Alexandre Vallaury for the Ottoman Exchange and Stocks Company [Société Ottomane de Change et de Valeurs], which was housed here until the firm's liquidation in 1901-3. The building then became the British Consulate, which was housed here from 1903 until well into the 1940s. It was purchased in 1959 by Demirbank, which still has its Karaköy branch office here.

Voyvoda Han: This modest neo-classical building, erected in 1903-4, has preserved its original architectural form unchanged since its erection. Among the enterprises that it housed was the British Post Office, as evidenced by the sign on the second floor bearing the British coat-of-arms and the insignia ER, for Edward Rex, i. e., King Edward VII (r. 1901-10).

Originally known as the Narlıyan Han, this neoclassical edifice was probably built in 1882. Its original occupant was the Water Company of Constantinople [Compagnie des Eaux de Constantinople]. In 1911 it became the main branch of the Russian Bank for Foreign Trade, after which it housed in turn the offices of the State Tobacco Monopoly, the State Monopolies, Tutum [Thrift] Bank, the Association of Controllers and Auditors, and various services of the Ministry of Finance. Among the private enterprises housed here was the office and archives of the famous photographers Abdullah Frères.

Şark Han: The first masonry building on this plot was the head office of Dersaadet Tramvay Şirketi [Streetcar Company of Constantinople], with the ground floor used as stable for the horses used to pull the trams. This was torn down and the present building erected in 1918, probably by the Armenian architect Michel Nouridjian. The ground floor of the new building was used by the National Credit Bank, founded in 1917, and, in the 1920s, by the Istanbul Commodity Exchange. The building was completely renovated in 1924, and within the next two years it was acquired by Şark [Orient] Insurance Company, founded in 1923 by the Riunione Adriatica di Sicurta. Şark Insurance Company used the building until 1976 and sold it in 1997, nevertheless it is still known as the Şark Han.

Akbank Binası: The history of this building, originally known as Baltazzi Han and later as Agopyan Han, goes back to at least 1868, when it is mentioned for the first time. The building was first modified in 1904, when the two upper stories were added. It was further modified in the decade prior to World War II, when, as Edhem Eldem writes: 'Its façade was redone in the characteristic Italian/German style of that time which has been preserved to our own day.' The *han* was used by Deutsche Orientbank until World War I. It took its present name in 1978 when it was acquired by Akbank.

Hidayet Han: This han, erected in the late 1970s at the corner of Ziya Paşa Sokak, stands on the site of an early twentieth-century building that on its ground floor housed a popular coffee-shop belonging to one Georges Douvardjioglu (Yorgo Duvarcıoğlu).

Vefai Han: This five-storied building is dated to 1900-1, its neoclassical façade is articulated by Corinthian pilaster that rise through the second and third stories, surmounted by Ionic pilasters on the fourth storey.

Burla Binası: The building was probably erected in 1883, the date of foundation of the Economic Cooperative Company, its first owner, which ran one of the most famous department stores in the city. The *han* takes its present name from Burla Biraderler (Burla Brothers), importers of electrical equipment since 1911, who acquired the business in the late 1930s and still do business there. Burla Biraderler have never received permission to elevate their building to the height of the adjacent buildings, so that it preserves its original structure other than a remodeling of its façade in the 1970s.

Bereket Han: The façade of Bereket Han was built in the 1880, when the laying of the tramway along Voyvoda Caddesi required the demolition of the front half of the original structure, Francini Han. Professor Semavi Eyice has shown that Francini Han was the Genoese Podestat, also known as Palazzo Communale. During late Byzantine times this was the headquarters of the Podesta, the official appointed yearly by Genoa to govern the city state of Galata. The original Podestat would have been erected soon after 1261, when the Genoese and Byzantines signed the Treaty of Nymphaion giving Genoa a trading monopoly in the empire and autonomy in Galata. The present Podestat, which survives as the rear half of the building, was erected in 1316, making it the oldest extant structure by far in Galata.

Pamukbank Binası: This building, used as a Pamukbank branch since 1991, was erected in the 1980s on the site of Laziridi Han, later known as Güzin Han. The han has housed a series of *muhallebi* shops, the earliest of which, owned by a certain Hüseyin Efendi, is mentioned as early as 1901, the latest being one of the Özsüt chain.

Mevag Binası: The first building on this site was Uzun [Long] Han, erected ca. 1899-1900 as an apartment house, most of whose tenants worked in the companies along Voyvoda Caddesi, as the avenue was then called. By 1911 the building changed character, housing offices rather than tenants. Among the establishments located here were the Chancery of the Latin Community, and two newspapers, *Moniteur Oriental* (in French) and *Tachydromos* (in Greek). From the 1930s onwards the building housed mostly companies dealing in electrical equipment.

Anadolu Finans Binası: Built in the early 1970s by Anadolu Finance Company, this building stands on the site of a narrow two-storied building that originally, in the 1890s, housed a pharmacy and a bakery, both owned by Greeks.

Yakup İş Merkezi: This building, erected in the early 1980s, replaced a two-storied stone and brick structure dating from the 1890s. All of the original tenants were Greek establishments, the most notable being a wine and *mastika* (*rakı* flavored with mastic) shop.

Ankara Sigorta Han: Previously known as Adalet Han, this was built in 1906-7 as a four-storey building, to which two additional floors were subsequently added. The building that previously stood on this site, Hamdi Paşa Han, may have dated back to the eighteenth century, as evidenced by photographs showing its resemblance to hans of that date that still stand on Perşembe Pazarı Caddesi.

Güven Sigorta: The present building was erected in the years 1975-7 on the site of Bağdat Han, which housed the offices of several railway companies, as well as the famous French-language newspaper *Journal d'Orient*.

Hezaren Han: This elegant art nouveau edifice was built in 1902 by the architect Alexandre Vallaury for the Ottoman Bank. The following year the bank rented the first three stories of the building to the Société du Tombac and another to the Greek banker E. Eugenides. Three years later the bank sold the building to Hamdi Bey, the governor of Pera. The appearance of the *han* has remained unchanged throughout its history.

Nazlı Han: This neoclassical building was erected in 1904, and in 1910 it became the head office of the Société Générale d'Assurances Ottomane, the first Ottoman Insurance Company. One of those who worked in the *han* was Mahmut Baler (1896-1987), an insurance broker who later became a famous journalist and story-teller under the nickname of *Bal*, or 'Honey,' because of the sweetness of the tales he told.

Emlak Bankası Binası: This was erected on the site of Keçecizade Apartmanı [Ketchedjizade Apartment], built in the 1890s by a member of the family of Keçecizade Fuad Pasha (1815-69). This building stood the very end of the oldest section of Voyvoda Caddesi.

Hüsnü Gök Han: Originally known as Asaf Han, this building was erected in the 1890s. The original owner was probably Asaf Pasha, commander of the Fourth Army, who used it as his residence. It took its present name in the 1950s, by which time it was an apartment building. It is presently occupied by shops and firms selling electrical equipment.

We now leave Bankalar Caddesi and take Eski Banka Sokak, a

very short L-shaped lane that turns in behind Hezaren Han. The street takes its name from the huge old building on its left side, just behind Hezaren Han. This is the Saint Pierre Han, which in the years 1856-92 housed the original Ottoman Bank before the erection of its later home on Bankalar Caddesi.

Saint Pierre Han, erected in 1771 by the Compte de Saint Priest, French ambassador to the Sublime Porte (the Ottoman Foreign Office) in the reign of Mustafa III (r. 1757-74), who built it as the 'lodging-place and bank of the French Nation', as recorded in his bequest. A plaque high on the side of the building bears the arms of the Compte de Saint Priest, and another at the angle of the street, has the arms of the Bourbons. A third plaque high on the façade notes that the *han* was built on the site of the house where the French poet Andre Chénier was born on October 30, 1762. Chénier left Galata with his parents when he was only three years old and spent the rest of his short life in France, where he earned the reputation as the finest poet of his era. He died on the guillotine on 25th July 1794, just two days before the Ninth of Thermidor would have saved him, with the famous remark –pointing at his head– 'There might have been something there.' A haunting line in one of Chénier's poems expresses his longing to see 'the Galata of his childhood: 'Galata, which my eyes have long desired....'

At the end of Eski Banka Sokak we cross Galata Kulesi Sokak and continue straight ahead on Kart Çınar Sokak. The building on the far corner to the right is the former Podestat, or Palazzo Communal of medieval Genoese Galata, whose façade we saw earlier on our stroll along Bankalar Caddesi. The part of the Podestat that we see here on Kart Çınar Sokak is basically the original structure of 1316. The building directly opposite the Podestat is Genoese as well, and has also been dated to 1316.

Continuing along Kart Çınar Sokak, at mid-block we see on our left Sankt Georg Avusturya Lisesi [Austrian Lycée], which also houses Latin Katolik Sankt Georg Kilisesi [the Roman Catholic church of St. George]. A Genoese document of 1303 refers to a church of St. George in this neighborhood, probably one that had been Greek Orthodox and was taken over by the Roman Catholic Latins after 1261. The church was served in turn by the Jesuits beginning in 1585, and then after 1626 by the Dominicans and the

French capuchins. It was destroyed by fire in 1660 and rebuilt in 1667. The church was burned down again in 1696 and its convent was destroyed by fire in 1731. Immediately after the 1731 fire the church and convent were rebuilt with a donation by King Louis XIV of France. The present church dates from this rebuilding, plus some modern restoration. The Capuchins sold the church to the Apostolic Vicarate, which in turn sold it to the Bosnian Franciscan Observants in 1853. In 1882 the Austrian Lazarists bought the church and founded the present Avusturya Lisesi next to it, while the convent became the present Avusturya Sen Jorj Hastanesi [Austrian Hospital].

Within the church there is a *hagiasma*, or holy well, of great antiquity, believed to have been sacred to Apollo. Early in the Byzantine era the *hagiasma* was rededicated to St. Eirene, not to be confused with Haghia Eirene, the Holy Peace, to which the famous church on the First Hill was dedicated. According to tradition, St. Eirene was a Christian maiden of Sycae who was beheaded here for refusing to worship Apollo at his sacred well. A modern painting shows St. Eirene standing beside the holy well, with her severed head on the ground beside her.

We now come to Midilli Sokak, where on our right we see Kamondo Merdivenleri leading down to Bankalar Caddesi.

We turn left on Midilli Sokak, which a short way along on the right is intersected by Felek Sokak. The building at No. 1 Felek Sokak is Schneidertempel Synagogue, known variously as Terziler Sinagogu [the Synagogue of Tailors], and Edirneli Sinagogu [the Edirneli Synagogue], and the latter name stemming from the fact that the original congregation was from Edirne. The synagogue was founded in 1894 by Ashkenazi Jews and is now used as an arts centre.

Continuing up Midilli Sokak, we soon pass on our right Avusturya Hastanesi, which, as noted below, was originally the convent of Sankt Georg Kilisesi. Beyond that, on the same side of the street, is Beyoğlu Hastanesi [Beyoğlu Hospital], formerly British Seamen's Hospital, originally built in 1855 during the Crimean War. The hospital was rebuilt in its present form by the English architect Percy Adams. It continued as the British Seamen's Hospital until 1924, when the British Government turned it over to the Red Crescent Society. The courtyard in front of the hospital is paved with a delightful mosaic of black and white pebbles, including a mixture of nautical and medical symbols, including a steering wheel, an anchor, and a caduceus, the wand of Asclepius, god of healing.

The building to the left of the hospital formerly belonged to the British Consulate, before the consular staff moved to the present British Embassy building at Galatasaray in 1923. The building is now part of Beyoğlu Hastanesi.

We now retrace our steps to the corner of Kart Çınar Sokak and Galata Kulesi Sokak where we turn right on the latter street.

A third of the way up the street on the left is the entrance to another of the surviving medieval Latin churches in Galata. This is Latin Katolik San Pietro ve Paolo Kilisesi [the Roman Catholic church of Saints Peter and Paul], whose monastery is just beside it on Galata Kulesi Sokak.

The outer gate leads to a narrow courtyard lined with old tombstones, a few of which are from the ancient Greek settlement of Sycae, others from the graveyard of the church in the Ottoman period. Many of the latter tombstones are engraved with Maltese names from the nineteenth century, when stonemasons were brought from Malta to work on the new British embassy building and Kırım Kilisesi [the Crimean Memorial Church].

The church was founded by Dominican teaching friars, known in English as the Black Friars because of the black cape worn over their white robe. The Dominicans first came to Constantinople during the Latin occupation of 1204-61, establishing themselves in Galata, where they built the church of St. Paul and St. Dominic, the present Arap Camii, at the foot of the hill. When the church was converted into a mosque in 1475, Dominicans built a new church farther up the hill on the present site, dedicating it to St. Peter. The new church was enlarged in 1603, but then in 1660 it was destroyed by fire. The church built to replace this burned down in 1731, forcing the Dominicans to rebuild once again. Then in 1841 the Dominicans decided to erect a new and larger church on the same site, commissioning Gaspare Fossati to design and build it. The new church, the one we see today, was dedicated to Saints Peter and Paul.

The rear wall behind the altar is built up against one of the towers of the Genoese wall that separated the enceinte of 1348 from the one added in 1387-97.

One enters the nave on the right through an ornate portal of polychrome marble, a work of the Genoese sculptor Drago. The main aisle is flanked by Corinthian columns coupled by pilasters carrying arches across the central axis, illuminated by a series of crystal chandeliers. Six small marble columns support the semidome in the apse, flanked by statues of two angels, one representing 'Justice' (the Old Testament), the other 'God's Love' (the New Testament).

The high altar is the work of the Carrarese sculptor Giovanni Isola, who designed the altar table in the form of a Roman sarcophagus. On each side of the tabernacle there are reliefs symbolizing the Eucharist, the Arch of the Alliance, and the Memorial of the Passion and Resurrection. The altar is flanked by two almost life-sized marble statues, the one on the left holding the Cross, symbolizing Faith, the other Justice, pointing to the Ten Commandments. Behind the high altar is a painting depicting the meeting of Saints Peter and Paul, done in 1847 by the Dominican Serafino Gudotti.

The choir is covered by a sky-blue cupola eight meters in diameter, studded with golden stars. On the four sides there are portraits of the Dominican Popes: St. Pius V, the Blessed Innocent V, Benedict XIII, and the Blessed Benedict XI. On the semidome above the high altar there are paintings of Our Lady of the Rosary and at her feet St. Dominic and St. Catherine of Siena. There are four side altars, above one of which a painting by Serafino Gudotti depicts the death of St. Dominic. Opposite a painting by Francesco Mauro depicts St. Vincent Ferrer. The other two altars are works in marble by Giovanni Isola. The polychrome wooden statue of the Virgin is by Drago. The wooden crucifix beside the entrance portal is by an anonymous nineteenth-century Italian sculptor. Opposite is a hexagonal baptistery in the form of a ciborium.

Above the entryway there are two galleries with decorative wooden balusters; an organ gallery, and a smaller upper gallery once used by pupils of İtalyan Okulu [Italian School]. The organ was built in 1875 by Camillo Bianchi.

The church's greatest treasure is an ancient icon of the Blessed Virgin known as the Hodegitria, 'the one who shows the way.'

According to tradition, the original icon of the Virgin Hodegitria was painted by St. Luke. This icon was considered to be the protectress of Byzantine Constantinople, and when the city was besieged it was carried in procession along the Theodosian Walls. During the Turkish siege of 1453 the icon was kept in the church of St. Saviour in Chora, near the Theodosian Walls. According to the Greeks, the icon disappeared after the conquest, but the Latins hold that it survived and was eventually taken to the present church. Only the faces of the Virgin and Child can now be seen, the rest of the icon being covered in a protective case of embossed silver plate, in which a relief shows the Virgin welcoming the Order of St. Dominic under her protective mantle.

We now continue up Galata Kulesi Sokak, passing on our left the entrance to San Pietro ve Paolo Manastırı [the monastery of Saints Peter and Paul], which continues to function.

The stone building directly opposite the monastery is the former British Jail, which was part of the British Consulate before it moved to Galatasaray. The building has been well restored by the Turkish architect Mete Göktuğ.

Continuing up Galata Kulesi Sokak, looking to our left we see the remnants of two towers of the Genoese wall that separated the enceinte of 1348 from the one added in 1387-97. The rear wall of San Pietro ve Paolo Manastırı is built up against the southernmost tower.

At the top of the street we finally come to the Galata Tower, the apex of the main land walls of Genoese Galata, where this stroll comes to an end.

CHAPTER 5
From The Galata Tower To Tünel

As mentioned earlier, the Galata Tower, originally known as the Tower of Christ, was erected in 1348 by the Genoese as the bastion of their defense system, which in its final form had outer walls going down from here to the Golden Horn on one side and to the Bosphorus on the other, and with cross walls forming five enceintes. Outside the outer walls there was a ditch 15 meters wide extending down from the Galata Tower to both the Golden Horn and the Bosphorus. The tower itself was protected on its outer side by a semicircular barbican with a single postern.

At the time of the Turkish conquest in 1453 sections of the defense walls were demolished, and since then most of the rest of the Genoese fortifications have disappeared, except for the two towers behind San Pietro ve Paolo Kilisesi, the fragment of the tower we saw in Tophane, and the short stretch of sea-wall along the Golden Horn we saw near Azapkapı Camii. But the Galata Tower remains virtually intact, the iconic image of the medieval Genoese city-state of Galata.

The tower was reconstructed on a number of occasions in the Ottoman period, most notably after the great fires that destroyed much of Galata in 1791 and again in 1832. After the first of these fires it was restored by Selim III, and after the second by Mahmud II. The tower's distinctive conical roof was blown off during a hurricane in 1875, and it was not replaced in a subsequent restoration. The conical cap was finally put back during a restoration in 1964-7, which gave the tower much the same appearance that it had in Genoese times, though retaining the fenestration and other structural aspects from the Ottoman period.

The dimensions of the Galata Tower are believed to be essentially the same as they were in the Genoese period. The tower is about 67 meters high, its base standing on a slope 35 meters above sea-level.

A look at the Galata Tower from Büyük Hendek Sokak [Büyük Hendek Street].

The external diameter of the tower at its base is 26.45 meters, the inside diameter is 16.90 meters, and the thickness of the walls 3.75 meters.

The entryway is on the south side of the tower, approached by a double curving stairway of Proconnesian marble. The inscription above the ornate entryway is a verse of sixteen lines written by the poet Şair Pertev, who praises Sultan Mahmud II for having restored the tower in the year AH 1248 (AD 1832). The entrance and the ornate steps leading up to it date from the restoration by Mahmud II. Prior to that time the approach to the entryway seems to have been via a wooden plank or drawbridge. The window above the door was probably a lookout for the soldiers of the garrison on duty.

There are nine floors above the lofty entrance hall. The windows on the lower floors are few in number and merely slits, increasing appreciably in size on the sixth and seventh floors. The eighth floor has huge round-arched windows, while the ninth floor has smaller windows with ogive arches.

During the first centuries of the Ottoman era the Galata Tower was occupied by a detachment of janissaries the elite corps of the Ottoman army, whose commander served as the military governor of Galata. During the sixteenth century the tower was used to house prisoners of war, who were usually consigned as galley slaves in the Ottoman arsenal at Kasımpaşa on the Golden Horn. One of these slaves, Michael Heberer of Bretten, who was imprisoned here during the years 1582-6, describes the tower thus: 'There is a very high and strong tower in the center of a large courtyard enclosed in high walls on the highest point of Galata and at the beginning of the moat. Fifteen hundred slaves of the Sultan who are made to work at various jobs shelter in this tower.' During the restoration in 1964-7 large quantities of human bones were unearthed in the dungeon beneath the tower, doubtless the remains of the slaves who were imprisoned there.

During the reign of Selim II (r. 1566-74) the Galata Tower was used as an observation point by the renowned Turkish astronomer Takiyüddin, who had his main observatory farther up the hill in Pera. During the reign of Mustafa II (r. 1695-1703 the Şeyhülislam Feyzullah Efendi tried to set up an observatory in the tower with the aid of a Jesuit priest. But the effort was cut short during an uprising in 1703, in which the Sultan was overthrown and Feyzullah Efendi killed.

Galata Tower became a fire-watch station in 1874, a function it performed until 1964, when it was closed to convert it into a tourist attraction. When we first visited the tower in 1960, ascending to the top floor by a series of stairs and then a ladder, the fire brigade was still stationed there, offering little glasses of tea or a shot of rakı to the few intrepid tourists who came up to take in the view. Sentinels were posted there day and night to give the alarm when they spotted a blaze, crying out 'Yangın var!' [There's a fire!], sounding alarms to alert the tulumbacıs, the men of the fire brigades. Edmondo de Amicis writes of this in his Constantinople

(1896), giving a dramatic description of a fire that took place early one morning in Galata during his stay in the city. He tells of being awakened at five o'clock in the morning by the commotion on the street outside the Hotel de Byzance in Pera. He went out into the hallway, where a waiter told him that there was a fire and shouted 'Look at the top of the Galata Tower!'

> We ran back to the window, and, craning our necks toward Galata, saw the upper part of the great tower illuminated by a brilliant red light, while a dense black cloud, issuing from some neighboring housed amid a vortex of flames and sparks, spread itself rapidly across the starlight sky....
>
> We flung on our clothes and ran down the Grand Rue de Pera as fast as our legs could carry us, but, happily our curiosity was not to be satisfied on this occasion. By the time we reached the Galata Tower the fire had been pretty nearly extinguished; only two small houses were actually burned; the people were dispersing and the

"Grand Rue de Pera" (İstiklal Caddesi) [İstiklal Avenue].

streets were flooded with water from the pumps and cluttered with furniture and bedding; men and women, shivering with fright and cold, were going about in their night clothes, talking and lamenting in a dozen different languages, nothing being distinguishable through the noise and confusion but the shrill note of terror and excitement which marks the near escape from some great danger.

The large entryway leads into the lofty main hall of the tower, now used as the entrance lobby, from where elevators ascent to the seventh floor. Above the elevator doors in the lobby there is a large bronze relief of Genoese Galata and its tower and defense walls, based on the miniature done in 1535 by Matrakçı Nasuh, court painter of Süleyman the Magnificent. On the seventh floor there is a marble relief depicting the exploit of Hezarfen Ahmed Çelebi, who in the mid seventeenth century fashioned himself a pair of wings and flew from the top of the Galata Tower across the Bosphorus to Üsküdar on the Asian shore, at least according to the story told by Evliyâ Çelebi in his Seyahatnâme.

A wooden staircase leads up from the seventh floor to the ninth, where there is a restaurant and night club, ringed by an open observation deck that commands a stunning view of Istanbul, surrounded by what the sixth-century historian Procopius called 'the city's garland of waters,' with the Bosphorus and the Golden Horn flowing together into the Sea of Marmara past the promontory at Sarayburnu.

During the Allied occupation of Istanbul after World War I, the tower was used as a prison by the British military police. From April to November, the niches in the walls are home to large colonies of alpine swifts, which towards sunset fly in noisy, joyful circles around the tower.

After descending from the tower we will walk around to its north side, where a short stretch of the barbican wall has been restored. The barbican consisted of this semicircular wall outside the tower on the north side, together with straight section of wall to the southeast to join up with the bastion known as the Tower of St. Nicholas. There were two gates in the barbican, the one on the northeast known as Kuledibi Kapısı, and another on the southeast called Küçük Kale Kapısı. There was also a gate known as Kuledibi

Kapısı in the main defense wall just to the west of the Galata Tower. The barbican formed a little citadel around the tower, which can be seen in views from as early as the sixteenth century. These gates and others in the defense circuit were still in use as late as 1856, when *Murray's Guide to Constantinople* advised tourists to pay *bahshish* [a gratuity] to the gatemen who still guarded these ancient portals.

The barbican was flanked on either side by a deep ditch, in Turkish *hendek*, which extended around the exterior of the main defense wall down to the Golden Horn on one side and the Bosphorus on the other. This ditch gave its name to the two streets that were laid out along its course when it was filled in, with Büyük Hendek Caddesi extending westward from the Galata Tower and Lüleci Hendek Caddesi eastward.

In Kule Meydanı, the little square beside the tower, there is a famous street-fountain fixed against the remnants of the barbican. The fountain in its present form dates from 1732, but it was originally constructed just after the conquest. Its founder was Bereketzade Hacı Ali Ağa, the first Turkish governor of the citadel of Galata. The fountain originally stood near Bereketzade Camii, which was located about fifty meters below the tower, but it was moved to its present site in 1950 when that was demolished.

Much of the area through which we will pass (known as Kuledibi, the Base of the Tower – the slope rising beyond the tower was known to the local Greeks as the hill of St. Theodore), particularly those parts of it that were outside the walls of Galata, was only sparsely populated, mostly by ship captains who were converts to Islam, until 1813, when the area along what is now Büyük Hendek Caddesi began to be developed. However, it was not until the late 1850s, when the walls of Galata were demolished, that this development began to gather pace, and not until the mid 1860s, when Jews began to move here from the districts of Balat and Fener, to be joined later by Greeks moving from the district of Fener, that it became densely populated. It was in this area that buildings of stone rather than wood and mud-brick, and multi-family rather than single family dwellings, began to be built.

The demographic makeup of the area, that is, mostly Jewish, with some Christians and Muslims, remained largely unchanged until the 1950s, when the Jews started migrating to Israel or moving

The Galata Tower and Kuledibi in the early 20th century.

to other neighborhoods such as Nişantaşı, and the Greeks began leaving for Greece. Sayım Çavuş, longtime *muhtar* of the Şahkulu district, tells us that traditionally the concierges of the Jewish apartment buildings were Turks from the province of Erzincan. As apartments became vacant, the concierges would fill them with their relatives, until the Erzincanlıs began to outnumber the Jews.

In the 1960s there was a huge wave of migration to Istanbul from the Eastern Black Sea region of Turkey, and in time these migrants, in this area mostly from the province of Rize, began to outnumber the Erzincanlıs. At the same time the local Roma community, some of whom claim to be descended from the Roma who lived here in Byzantine times, was augmented by an influx of their kin from the Çukurova region of southern Turkey. By 1970, the area had taken on a distinctly Anatolian character.

During the anarchy of the late 1970s, this area, along with much of the rest of Beyoğlu, fell into decay and developed a reputation for lawlessness. Then, in the late 1990s, a number of Turkish intellectuals and artists, as well as a fair number of foreigners, began to buy property in the area, and by 2005 it had once again begun to change rapidly. There are hardly any Jews still living here. However, some of the older Erzincanlıs still remember the Ladino (a Spanish dialect spoken by many of Istanbul's Jews) they learned as children, and are able to converse with the Spaniards and South Americans among their new neighbors.

We now take an excursion from Kule Meydanı along Büyük Hendek Caddesi, which on its left side near its far end brings us to Neve Şalom Sinagogu [Neve Shalom Synagogue]. This is the principal synagogue of modern Galata, with a large congregation drawn from all over the city. Although the present building was erected only in 1952, there was already a synagogue on this site as early as the fifteenth century. The synagogue was the scene of a horrific atrocity on 6 September 1986, when terrorists broke in during the Sabbath service and killed 21 worshippers. There was another bomb attack in 1992, in which fortunately no one was killed. Then, at 9:29 am on November 15, 2003, when the street was crowded with shoppers and the synagogue itself was packed with worshippers, a suicide bomber in a red panel truck detonated 400 kg of explosives outside the front door. The blast, which destroyed the façade of the synagogue and left a two-meter deep crater in the street, damaged 70 buildings, including a nearby mosque, 6 of them so severely that they had to be demolished. There was an almost simultaneous truck bombing outside Beth İsrael Sinagogu [Beth Israel Synagogue] in Şişli. 30 people were killed and over 300 were injured in the two bombings.

At its far end, after crossing Ziya Paşa Caddesi, Büyük Hendek Caddesi comes to Şişhane Meydanı. The huge building on the left is Frej Apartmanı, one of Galata's first modern luxury apartment houses. This area has for some years been the center of Istanbul's chandelier trade, though with gentrification and the subsequent rise in rents, some of the chandelier shops have begun moving elsewhere.

We now turn the corner and walk down Okçu Musa Caddesi,

the Avenue of Musa the Archer. A short way along, at the second intersection on the right, we make a short detour that takes us to the intersection of Tutsak Sokak and Yüksek Minare Sokak. There we see a little mosque call Emekyemez Mescidi, founded in 1590 by one Hüsameddin Efendi. The mosque was completely rebuilt in 1884 and is now of no architectural interest.

Continuing along Okçu Musa Caddesi we come on our left to Midilli Sokak, where we see an old mosque called Okçu Musa Mescidi, from which the avenue takes its name. The mosque was built during the reign of Mehmed II (r. 1451-81) by one Okçu Musa. The mosque was completely rebuilt in 1939 and now is of no arehitectural interest.

At the far end of the short Midilli Sokak we come to Şair Eşref Sokak, where we turn right and after a few steps come to Ziya Paşa Caddesi. A short way down Ziya Paşa Caddesi, on the opposite side, we see İtalyan Sinagogu [the Italian Synagogue], founded in 1887 and still functioning. Its founding stemmed from a dispute in the mid-19th century between the leaders of the Jewish community and Daniel Farandi, head of the Italian congregation. Acting on a request by the Italian government, Sultan Abdülaziz in 1866 granted the Italian Jews a plot of land in Galata, on which they eventually was built the present synagogue. Until the 1960s this part of Ziya Paşa Caddesi popularly known as 'the Jewish slope,' because of the large number of Jews who lived along it.

We now make our way up Ziya Paşa Caddesi, which at the next intersection brings us to a small mosque called Şehsuvar Mescidi. This mosque was built during the reign of Mehmed II by one of Fatih's naval commanders. This would have been one of the first mosques built in Galata after the Turkish conquest of 1453. Its proximity to the Galata Tower means that it would have principally served the janissaries who were on garrison duty there. The mosque was rebuilt in 1954 and now is of no architectural interest.

Returning to Kule Meydanı, we now take an excursion on Şah Kapısı Sokak, which crosses Galip Dede Caddesi, the upper extension of Yüksek Kaldırım. After the first turning on the right Şah Kapısı Sokak changes its name to Serdar-ı Ekrem Caddesi, which soon passes on its right the famous Doğan Apartmanı. This was the site of Mehmed Paşa Konağı, a two-storey mansion in the Turkish style that

Doğan (Helbig) Apartmanı [Doğan Apartment] (on the top and bottom).

for a time was the residence of the Prussian Ambassador. Mehmed Paşa Konağı was destroyed by fire in 1870, and the present building, the first of Galata's deluxe apartment houses in the European style, was erected in 1892-5 as Helbig Apartmanı. It changed owners and name several times, becoming in turn Nahid Bey Apartmanı, Botton Apartmanı and Victoria Han. In 1942 it was bought by Kâzım Taşkent, founder of Yapı Kredi. The building's tennis courts are now used as a parking lot.

Continuing along Serdar-ı Ekrem Caddesi as it veers to the right, near the end of the street we come to the largest and most handsome of the western churches in the city, looking as if it belonged in England rather than Turkey. This is Kırım Kilisesi, built between 1858 and 1868 under the aegis of Stratford Canning, Lord Stratford de Redcliffe, Great Britain's Ambassador to the Ottoman Empire during the period 1810-56. The church was designed by George Edward Street, the architect of the London Law Courts; it is built in the neo-Gothic style with a cavernous porch, like the Law Courts themselves. The church was abandoned for a time, but recently it has been well restored through the efforts of Father Ian Sherwood, and is once again in use as an Anglican church.

If one were to climb a little way up the cul-de-sac known as Seraskerci Çıkmazı, one would come to the gate of the Swedish chapel. This tiny chapel in its own enclave at the back of the grounds of the Swedish Embassy was originally built in 1748 and restored in 1818 after it was damaged by fire. The chapel was used by Swedish Lutheran missionaries who hoped to bring salvation to seamen visiting the port. Though they never had much success with the seamen, who tended to prefer the taverns and brothels of Galata, they did find unexpected converts among the local Greek population, and from about 1880 until the late 1950s the church housed several congregations of Greek-speaking evangelical Protestants. During the 1960s and 70s it was home to a congregation of Armenian Protestants. From the early 1980s, it was used off and on by a congregation of Turkish Protestants, mostly converts from Islam, and for a time it was home to the tiny Turkish Anglican church, whose pastor, Father Engin Yıldırım, became, when he was consecrated by the Bishop of Gibraltar in January 2008, the first Turk since 1850 to be ordained an Anglican priest.

We now retrace our steps to Galip Dede Caddesi, where we turn right to walk uphill toward the heights of Pera. As we do so we pass on our right one of the oldest mosques in Galata. This is Müeyyedzade Camii, formerly known as Yazıcı Camii, a late 16th century mosque that still retains its original structure except for a modern façade. The mosque was built in 1582 by kadi [judge] Müeyyedzade Mehmed Efendi, who died during the reign of Ahmed I (r. 1603-17), under whom he held high office. Evliyâ Çelebi tells a strange story about the founder, whom he calls 'Meyyit Zade', which means 'Son of the Dead,' a play on his real name:

His father, going to the siege of Erla recommended the child, then in his mother's womb, to the care of God Almighty. Soon after his departure the woman died and was buried; she was then delivered in the womb and nourished the child by a miracle. The father, on his return, having heard of his wife's death, desired to be shown the grave, where he found the child suckled by the mother's breast, which had not perished. He praised God and took the child home, who became a great and learned man and died at the time of Ahmed I, and was again buried close to his mother. A cupola was erected over his grave, which is a place of general pilgrimage.

Just across the street from the mosque, until the early 1970s, was Sancak Sineması [the Sancak Cinema], one of the least reputable local cinemas of Beyoğlu. Giovanni Scognamillo describes a visit there in about 1960 (despite his mother's warning not to go because he might get lice). 'Next to us were several *hamals* who had taken off their shoes, filling the place with the smell of feet, people were smoking hashish behind us, towards the front several men were passing around a bottle, and an elderly prostitute was walking up and down the aisle looking for customers.' The films were Fritz Lang's *Doktor Mabuse, der Spieler* (1922) and Joseph von Srenberg's *Der Blaue Engel* (1929).

Continuing up Galip Dede Caddesi, we now pass on our left Şahkulu Camii, the mosque for which the surrounding quarter is named. The mosque was founded in the reign of Mehmed III (r. 1595-1603) by the Sultan's boon companion Mehmed Çelebi; however the present structure dates from a complete rebuilding in recent years.

Directly across the street, until quite recently, was the shop of Monsieur Pepo the hat-maker. From the early years of the Turkish Republic until the 1950s, this street was known for its hat-makers. Monsieur Pepo was the best known of these, and after his death the shop was taken over by his assistant of many years, Osman Ibıl, a native of Erzincan. The shop closed in 2009 and was replaced by a touristic boutique.

Farther up the street we pass on our right the German Cultural Club Teutonia, founded in 1847 and still functioning. The present building was erected in 1875. Among those who paid visits to the

German Cultural Club Teutonia on Galip Dede Caddesi [Galip Dede Avenue].

club were Kaiser Wilhelm II and Joseph Goebbels, Hitler's propaganda chief.

This was previously the site of what is thought to have been Beyoğlu's first bookstore, J. J. Wicks, which opened here in 1848. During the last half of the 19th century and the first half of the twentieth century, the upper half of Galip Dede Caddesi was known for its bookstores, only one or two of which are left. During the late 1950s this area became a center for shops selling musical instruments. As a result of this, many nearby apartments have been converted into music studios, where the bands that play in Beyoğlu's countless bars and nightclubs practice their repertoires.

Near the upper end of the street we come on our right to the entrance of Galata Mevlevi Tekkesi [Lodge of the Mevlevi]. The *tekke*, which also houses Divan Edebiyatı Müzesi [the Museum of Turkish Court Poetry], is open 09.30-16.30; closed Monday.

The *tekke*, or dervish monastery, was built in the last decade of the fifteenth century by Şeyh Muhammed Semai Sultan Divanî, a descendant of Mevlanâ Celaleddin Rumi, the great divine and mystic poet who in the thirteenth century founded the religious brotherhood known as the Mevlevi. The *tekke* was one of the sights that foreign tourists were shown in the nineteenth century, as John Cam Hobhouse writes in the journal he kept during his travels through Greece and Turkey with Byron in 1809-10: '... the people of Constantinople run in crowds to amuse themselves (for no other motive can be assigned to them) at the exhibition of the turning... Dervishes, to which all strangers are carried, as to the theatre or other places of entertainment in the cities of Christendom.'

The *tekke* was closed in the 1920s when all of the dervish orders were banned early in the Turkish Republic; it was then virtually abandoned until it reopened in 1975 as a museum, having been well restored in the interim. Until the 1940s, part of the *tekke* was used as a police station, whose main function seems to have been to

Galata Mevlevihanesi [Galata Dervish House] also houses Divan Edebiyatı Müzesi [the Museum of Turkish Court Poetry].

keep the riffraff of Galata out of Beyoğlu. During the Crimean War and again during the Allied occupation, British soldiers were posted here for the same purpose. The central structure of the complex now houses Divan Edebiyatı Müzesi, devoted to the mystical writings of the Mevlevi and other Sufi poets and philosophers of the Ottoman era and even as far back as that of the Selcuks in the thirteenth century, when the dervish movement first flourished in Anatolia.

The structure to the left of the entrance, an ornate marble kiosk with round-arched windows screened by decorative iron grills, is the *türbe* of one Halil Efendi, built in 1816 by his son Haled Said Efendi. The two-storied structure to the right of the entrance is also dated 1818, another element of the *külliye* founded by Haled Said Efendi in memory of Halil Efendi. The building on the ground floor is a *sebil*, or fountain-house, where attendants once handed out cups of water to passersby. The word 'sebil' also means 'path,' and the Islamic tradition is that endowing a *sebil* helps pave the donor's path to paradise. Next to the *sebil*, just inside the entryway, was the library of the *tekke*, with an arcadia loggia on the upper floor. Above the sebil was the *muvakkithane*, the house and workshop of the resident astronomer. The astronomer's duties included the determination the times for the five occasions of daily prayer and the dates for the beginning of the lunar months, particularly Ramadan, as evidenced by the appearance of the first crescent moon on the western horizon shortly after sunset.

The alleyway inside the entrance leads to the central courtyard of the *tekke* complex. At the near right-hand corner of the courtyard there is a classical Ottoman fountain, with an ogive-arched recess where the faucets once poured water into the marble basin below. The inscription above the basin records that the fountain was built in 1649 by one Hasan Ağa.

Just beyond the sebil of Haled Said Efendi we see the *türbe* of Galib Dede, the renowned mystical poet who headed the tekke in the late seventeenth century, and for whom the street outside is named. The *türbe* in its present form dates from 1818, another benefaction of Haled Said Efendi.

Other members of the dervish brotherhood are buried in the picturesque graveyard to the left of the central courtyard, their tombstones surmounted by the distinctive headdress of the

Mevlevi, a tall and slightly tapering cylindrical cap with a rounded top and barely upturned brim. The Mevlevi community also included women, whose tombstones are usually surmounted by a representation of a vase of flowers and with a floral relief decorating the stone itself. The inscription on one such tombstone records the grave of a lady known as Dervish Emine Hatun, who died in AH 1280 (AD 1864).

At the far left corner of the graveyard we find the large funerary monument of Count Bonneval, known to the Turks as Kumbaracı Osman Ahmed Pasha. Bonneval was a French nobleman who enrolled in the Ottoman army during the reign of Mahmud I (r. 1730–54) and was made Commandant of the Corps of Artillery [Kumbaracıbaşı]. He became a Muslim, changed his name to Kumbaracı [the Bombardier] Osman Ahmed, and spent the remainder of his life in the Ottoman service. He died in 1747 after having spent the last years of his life as a dervish in Galata Mevlevihanesi [Galata Dervish House]. A French contemporary of Bonneval wrote of him that he was 'a man of great talent for war, intelligent, eloquent with charm and grace, very proud, a lavish spender, extremely debauched, and a great plunderer.'

At the left rear of the courtyard we come to the heart of the *tekke*, its *semahane*, or dancing-room, a beautiful octagonal chamber that was splendidly restored in the early 1970s. The *semahane* and its adjacent chambers now house Divan Edebiyatı Müzesi. The collection includes manuscripts of the works of Galib Dede and other mystic poets, as well as examples of Ottoman calligraphy and other memorabilia of the Mevlevi dervishes who once lived here. Performances of the ethereal Mevlevi dance and the hauntingly beautiful music of the *ney*, or Turkish flute, that accompanies it are given here and in Konya each year on the feast day (December 17) of Mevlana. The archaeologist Gertrude Bell visited the tomb of Mevlana at his shrine in Konya on 13 May 1905, and her description of the ceremony she witness evokes the soulful scene:

> Beyond the tomb are two great dancing halls with polished floors and the whole is enclosed in a peaceful garden, fountains and flowers set around with the monastic cells of the order. So he lies, Jelal et din Rumi, and to my mind the whole quiet air was full of the music of his verse: 'Ah listen to the reed as it tells, ah listen, to the plaint of the reed.' 'They reft me from the rushes of my home,

my voice is sad with longing, sad and low.' But the Persian is the very pipe, the plaintive pipe of the reed, put into words, and there is nothing so invades the soul.'

We now continue up the last stretch of Galip Dede Caddesi, which is here lined with shops selling musical instruments and recordings of music of all types, including that of the Mevlevi. At the upper end of Galip Dede Caddesi we come to Tünel Meydanı, the square in front of the upper terminus of the funicular railway, where this stroll ends and the next one begins.

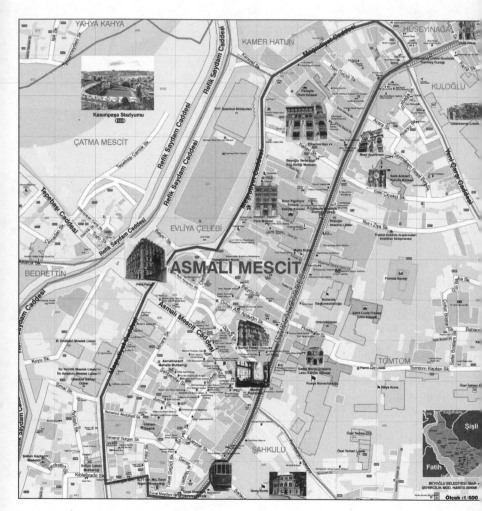

© Beyoğlu Belediyesi Emlak ve İstimlak Müdürlüğü

CHAPTER 6
From Tünel to Galatasaray

This stroll begins where the last one ended, in Tünel Meydanı, the square in front of the upper terminus of the funicular railway. Many of the victims of the city's first plague epidemic in the sixth century were buried here, under the direction of Theodore after whom this hill was named. He hired men to dig the mass graves, and then, when the dead kept arriving, ordered them to jump on the bodies to pack them down so that more could be fit in. In late Byzantine times, this was the site of a hamlet called Elaias and the church of SS. Archippos and Philemon, with, nearby, the largest poorhouse of Constantinople. Beyond were farms, orchards, vineyards, cemeteries, scattered hamlets and a narrow road, not much more than a path, following almost exactly the same course as the present Istiklal Caddesi. The area remained mostly unchanged until the later part of the sixteenth century, except for the appearance after the Turkish conquest of a few small Muslim settlements outside the walls of Galata, along the ridge, and in the area now known as Tarlabaşı, and a few settlements of mostly Greek workers and servants in Tarlabaşı, Dolapdere and around the church of Haghios Dimitrios in the area that came to be known as Tatavla [Kurtuluş].

As the port of Galata became busier and more crowded, wealthy merchants began to flee disease, foul smells and the taverns and brothels, converting their homes into warehouses and moving to roomier and airier homes uphill. By the end of the sixteenth century, they had begun moving outside the walls of Galata, at first to the slopes overlooking the Bosphorus, and later on the ridge, along the road that would become Grand Rue de Pera.

Among the first to move out of Galata were the Genoese Adorno, Doria, Ocase, Boteghe and the Venetian Boroni, Lorenzi and Andria families, who by this time were speaking a dialect that mixed Italian with Greek. After the Genoese lost their colonies on the Black Sea

By the end of the sixteenth century, denizens of the port of Galata had begun moving outside the walls, at first to the slopes overlooking the Bosphorus, and later on the ridge, along the road (above) that would become Grand Rue de Pera.

and the Venetians lost their dominance of the Aegean, and after the French became the principal traders in the area, leading members of the growing French community also began to move outside the walls, one of the first being the French Ambassador Jaques de Germigny, who used to sign his letters, 'from the vineyards of Pera'. After the founding of the Levant Company, the English too began to build houses in the area, to be followed by Dutch, Germans and Scandinavians.

By the beginning of the seventeenth century, the area along Grand Rue de Pera between what is now Tünel and Galatasaray had become a distinct entity centered on the Crossroads (referred to as *Dörtyol* in Turkish and Stavrodromi in Greek) formed by the intersection of the avenue with what is now Asmalımescit Sokak and what is now Kumbaracı Yokuşu. The district was divided into five neighborhoods, Dörtyol, Tomtom and what was later to become known as Polonya to the right of the avenue, Asmalımescit to the left and Galatasaray at the end. Development to the left of the avenue, in the area now known as Tepebaşı, was restricted by a cemetery known as Petits Champs des Morts; a larger cemetery, Grands Champs des Morts, occupied the area around what is now Taksim Meydanı. Except for small Muslim settlements in Asmalımescit and Galatasaray, it was a completely European and Christian entity, differing in architecture, customs and atmosphere from any other neighborhood of Istanbul.

The European embassies were established more or less where they are now in the course of the sixteenth to eighteenth centuries, generally by grants of land bestowed by the Sultans, and each formed the center of its 'nation,' as it was called; that is, of the community of resident merchants and officials of the various countries. These embassies came to exert a growing influence on the Ottoman Empire as its powers declined, and collectively they dominated the life of Pera until the establishment of the Turkish Republic. Near the embassies various churches were established, more or less under their protection, and some of these survive in a modern form. They are all situated along Istiklal Caddesi between Tünel and Galatasaray Meydanı, the square midway along the avenue, some of them standing next to the old ministries to whose 'nation' they once ministered.

Pera was, however, a far from cohesive entity, made up as it was of merchants, priests and diplomats from nations that were in constant and fierce competition with each other, and indeed often at war with each other (more than once, the Ottomans found it necessary to exert pressure to prevent British and French ships from attacking each other in the harbor). The status of each community in relation to that of the others was constantly shifting. The once wealthy and powerful Genoese and Venetians, stranded by the receding tide of the fortunes of their native Republics, were sometimes reduced to working as tradesmen and translators (Marini, Silvestri, Paradi, Orlandi and Gritti families, once of the Venetian aristocracy, took Austrian, French or German citizenship and in time became famous 'dragoman families'). Occasionally, too, communities experienced internal divisions due to strife in their native countries, as was the case with the English during the English Civil War and the French during the French Revolution. The Austrian historian Joseph von Hammer, writing in the second quarter of the nineteenth century, wrote sarcastically of Grand Rue de Pera that 'it was as narrow as the comprehension of its inhabitants and as long as the tapeworm of its intrigues.'

Pera of this time bore little resemblance to the Beyoğlu of today. The avenue was not an avenue but a narrow lane that was muddy in winter and dusty in summer. Except for the embassies and the mansions of the wealthiest merchants, most of the houses were built of mud-brick and wood, crowded together, and neither adequately heated in winter nor properly ventilated in summer. There were frequent fires and epidemics. In 1673 the area was almost completely depopulated by an outbreak of the plague.

However, the district rebounded from each disaster, and each time it was rebuilt, it was with somewhat better planning. By the beginning of the 19th century, thought still not yet fully urbanized, it had begun, as foreign clockmakers, doctors, pharmacists, tailors, tradesmen and artisans came to serve the foreign merchants, and with the opening of hotels, shops, theaters and restaurants and the building of churches, to resemble a European city. To the optimistic it was a "Little Paris", and to the pessimistic a "2nd class Paris".

This Pera was devastated by the Great Fire of 1830. As *Gentleman's Magazine and Historical Chronicle* reported at the time:

Pera, the suburb of Constantinople, was destroyed on the 2nd of August by a conflagration. The residences of the French and British Ambassadors became a prey to the flames. Everything was consumed except the Austrian Palace and the Russian Chancery. Many foreign merchants voluntarily threw themselves into the flames in despair at having lost all their property. The fire broke out in several places at the same time; 18,000 houses have been destroyed, and no less than 60,000 persons rendered houseless.

After the fire, the population of foreign Christians, or, more precisely, those under the protection of foreign embassies, was 13,000 but by 1848 it had reached 25,000. This population was augmented by 15,000 Greeks who moved to Pera from the district of Fener and by several thousand Jews who moved to the area now called Şişhane from the districts of Balat and Hasköy.

Albert Richard Smith's description of Grand Rue during his visit in 1849 illustrates the process of change that was beginning to occur. His first impressions were not favorable:

> The miserable, narrow, ill-paved thoroughfare did not present one redeeming feature – even of picturesque dreariness. The roadway was paved with all sorts of ragged stones, jammed down together without any regard to level surfaces; and encumbered with dead rats, melon-rinds, dogs, rags, brickbats and rubbish that had fallen through the mules' baskets as they toiled along. The houses were of wood – old and rotten; and bearing traces of once having been painted red. Here and there, where a building had been burnt, or tumbled down, all the ruins remained as they had fallen. Even the better class of houses had an uncared-for, mouldy, plague-imbued, decaying look about them.

However he later adds that, 'The main street of Pera is to be much wider; and in some parts handsome European edifices are rising, built entirely of stone, or with party walls. Here and there are houses, at present in the course of erection, which might rank with many on the Parisian boulevards.'

European symphony orchestra and opera companies were brought to Istanbul by Giuseppe Donizetti, whom Mahmud II had hired as his musical director in 1828, making him a pasha. Donizetti Pasha, elder brother of the famous composer Gaetano Donizetti, trained the imperial band in music *alafranga*, i. e., 'in the manner of the Franks,' or Europeans. Donizetti later built Istanbul's first opera house in Pera, bringing foreign musicians and singers to perform there. The first European-style theater in the city was founded in 1840 in Pera with the support of the Ottoman government together with the foreign embassies. The theater was erected by a Genoese named Giustiani, whose successor, the Italian magician Bosco, put on his own magic shows as well as bringing in European plays and operas. Several other theaters soon opened in Pera, all of them catering principally to foreigners and the non-Muslim minorities, with the Sultan himself often attending premier performances.

Nur Akın's thorough examination of the newspapers of the time shows us that the average Periot family spent three evenings a week at the theater or at concerts, and the remaining four evenings attending balls, salons and informal social gatherings. *Apokrias*, or Greek carnival, when people of all faiths and denominations donned costumes and caroused in the streets, was the high point of the year. The Latin and Orthodox Easter celebrations were taken very seriously by all, as was the Spring Festival on May 1st, when all of the Greek and Armenian families departed for picnics in the countryside, returning with wreaths of wildflowers with which they decorated their doors. The Sultan's birthday and the anniversary of the Sultan's accession to the throne were also cause for jubilant celebration. The streets would be lined with flags, and merchants tried to outdo each other with displays of lights or arranged flowers. In summer, however, when all of the embassies and wealthy households moved to summer residences on the Bosphorus, Pera would have a deserted air. All of the theaters and ballrooms and many of the better restaurants and cafes closed, though there were outdoor circuses and displays of equestrian skill to entertain the less fortunate who remained behind.

In 1855 the Beyoğlu Municipality was established, and though it was the first local municipality in Istanbul, it designated itself Altıncı Daire-i Belediye [6th Municipal Division] after the 6th arrondisement of Paris. The mayor, or director [*müdür*], and the seven member council were appointed by the grand vizier, and all members were required to own property valued at a minimum of 100,000 *kuruş* and to have lived in the district for at least ten years. The government encouraged the involvement of foreigners in the council, because, as they lacked sufficient funds for urban improvement projects, they hoped these foreigners would provide loans and contributions. Hence (with a few notable exceptions, such as the much respected Server Efendi) most of the directors were foreigners or Levantines. Regulations concerning public order and the cleanliness of streets were enacted, itinerant peddlers were banned, the main streets were widened and paved (Apparently the winter of 1855-6 was a nightmare for residents of Beyoğlu, as the streets became impassable because of the digging and the piles of earth, cement and paving stones. Ever since then, Beyoğlu has relived this nightmare every decade or so. In the past decade, in 2005 and 2006, it happened two winters in a row. The repaving of the main streets had just been finished when there was a public outcry that Chinese rather than Turkish marble had been used, so the then mayor, Kadir Topbaş, promptly had the Chinese marble ripped up and replaced with Turkish marble) and illuminated by gas lamps (fed by the gas house near Dolmabahçe, which was originally established to illuminate the palace), the walls of Galata were demolished, Grands and Petits Champs des Morts were razed to make room for further development, horse-drawn trams were introduced, theaters, opera houses and grand hotels with ballrooms were built, and the streets filled with carriages imported from Europe. (These services and improvements did not benefit the poor Greeks, Armenians and Turks living in the areas of Tarlabaşı, Tophane, Kasımpaşa and Pangaltı. This may have contributed to the alarming increase in crime in Pera.) In the 1850s, a French restaurant opened in what is now Tünel Meydanı (Tünel had not yet been built) to cater to the crowds of tourists who came to see performances of the 'whirling dervishes' at Mevlevihane, and soon afterwards an Italian circus and a French theater opened nearby. An English cricket club was established, and Sultan Abdülaziz, who frequently attended the opera there, decreed that Naum Tiyatrosu [the Naum Theater] be gas-lit. Meanwhile, rents and property taxes rose astonishingly. Between 1838 and 1847, property prices rose by 75 percent, and continued to rise in the following two decades. In 1868, foreigners were given the right to buy property, and subsequently the Muslim population decreased. By this time, French had become the language of Pera.

In 1851 a commission was appointed to name and number the streets, taking seven years to complete the task (almost all streets, except for those in Perşembe Pazarı district, were given French names), and in 1867 the avenue, now 1607 m long, between 3.75 and 10.5 m wide and lined with 470 buildings, was officially named Grand Rue de Pera (previously various stretches of the avenue had been known by separate names).

The reforms in Ottoman government instituted by Mahmud II (r. 1808-39) and his son and successor Abdülmecid (r. 1839-61) greatly increased the foreign trade of Turkey, bringing a large number of Europeans to Istanbul. Zeynep Çelik writes of how this led to the establishment of many Western-style hotels in Pera. One of the first was the Hotel des Ambassadeurs, whose elegance and comforts were praised in 1855 by *Journal de Constantinople*, which noted that it had a dining-room of '*le plus grand luxe*'.

Then, on the June 5, 1870, disaster struck again, in the form of a fire even greater than that of forty years earlier. More than two-thirds of the district was destroyed, and thousands were killed.

On the June 5, 1870, a disaster struck, in the form of a fire, and more than two-thirds of the district was destroyed, and thousands were killed.

The city's first fire brigade was established on the Hungarian model.

(Soon afterwards the city's first fire brigade was established, on the Hungarian model, headed by Count Sachany.)

Sultan Abdülaziz quickly turned his thoughts to the rebuilding of the district, and, envisioning a modern city to rival the capitals of Europe, commissioned a team of architects and engineers to produce a grand plan for a 'nouvelle ville' with great squares, broad boulevards and monumental buildings. The initial plan they presented was immediately deemed beyond the financial means of the government, but even the more modest second plan proved to be impossible to implement because it ignored the topography of the district. The engineers and architects, never having visited Istanbul, assumed that the area was flat, rather than the fish skeleton of ridges and valleys that it is. One of the great squares would have been at the bottom of a ravine (Bülbül Deresi), and several of the broad boulevards would have been on impossibly steep slopes (e.g. Kazancı Yokuşu). Property owners were also quite opposed to surrendering their land to these squares and boulevards. So, except for the widening of the avenue, the straightening of some of the side streets and the elimination of a number of culs-de-sac, Beyoğlu was left to develop on its own, with no master plan except that imposed by nature, and soon came to resemble the district as we know it.

This period saw an increase in the number of European style multistorey apartment buildings. Zeynep Çelik tells us that in its issue of February 8, 1875, the publication *La Turquie* pointed out that the number of 'comfortable' flats with 'commodious plans and well-studied façades' was very small in Pera, but now a number of skilled French architects were arriving who would be designing apartment buildings comparable to those in Europe. During this period, and even still at times today, frequent and lengthly water cuts became a problem, and the most prestigious buildings boasted their own wells and cisterns.

The cosmopolitan atmosphere of late Ottoman Pera is vividly evoked by the Italian writer Edmondo de Amicis in his *Constantinople* (1896), where he describes the scene as he emerged from the Muslim cemetery by the Galata Tower, walking up along Galip Dede Caddesi and then strolling along Grand Rue de Pera:

> Coming out of the cemetery, we passed once more close to the base of the Galata Tower, and took the principal street of Pera. Pera lies more than three hundred feet above the level of the sea, is bright and cheerful, and overlooks both the Golden Horn and the Bosphorus. It is the 'West End' of the European colony, the quarter where are to be found the comforts and elegancies of life. The street which we now follow is lined on both sides with English and French hotels, cafés of the better sort, brilliantly lighted shops, theatres, foreign consulates, clubs, and the residence of the various ambassadors, among which tower the great stone palace of the Russian Embassy, commanding Galata, Pera and the village of Findukli on the shore of the Bosphorus, for all the world like a fortress.

He goes on to describe the pedestrians he saw along Grand Rue de Pera, mostly Europeans or Levantines, as contrasted with what he had seen below in Galata or across the Golden Horn in the old city.

> The crowds which swarm and throng these streets are altogether unlike those of Galata. Hardly any but stiff hats are to be seen, unless we except the masses of flowers and feathers which adorn the heads of the ladies: here are Greek, Italian and French dandies, merchant officials of the various legations, foreign navy

officers, ambassadors' equipages, and doubtful physiognomies of every nationality. Turkish men stand admiring wax heads in the hairdressers' windows, and the women pause open-mouthed before the showcases of the milliners' shops. The Europeans talk and laugh more loudly here than elsewhere, cracking jokes in the middle of the street, while the Turks, finding themselves, as it were, foreigners, carry their heads less high than in the streets of Istanbul.

Horse-drawn trams were introduced to Istanbul in 1869, one of them running the entire length of Grand Rue de Pera. Then in 1913 the horse-drawn tram-service along Grand Rue de Pera was replaced by an electric trolley line, so that the Periots could ride comfortably all the way to Taksim.

After World War I thousands of White Russian refugees came to Istanbul, many of them settling for a time in Pera and finding work there as restaurateurs, waiters, singers, dancers and musicians, giving a new infusion of life to the district. The cosmopolitan character of the district, now more generally called Beyoğlu, lasted until the early years of the Turkish Republic. After Ankara became the capital of Turkey in 1923 the foreign powers moved their embassies there from Istanbul. The former foreign embassies in Istanbul were reduced to the status of consulates, but the buildings are so palatial that even today they are still referred to as 'embassies'.

Thus today the population of Beyoğlu is predominately Turkish, though the presence of non-Muslim minorities and an increasing number of foreigners have restored something of the former cosmopolitan atmosphere of the district. During the past decade Beyoğlu has experienced a tremendous revival, and in many ways recalls old Pera in the extent and variety of its cultural activities and the vigor of its night life. As the Turkish writer Sait Faik remarked in 1954, words that are still true today: 'Beyoğlu is a world of its own kind. It is an exquisite road full of life, music, entertainment, gaiety, glitter and light, teeming with carefree laughing, friendly people. One cannot visualize an Istanbul without Beyoğlu.'

The whole length of Istiklal Caddesi is now a pedestrian mall, with an old-fashioned tram running from Tünel to Taksim Meydanı, the square at the upper end of the avenue, stopping halfway along at Galatasaray. Our present stroll will first take us down the right (east) side of Istiklal to Galatasaray, then back along the west side

In 1913 the horse-drawn tram-service along Grand Rue de Pera was replaced by an electric trolley line.

to Tünel, then back to Galatasaray by streets to the west of Istiklal. The following stroll will take us from Galatasaray to Taksim by along a similar back and forth itinerary.

We now turn our attention to the terminus of the funicular railway, housed in Metro Hanı, the large building on the southern side of the square. The building was designed by a Belgian firm for the Istanbul Electric Company and built in 1912-13, with a seven-storey addition erected in the 1930s.

Tünel, the underground funicular railway, was built by the French engineer Eugéne-Henry Gavand in the years 1871-6; it was the world's third subway after those of New York and London, designed to take passengers from the shore of the Golden Horn to the heights of Pera. The story goes that Monsieur Gavand came to Istanbul as a tourist in May of 1867, and was inspired with the idea for the funicular one warm day as he was struggling up the steep hill. He spent several years travelling between Paris, London and Istanbul, working out the technical details of the project and arranging for its financing, before being granted an audience with Sultan Abdülaziz, who, being in favor of modernization, and pleased with the idea of having an underground railway before many other

European capitals, approved at once (when the railway station at Sirkeci was being built, and there was opposition to allowing tracks to pass though the grounds of Topkapı Sarayı, the Sultan is said to have declared 'let them pass over my back if they must, but let them pass') and the Metropolitan Railway of Constantinople, from Galata to Pera, was formed.

There was opposition to the funicular at first, with critics referring to it as 'the mouse's hole,' one of them saying 'Why should a man go underground before he dies?' Indeed work was delayed for some time because of objections to the razing of a small cemetery where Metro Hanı now stands (it seems a local folk saint whose name is now long forgotten was believed to be buried there), and because of the protests of the owners of buildings over the route of the proposed tunnel, who feared the weakening of their foundations, and their possible collapse.

An unforeseen problem occurred during construction of the tunnel. It seems that no one had given any thought to what would be done with the tons of earth and rock that would be excavated, and for several years it was simply dumped in a huge pile in the middle of the street, to the great inconvenience of local residents, especially as, whenever it rained, rivers of mud flowed into the surrounding streets. In the end it was used to fill in the area now occupied by Tepebaşı Parkı (for years Les Jardins des Petits Champs), which until recently had been part of Petits Champs des Morts, and the area of what is now Tel Sokak.

> The railway was completed in the spring of 1874, and for six months its safety and operation were tested by transporting cattle. It was finally inaugurated on the 18th of January 1875 with a grand ceremony attended by the Sultan himself and everyone of note in Pera. The ceremony began with the conveying of distinguished guests up and down between Pera and Galata. A band playing Western music accompanied each train. The *Levant Herald* tells us that, 'Shortly after one o'clock, the assembled guests sat down to a sumptuous *dejeuner a la fourchette*, with champagne and other choice wines, served by Messieurs Vallauri, the Pera confectioners, on several elegantly arranged tables on both sides of the Pera station. At the dessert, Mr. Albert, the general manager, proposed the Health of his Imperial Majesty Sultan Abdülaziz...'

and followed with a speech praising the Sultan's dedication to the development of roads and railroads, and expressing the hope that the new railroad would 'prove a new link of fraternity to cement the friendship between the Eastern and Western elements which meet in Constantinople. The band played the Sultan's Anthem, and then Baron Foelckershamb, a representative of the company, proposed the Health of the Queen of England, the most ancient ally of the Sultan. The band then played God Save the Queen.' The Baron also proposed the Health of all other Sovereigns who had representatives there.

These carriages, which were quite primitive at first (and apparently a whiff of cattle remained in the air for some time), were eventually fitted with seats, glass windows and gas lamps brought from London. Initially there was a two-car train on each of the tracks. One of the cars was reserved for passengers and divided into two classes: each class had in turn two compartments, one for men and the other for women. The second car carried goods, animals and horse-drawn carriages. Tünel soon became very popular among the Periots, sparing them the long and arduous climb up the step-street known as Yüksek Kaldırım.

In 1911 operation was transferred to Dersaadet Mülhakatından Galata ve Beyoğlu Beyninde Tahte'l-arz Demiryolu Şirketi, and in 1939 the railway was nationalized to become part of İ.E.T.T. (İstanbul Elektrik Tramvay ve Tünel) and the steam engines were replaced by electric motors. In 1971 the original wooden carriages were replaced with metal carriages, and in 2007 another major renovation was completed. The building across the square to the left with the large smoke-stack contained the steam engines that pulled the trains, and was for years used for the repair and maintenance of the carriages. It continues to house the administration of the funicular.

Looking down to the left we see the very handsome six-storey Beyoğlu Municipality building, the town hall of Beyoğlu. This was commissioned in 1880 by Edouard Blacque Bey when he was the mayor of this part of Istanbul. Designed by the Italian architect Barborini and completed in 1883, it was the first town hall in the city. The central part of the façade, which projects slightly from the two symmetrical wings, is in the neoclassical style. According to

Said Duhani, 'If Monsieur Barborini's daughter is to be believed, her father forgot to put in the front door, and later, to make up for his forgetfulness, added two side doors.' A front door was added at some point during the early years of the Republic. For many years an iron bridge led from the fourth floor of the building to what was then called Karanfil Sokak, almost to the door of Stavros' tavern, a fondly remembered establishment that has long since vanished. The gate that once opened onto the bridge is still standing. Since 1984 the building has been the headquarters of the Beyoğlu Municipality and is currently under restoration.

To the right, in front of where the public toilets now stand, was once the terminus of Maçka-Tünel, Kurtuluş-Tünel and Şişli-Tünel tram lines (and until recently a stop on the Şişli-Şişhane *dolmuş* line), and on Ensiz Sokak was the famous music school, established by Paul Lange in 1884, and Ensiz hat shop. The twin buildings on the right side of Ensiz Sokak were originally owned by English families, and each had a mailbox marked 'Letters' (at one time, each of the foreign communities in Pera operated its own postal service). Across the street was the home and clinic of the Italian pediatrician Dr. Violi, whose annual charity balls at the Pera Palas Hotel were among the most anticipated events of Pera's social calendar.

The large building across the square is Tünel Apartmanı, a luxury apartment built at the same time as the funicular railway. An ornate gateway leads into a picturesque passageway called Tünel Geçidi, flanked by cafés, restaurants, and an old bookshop. The latter is Cohen Sisters Kitabevi, the oldest bookshop in Beyoğlu, which was originally located near the southern end of the Grand Rue de Pera.

During the 1960s and 70s, Tünel Geçidi fell into a neglected and semi-abandoned state, but in the early 1990s a number of pricey and rather precious cafés opened there, the first sign of the gentrification, or rather re-gentrification, that would gather pace in the area over the next two decades.

In his *Vieilles Gens, Vieilles Demeures*, Said Duhani recalls some of the establishments in Tünel Meydanı at the end of the nineteenth century, during the reign of Abdülhamid II. Among them were Loeffler's printing shop, where the gold lettered menus used at Yıldız Sarayı were printed, Monsieur Baudin's second hand bookstore and Verdoux the optician's. Next to Verdoux's shop was the photographic studio of Kargopoulos, Abdülhamid II's personal photographer, one of the very few people allowed to photograph the Sultan and his palace. His trusted position did not prevent him from being subjected to a long and arduous investigation when a police spy noticed a portrait of the deposed Murad V that he had forgotten to take down from the wall of his studio.

Behzat Üsdiken recalls some of the establishments in the square in the 1930s and 40s; Arif Aydın's pudding shop, famous for its ice-cream, at the entrance to Tünel Geçidi; Jean Russel's corset shop; Samuel the watchmaker's; Süreyya Photography Studio (later the Four Seasons Restaurant and now a Gloria Jean's coffee shop); Vasili Guliadis butcher shop; and, with its entrance on Sümbül Sokak (now General Yazgan Sokak) and windows overlooking the square, the original incarnation of the famous Fischer Restaurant, opened in 1931 by Rudolph Fischer, an Argentinean of German descent. In 1930, Rudolph decided to migrate with his family from Tierra del Fuego to Baghdad, and though he intended to make only a brief stopover in Istanbul, ended up remaining here for the rest of his life. The Fischer Restaurant operated in Tünel until 1960, when it moved to the corner across from the British Consulate. The restaurant closed in 1978, but was reopened in 1983 in Gümüşsuyu, across from the German Consulate, by Rudolph's daughter, who still runs the restaurant today.

From much more recent times, many remember Gramofon Jazz Bar, which operated in Tünel from the beginning of the 1990s until about 2008, and Dürüm Kafeterya on the corner of General Yazgan Sokak, which was perhaps the last place in Beyoğlu where *döner kebab* was cooked with charcoal rather than with an electric fire.

Said Duhani also recalls that until the turn of the twentieth century, there was a pool with a fountain in the center of Tünel Meydanı. Today in the spot where the fountain once was stands a sculpture that has been described as 'a sort of obelisk of wrought iron'. This sculpture, by Ayşe Erkmen, and enigmatically titled 'Mutual Assistance', was erected in 1993. Apparently the six patterns used in the sculpture were taken from wrought-iron balcony railings, window-grilles and fences in the immediate area.

In 2007 the sculpture was so badly damaged by vandals that it had to be removed for repair. The vandals' motive remains a mystery. We now make our way back from Tünel Meydanı to Istiklal Caddesi, which begins at the upper end of Galip Dede Caddesi.

The first turning on the right off Istiklal Caddesi is Şahkulu Bostanı Sokak. This street, built in 1920 on what had until then been a small Catholic cemetery, was originally called Yeni Yol, or the New Road. On the right side of the street is Tarık Zafer Tunaya Kültür Merkezi [Tarık Zafer Tunaya Cultural Institute]. This building, built in 1947 on what had been part of the cemetery of Mevlevi Tekkesi, served for years as the Beyoğlu Marriage Bureau, and was converted into a multi-purpose cultural center, named after a distinguished jurist and former dean of Istanbul University Law and Social Sciences Faculties, in 1993. Beyond that the right side of the block is largely taken up with the buildings and grounds of Alman Lisesi [German Lycée], one of the oldest and most prestigious foreign schools in Istanbul, founded in 1868. For the first few years the school operated out of rented quarters, and in 1872 a school building was constructed near the Galata Tower by the German architect F. M. Cumin. It quickly outgrew this building (which afterwards housed a Turkish primary school for many years and is now a parking lot), and the present school buildings were completed in 1897 by Otto Kapp.

On the next block along Istiklal Caddesi we see on our right a gateway opening off Istiklal Caddesi to the grounds of the old Swedish Embassy, now the Swedish Consulate and Cultural Institute. The first Swedish envoy to the Sublime Porte, the foreign office of the Ottoman Empire, arrived in Istanbul in 1750 and took up residence in a wooden mansion that already existed on this site. This burned down in 1818. A garden kiosk spared by the flames served as a temporary home for the legation until the completion of the present edifice, which was designed by the Austrian architect Pulgher and completed in 1870. The furnishings in the public rooms of the embassy date from the period 1790-1810.

Until 1934, the front of the grounds, along the avenue, was lined with shops that the Swedish Government rented out. Among these shops was Cohen Kitabevi, which, as we saw earlier, later moved to Tünel Geçidi. Others, as Said Duhani tells us, included Vodovinch

119

the tailor (whose most illustrious customer was Mehmed Reşad Efendi, Abdülhamid II's brother, who succeeded him as Sultan in 1909 as Mehmed V, and who, as Caliph, declared Jihad [Holy War] against the allies on November 11, 1914); Heidrich Bookstore, and the famous gentlemen's shoemaker Burguy.

Just beyond the Swedish Consulate we see Botter Apartmanı. The house was designed and built in 1900 by the Italian architect Raimondo D'Aronco as the home and workplace of J. Botter, the palace couturier (his shop occupied the ground floor). This is one of the best-known examples of art nouveau architecture in Istanbul, its most distinctive features being the decorative stone carvings and ironwork on the façade and the elliptical stairwell, curved stairs and landings.

Next to Botter Apartmanı stands Testa Apartmanı, the ground floor of which was once occupied by the shop of Sigmund Weinberg, the local representative for the Pathé company who brought the first kinematograph projector to Istanbul. The first private demonstration of this device at the home of İzzet Pasha ended in disaster (the film caught fire and the pasha's mansion burned down), but Weinberg went on to achieve great success, and we will encounter him again several times. These premises were later occupied in turn by Mondiale and ABC bookstores, and now house a branch of the Starbucks chain.

The last building on the block is Hidiviyal Palas. This stands on the site of the famous Hotel d'Angleterre, Pera's first European-style hotel, opened by J. Missire in 1841. The hotel changed names several times before it became Hidiviyal Palas, which in 1950 ceased to be a hotel and became a business center. Among those who stayed in the hotel were the French writer Pierre Loti. Part of the ground floor of this building is occupied by the present incarnation of Lebon Patisserie, which originally opened across the street in the premises later occupied by Markiz Pastanesi [Markiz Patisserie] and about which we will learn more later in this chapter.

The next side street to the right off Istiklal Caddesi is Kumbaracı Yokuşu, named for Kumbaracı Ahmed Pasha, Count Bonneval, who had a mansion there during the years he was a member of Galata Mevlevihanesi community.

On the right side of Istiklal just beyond Kumbaracı Yokuşu is the modern Richmond Hotel. Just beyond that is the entrance to the Russian Consulate. The consulate is housed in the old Russian Embassy, one of the most splendid of all the embassies that were erected on or near Grand Rue de Pera. This was built in the years 1837-45 by Giuseppe Fossati, replacing the original embassy, which had been destroyed by fire in 1831. The building was damaged in the 1894 earthquake and even more by a storm in 1905, after which it was restored by the Italian architect G. Semprini. It has been used to house the Russian Consulate General since 1924. Patricia Daunt, writing in the winter 1993-4 issue of *Cornucopia* magazine, describes the new embassy building erected by Giuseppe Fossati:

> Only in 1837 did work on a new Russian Embassy begin. Plans for an immense neoclassical palace were prepared by a young Swiss architect, who had won his spurs in St. Petersburg with his design for the Chamber of Nobility. The best Russian craftsmen were brought in, the iron gates, the imperial gates and window grilles were specially cast by the famous Russian ironworks at Lugansk, and a team of Italian artists commissioned to paint the ceilings and walls. A palace of no uncertain grandeur arose from the ashes of its wooden predecessor, the height of the ceiling in the columned ballroom was thirteen metres, with the adjacent loggia commodious enough to receive all Pera in comfort.

Russian Embassy.

The embassy building has recently been superbly restored, and has regained all of its former grandeur.

Just beyond the Russian Embassy on the same side of Istiklal Caddesi we come to a five-storey building known as Santa Maria Hanı. This takes its name from the Roman Catholic church of Santa Maria Draperis, whose outer entryway is in the arcade at the center of the façade. A stairway leads down to the church entrance, above which there is a large mosaic of the Virgin, who is shown standing on a cloud held aloft by two cherubs.

The history of Santa Maria dates back to the beginning of 1453, when the Franciscans erected a church dedicated to her near the present site of Sirkeci Station in what was then Byzantine Constantinople. After the Turkish conquest on 29th of May of that year the Franciscans abandoned the church and moved across to Galata, where in 1585 a pious Genoese lady named Clara Draperis gave them a house on or near the site of the present Cité Française, including a chapel with a sacred icon of the Virgin. The house and chapel burned down in 1659 but the icon was saved by a member of the Draperis family. The Franciscans then built a church in 1678 on the present site in Pera, enshrining the icon of the Virgin there. This church was burned down in 1697, its successor was ruined by an earthquake in 1727, and a third church was destroyed by fire in 1767. A new and larger church was erected in 1789, while the present edifice is due to a complete rebuilding in 1904 by G. Semprini.

The sacred icon of the Virgin survived all these catastrophes, and today, encased in silver plate that covers all of the portrait except for the features of the Virgin and Child, it hangs above the main altar of the church. The main altar itself, along with the surrounding chancel area, were done by the Italian sculptor Lorenzo Cerotti in the years 1769. The Italian architectural historian Paolo Girardelli points out some Ottoman Baroque features in the present parish office:

> An inner wall of the present parish office of Santa Maria, constructed later than the eighteenth-century building phase, contains and fills three bays of an originally open arcade with an unmistakable 'Ottoman Baroque' appearance. Its multicentered arches, slender quadrangular columns on high plinths with torus moldings clad

in metallic collars, and fluted palmette capitals, share the stylistic features of many coeval Ottoman structures, from the Madrasa of Seyyid Hasan Pasha, built in 1745, to the small complex of Beşir Ağa of the same period, and even to some parts of the complex of the Nuruosmaniye, completed only twelve years before the completion of the church... A process of stylistic redefinition and renovation begun in Ahmed III's reign (r. 1703-30) (the so-called *Lale Devri* or Tulip Period) had reached maturity by the first half of the eighteenth century, supplanting almost completely the classical Ottoman vocabulary of the mid-sixteenth and seventeenth century. By the time Santa Maria was being rebuilt, the landmarks of this new sensibility had been disseminated in the imperial capital in the form of fountains, *sebils* (fountain kiosks), libraries, schools, and imperial mosques.

In 1763 the church had a registered congregation of 261. Of these, 60 were defined as 'local Catholics' who owned their own homes, 134 as 'foreign Catholics' and 67 as 'foreign Catholic servants'. Of the total congregation, including those 'local Catholics' who did not own their own homes, 73 were born in Pera, 17 in Germany, 33 in France, 13 in Italy, 4 in Jerusalem, 4 in Ragusa and 50 on the Greek islands.

Among those buried in the crypt are Karl Ambros Bernard (1808-44), an Austrian physician who is honored as the father of modern medical education in Turkey.

The ground floor of Santa Maria Hanı housed the Armenian newspaper *Jamanak*, the oldest daily paper in Turkey, which was originally in Narmanlı Yurdu near the Tünel end of Grand Rue de Pera. It once also housed a Turkish Post Office.

Just beyond Santa Maria Hanı we come to Borusan Kültür ve Sanat Merkezi [Borusan Center for Culture and Art], which opened on 17 October 1997. The center, which has Turkey's first privately owned music library, is a venue for concerts, exhibitions and conferences, and also has a publishing house. Borusan Istanbul Philharmonic Orchestra and Borusan Chamber Orchestra give regular concerts.

The next turning on the right is Postacılar Sokak, the Street of the Postmen, formerly the Rue des Postes (so named because there was once a French post office here), which leads to a number of old European embassy buildings and churches.

A short way down and on the left is the entrance to the Dutch

Chapel. This was originally the chapel of the Dutch Embassy, which was founded on Grand Rue de Pera in 1612. The original chapel was destroyed when the embassy burned down in 1831. This was replaced by the present Dutch Chapel, which since 1857 has housed the Union Church of Istanbul, an English-speaking congregation from many lands. The chapel dates from the late seventeenth or early eighteenth century. The basement rooms of the chapel, now used as a Sunday school, have in the past served as a prison. The building is basically a single massive barrel-vault of heavy masonry; the brickwork of the façade, newly exposed to view, is particularly fine.

A frequent visitor to the Dutch Chapel in the early years of its existence was Cyril Lucaris, six times Greek Orthodox Patriarch of Constantinople and once of Alexandria. Deeply influenced by his conversations with Dutch theologians, Lucaris in 1629 published his *Declaration of Faith*, in which he proclaimed his belief in the basic principles of Calvinism. This brought about consternation in the Greek Orthodox Church, the hierarchy of which denounced the patriarch to Sultan Murad IV as a Russian spy. On 25 June 1638 Lucaris was executed by the janissaries, bringing to an end the remarkable career of the man whom Pope Urban had called 'the son of darkness and the athlete of hell.'

At the end of the block, where the street makes a dog-leg to the right, an alley on the left leads to Fransız Saint Louis Latin Katolik Kilisesi [Roman Catholic church of St. Louis des Français]. This was originally the chapel of the French Embassy, originally built on Grand Rue de Pera in 1581. The original chapel of the French Embassy was also destroyed in the 1831 fire, and the present church was built immediately afterwards. Many of the French ambassadors to the Sublime Porte are interred here.

Next to the church is Glavani Apartmanı, built by the influential Glavani family, who came to Istanbul from Genoa by way of the island of Chios in the 1890s. This building has been the home for many years of one of our companions on these walks, Giovanni Scognamillo, and also for a time housed a Vampire Museum. Postacılar Sokak was also the site of the famous Hristaki Meyhanesi.

Below the dog-leg turn the name of the street changes from Postacılar Sokak to Tomtom Kaptan Sokak. A short way down the latter street we see on the right the Spanish Consulate, no longer functioning, a small chapel attached to it. This little church, dedicated to Our Lady of the Seven Sorrows, was originally founded in 1670 by the Spanish Franciscans of the Observance; the present building dates from 1871.

At the bottom of the street is a small square flanked by two large old buildings. The one to the left, at the top of the square, is the former French Tribunal of Justice, a nineteenth-century structure in which the legal affairs of the French 'Nations' was handled in late Ottoman times. The handsome old building on the right side of the square is Palazzo di Venezia, now the Italian Consulate. The present building is believed to date from ca. 1695, though it was completely rebuilt around 1750. In Ottoman times this was the residence of the Venetian bailio, the ambassador of the Serene Republic and one of the most powerful of the foreign legates in the city. We learn from his *Memoirs* that Giacomo Casanova was a guest here in the summer of 1744; in his three months in the city this great lover did not make a single conquest but was himself seduced by one İsmail Efendi.

When Napoleon captured Venice in 1797, his ambassador to the Sublime Porte, the Corsican General Horace François Bastien Sébastiani de La Porta, moved into Pallazo di Venezia (the French embassy building was at that time occupied by the British). After the defeat of Napoleon and the Austrian occupation of Venice, the building served for many years as the Austrian Embassy. Then, at the beginning of the Allied occupation of Istanbul that followed World War I, Italian soldiers ejected the Austrians and reclaimed the building.

The huge building that takes up most of the right side of the street on the next block is the former Scuola Media e Liceo Scientifico Italia, founded in 1885, and now housing İtalyan Lisesi [Italian Lycée].

Returning to Istiklal Caddesi, after a few steps we see on our right the Embassy of the Netherlands, a handsome neoclassical building that looks rather like a small French château. This now houses the Consulate of the Netherlands.

The original Dutch Embassy, built in 1612 on the site of what had been a warehouse of the Dutch East India Company, was burned down twice, but parts of the substructure of the earlier buildings were preserved and incorporated into the present embassy. The present building was designed by Fossati brothers and completed in 1855; the lower structure, visible from the garden, goes back two centuries or more. Fossati brothers, of Italian Swiss origin, had been in Moscow for several years as official architects of Czar Nicholas I, who sent them to Istanbul to build his new embassy in Pera. Here they remained for twenty years or so as official architects for the Sultan, restoring Haghia Sophia in 1847-49 and building several other structures, including the Russian and Dutch embassies and San Pietro ve Paolo Kilisesi.

Beyond the Dutch Embassy there is a cul-de-sac called Muammer Karaca Tiyatro Çıkmazı, named for the theater on its right side. The theater was established in 1955 by the esteemed playwright and actor, and comrade-in arms of Atatürk, after whom it is named. A gate at the end of the street formerly led to the precincts of the French Embassy.

The French Embassy is situated in a fine French garden with views of the Bosphorus and the Sea of Marmara. France was the first European nation to establish formal diplomatic relations with the Ottoman Empire, beginning with the envoys sent by François I to Süleyman in 1525. The original French Embassy, Palais de France, was erected on the present site in 1581 by the French ambassador, the Chevalier de Germigny, Baron de Germoles. The embassy was destroyed in the 1831 fire, and the present building was erected in the years 1839-47 by Pierre Laurecisque. After the founding of the Turkish Republic in 1923 the embassy staff moved to Ankara, while the consular section moved to the old French Hospital farther up Istiklal Caddesi near Taksim. Palais de France now serves as the consul's residence, and it also houses Fransız Anadolu Araştırmaları Enstitüsü [French Institute for Anatolian Research]. This is the most sumptuously decorated of all the old European embassies along the old Grand Rue de Pera. Patricia Daunt describes its splendors in her *Cornucopia* article:

> A magnificent stairway sweeps up to the ambassador's apartment on the second floor, which houses a fine collection of portraits of kings of France and sultans of Turkey, history paintings, firmans [imperial Ottoman decrees] and rare furniture. The columned

drawing room is hung with tapestries bearing the arms of France and Navarre, specially woven for the palace by the Gobelin workshops. The paneled ballroom is decorated with a Restoration carved frieze of alternating swans and musical instruments. Both 'Empire Blue' boudoirs are lined with Louis XVI furniture and porcelains from the factory at Sèvres. The dining room, giving on to a terrace overlooking the garden, is hung with tapestries based on cartoons by Lebrun.

The French Embassy was left unoccupied for some years after the French Revolution, when the French community in Pera was deeply divided and in disarray. According to Akylas Millas:

> When news of the fall of the Bastille finally reached Pera the French Republicans and the Levantines who shared their beliefs quickly gathered outside the palace of the French Embassy, crying out and accusing the French Ambassador Count Choisel-Gouffier of being a royalist. They managed finally to expel him (the Count fled to Moscow) and planted, just as in France, the tree of liberty in the garden of the abandoned embassy, around which the Republicans would gather and celebrate. Many French, particularly the priests and friars, who were denounced as enemies of the Republic, and those of the merchants whose sympathies remained Royalist sought the protection of other embassies. Those who supported the Revolution were considered dangerous by most of the other foreign communities, and some were expressly forbidden to associate with them. A German who opened a theater on the avenue during this period was pressured by the German Ambassador into refusing entry to those wearing the Revolutionary tricolor rosette. The Austrian Embassy's chief dragoman appealed to the Foreign Minister Raşit Efendi to at least discourage the wearing of the tricolor rosette. Raşit Efendi replied, 'The government is not particularly interested in whatever signs the Franks wear or bear. They are considered the government's guests and they are free if they so wish to wear a basket of grapes on their heads.' French trade was disrupted, and many of those local Levantines and Greek Catholics who earned their living as translators for the French merchants found themselves in difficult circumstances.

A 'Citizen Ambassador' by the name of Descorches (whose Jacobin ideals had led him to renounce his title of Marquis de Ste-Croix) was allowed to come to Istanbul (after being detained for a time in Bosnia), but did not occupy the embassy and was not officially recognized by the Sublime Porte. Those French merchants who remained in business conducted their own relations with the Ottomans. And, oddly, an agreement between the Ottoman and French militaries that predated the Revolution remained unchanged, with the result that French officers continued to enjoy their leisure time in the taverns of Galata and the cafés of Pera.

Meanwhile, Descorches and his colleagues, to the alarm and consternation of the Grand Vizier and many of the ambassadors, began printing revolutionary pamphlets and newspapers in a number of languages, including Turkish and Greek. It seems that Descorches had made contact with a number of young Turkish intellectuals, among them İbrahim Müteferrika, who would later establish the first Turkish printing press, as well as with young Greek intellectuals, sowing the first seeds of the Greek Revolution (and also, it is rumored, gathering a great deal of information about Ottoman military installations in Greece). Descorches employed a number of spies, the most useful of whom was a deaf mute in whose presence no one hesitated to speak freely, and who was accepted everywhere. However, this man was an expert lip-reader and would communicate what he learned to Descorches by means of sign language. Another of Descorches supporters was Mouradgea d'Ohsson (originally Muradcan Tosunyan), chief dragoman and later chargé d'affaires at the Swedish Embassy, though later it was rumored that Mouradgea was actually spying on Descorches for Sultan Selim III, whose biography he was writing at the time.

The situation of the French in Pera improved slightly at the beginning of Napoléon's reign. However, when Napoléon invaded Egypt, the French found it necessary to flee. (It was at this time that the French Embassy was occupied by the British.) Those who did not manage to flee, including the translators who had worked for the French diplomatic staff, were imprisoned at Yedikule. Thus, for a time, not a single Frenchman was to be seen in 'Little Paris.'

Returning to Istiklal Caddesi, we soon come to a modern building known as Beyoğlu İş Merkezi [Beyoğlu Business Center], which is of no interest except for a terrace on the first floor that offers a magnificent view.

The next side street to the right is Nur-i Ziya Sokak. This street was formerly called Polonya Sokak [Poland Street], because the Polish Embassy was located there (the name Nur-i Ziya is believed to be associated with the Grand Lodge of the Free and Accepted Masons [Hür ve Kabul Edilmiş Masonlar], also known as the Nur Lodge – one of two distinct Masonic lodges in Beyoğlu, down the street on the left.) On the right side of the street is the building built in 1858, on the site of the former Polish Embassy and part of the grounds of Franchini-Longueville house, as English High School for Girls, which had been established elsewhere in Beyoğlu in 1849. Except for brief periods during the Crimean War and World War I, the school remained in operation until 1979, when it was nationalized to become İngiliz Kız Ortaokulu. In 1980 the school began accepting boys, and became Beyoğlu Anadolu Lisesi.

Just below Beyoğlu Anadolu Lisesi stood the building once occupied by the Embassy of the Republic of Ragussa. After this republic ceased to exist, the building was occupied by a dance school operated by a certain Professor Copello. Professor Copello was replaced in turn by Professor Psalty (whose waltz lessons were accompanied on the piano by Maestro Selvelli) and Professor Panosyan, thought to be the first teacher in the district of the tango that became so popular in the early years of the Turkish Republic. (Beyoğlu, whose social calendar was once crowded with balls and which is now home to countless dance bars, has a long and unbroken tradition of dance schools. Today there are dozens of dance schools operating, and on any evening of the week one can take classes in almost any type of dance imaginable.) This building was demolished and replaced in the 1940s. Just below, reached through a discount clothing market in what is a basement of Beyoğlu İş Merkezi, is a café bar, which changes management and décor quite frequently, that has a terrace overlooking the gardens of the French Embassy.

Across the street on the left, at No. 11 (formerly No. 19; the streets of Beyoğlu were renumbered in 2008, causing considerable confusion), we see a modern building bearing a commemorative plaque. The plaque commemorates the residence in a house on this site of Ferenc (Franz) Liszt, the renowned Hungarian composer and pianist who came to Istanbul in 1847 as a guest of Sultan Abdülmecid. The house belonged to the piano-maker Alexandre Commendinger (about whose shop on Istiklal Caddesi we will learn a little later in this chapter). In 1849 this house, along with many other houses on the street, was destroyed by fire and replaced by a larger building. Said Duhani tells us that it was in this building, at 9:25 pm on July 28, 1911, at a meeting of the *Cercle de l'Union* (a club for high ranking diplomats), as he was playing bridge with the American ambassador to Russia, the Romanian ambassador to France and the Duke of Gramont, Naum Pasha, the Ottoman ambassador to France, suddenly dropped dead at the very moment he was dealt the ace of spades. As the ambulance carrying his body passed Chez Maxim's nightclub, the conductor of the Lionel-Herpin orchestra raised his baton to command a moment of silence out of respect for the pasha. Then, immediately afterwards, the orchestra began to play *"Tout Paris qui chante et qui s'amuse"*.

The street was also home for a time to the Cercle Byzantin, a club whose membership was composed mostly of wealthy Greeks.

The next building on the left was the original location of Scuola Media e Liceo Scientifico Italia, which later moved to Tomtom Kaptan Sokak. It served briefly as the Italian Consulate, and in 1928 was bought by the Free and Accepted Masons, who converted it into their Grand Lodge. The lodge was closed in 1935, when Atatürk banned all Masonic groups, and reopened in 1948.

A short way farther along on the right side of Nur-i Ziya Sokak we pass the side gate of the French Embassy and its beautiful garden. It was on this site that the great Turkish astronomer Takiyüddin built his observatory in 1570, only to have it destroyed by the Islamic religious authorities in 1579. Ohannes Alacaoğlu, owner of Pars Fur Shop, recalls how when he and his friends used to play football on the street, their ball would often go over the embassy garden wall. As they were retrieving the ball they noticed a number of handsome fig trees, so when the figs were ripe they returned to pick them, and sell them to the local Greek housewives who made fig jam. (These fig trees may be the last surviving of the fig trees from which Sycae derived its name.)

If one were to continue to the end of Nur-i Ziya Sokak, turn right on Yeni Çarşı Caddesi, and then immediately left onto Hayriye Sokak, one would come to Cezayir Sokak, a steep, stepped alley leading down to the right. Many of the buildings on the street were built by the same Marius Michel Pasha who was involved in the construction the docks in Karaköy, and until the 1960s it was inhabited mostly by Greek-speaking Catholics of Venetian and Genoese descent from the island of Chios (*Franco-Chiotis* or *Frankiotis*) and the families of the Genoese stonemasons who were brought to work on Dolmabahçe Sarayı. Cem Örter, owner of the Korpi Fur Shop, remembers how every Saturday the residents would put tables out into the street for a communal meal of Greek and Italian food, and that his grandmother Evangelia Gennerini's pasta and roast were everyone's favorite. In 2004 the entire street was bought by a group of entrepreneurs with the idea of creating a street of cafés and restaurants reflecting Beyoğlu's French heritage. A team of Turkish and French architects headed by Mehmet Taşdiken spent two years completing the project, and no expense or effort was spared in producing a Disneyesque caricature of nineteenth-century Paris. When this new 'entertainment street' first opened in 2006, it was named Fransız Sokağı, or French Street. Not long afterwards, however, when a diplomatic incident resulted in considerable public anger at France and the French, the name was changed back to its original Cezayir Sokak, or Algeria Street.

Returning to Istiklal Caddesi, we pause for a moment to catch our breath outside a branch of Ziraat Bankası [Agricultural Bank] just to the right of the entrance to Nur-i Ziya Sokak. These premises were once occupied Monsieur Mulatier's patisserie, whose cakes, Said Duhani recalls, were far superior to those of the better remembered Tokatlıyan and Lebon patisseries, and whose chocolate cakes in particular were a favorite of Fehim Pasha (Sultan Abdülhamid II's feared and hated chief of the secret police, who in 1907, at the request of the German Ambassador, who called him 'a brigand and a notorious thief,' was exiled to Bursa, where a short time later he was lynched by an angry mob. He was described elsewhere as a "baby-faced psychopath", and he and the thugs under his command were frequently guilty of murder, rape and extortion. Fehim Pasha occasionally shot random passersby in the street to demonstrate that he could do so and get away with it). Fehim Pasha would frequently send an aide in his yellow satin lined carriage, which would be loaded down with 'piles of chocolate cake.' The premises were later occupied by an antique furniture store called Dekorasyon, and some still remember that many of the girls at the

English High School across the street were madly in love with the handsome young architecture student who worked there as a shop assistant.

The next building is the recently restored Merkez Han, which houses Koç Üniversitesi Anadolu Medeniyetleri Araştırma Merkezi [Koç University Institute for the Study of Anatolian Civilizations] and the Netherlands Institute in Turkey.

The next street on the right is Eski Çiçekçi Sokak, formerly Linardi Sokak. When Giuseppe Garibaldi lived here as a lodger with the French teacher Madame Sauvagio during his first stay in Istanbul in the 1830s, it was still a street of genteel and respectable poverty on what would then have been the fringe of the developed part of Pera. However, after the Crimean War, when the newly established Beyoğlu Municipality hired British policemen to clean up Galata, the displaced prostitutes, pimps and brothel owners moved here, and remained until about the end of the first decade of the twentieth century. Still remembered from this period is a *koltuk meyhane* on the corner of Eski Çiçekçi and Yeni Çarşı Caddesi called Çiçek, a hangout for streetwalkers and their pimps run by one Stelios, known as the Doctor. This establishment was closed down in about 1900 when the Doctor was deported after being investigated for murder.

Though murders seem to have been fairly common on this street at that time, one murder in particular, 'Çiçekçi Sokak Murder', has remained a part of Beyoğlu folklore for over a hundred years. There are, of course, several versions of the story, but the gist of it seems to be as follows.

A pretty 17 year-old boy named Yanni and his partner, a *kayıkçı* named Pericles with whom he shared a room, went to one of the brothels on the street. Yanni was entertained by a prostitute twice his age named Violeta (better known on the street as Despoina the Mermaid), and during the course of the night they fell passionately in love with each other. It was not until three months later, however, when they began telling each other their life stories, that they discovered they were in fact brother and sister (Violeta having left their family home in Arnavutköy in shame either before Yanni was born or when he was still an infant). Violeta also realized that Yanni's 'friend' Pericles had been the cause of her shame and her descent into prostitution. So one night Yanni and Violeta got

Pericles drunk, and after he passed out they strangled him with his own cummerbund. After a two year investigation, Yanni was charged with the murder and sentenced to seven years in prison. Violeta's name was not even mentioned during the trial.

Hakkı Sabacanalı informs us that from about 1910 until the mid 1920s, the street was home to a number of actors, variety artists, *kanto* singers and composers and musicians, the best known of these being the *kanto* singer Şamran Hanım. Though most of the brothels were gone by this time, there were still a number of *randevuevi*, or houses of assignation, an institution in Beyoğlu throughout the nineteenth and part of the twentieth centuries, where rooms could be rented in which to conduct illicit affairs.

In the 1930s, 40s and 50s, when the street had a mixed population of poor Italians, Greeks, Russians and Turks, it continued to have an unsavory reputation. Even though it was the quickest route between Yeni Çarşı Caddesi and Istiklal Caddesi, most people preferred to take the longer and steeper Nur-i Ziya Sokak, because the youths of Eski Çiçekçi were rumored to threaten passersby with razors and relieve them of their wallets and watches. During this period a gang operating from this street used to buy up all of the cinema and theater tickets in Beyoğlu and then scalp them. Former residents remember a back door of San Antuan Kilisesi [St. Anthony's church] through which the priests would distribute food to the poorest families and take delivery of the grapes from which they made their own communion wine.

Some of the better remembered characters of this time were Madame Shura, the widow of a Tsarist general, who manufactured cosmetics at home and sold them from door to door in wealthier neighborhoods, Arap Zehra and her husband Selahattin, who used to share their wine with the rooster who lived with them (the neighbors could always tell when the rooster was drunk from the way it crowed), and the accordionist Takis Gennarini, who began by playing for coins on the avenue, moved up to a gig at a classy *gazino,* and later gave live performances with his musical group on Radio Istanbul.

Today Eski Çiçekçi Sokak is home to a school for those who wish to become professional DJs, a profession much in demand in Beyoğlu now.

Just past Eski Çiçekçi Sokak we come to entrance to San Antoino di Padova, San Antuan Kilisesi [Franciscan church of St. Anthony of Padua], the largest Roman Catholic sanctuary in the city. This traces its origins back to the original church of St. Francis built in Galata in 1626. This was destroyed by fire in 1696 and its land confiscated by the government. The Franciscans then moved up to Pera, where they first arranged a small chapel within the house in which they were living on Grand Rue de Pera. Then in 1724 they built a wooden church dedicated to St. Anthony. This was burned down and rebuilt the following year in stone. The stone church was restored after the 1831 fire, but it had to be demolished in 1911 when the avenue was widened, whereupon the present church was erected farther back on the same site and rededicated on November 16, 1913. The church is a good example of Italian neo-Gothic architecture in red brick, was designed by the Istanbul-born Italian architect Giulio Mongheri. A plaque on the wall of the chapel in the south (right) chancel commemorates the visit of Pope Paul VI to Istanbul in 1967, when he said mass in San Antuan. Masses are celebrated on Sundays in English, Italian, Polish, Aramaic and Turkish.

During the 1970s and 80s the congregation dwindled to a small handful of aging Levantines, but today there is barely enough room for the crowds who attend the services. The congregation is now made up largely of African and Philippino immigrants, Arabic and Aramaic speakers from various regions of southeastern Turkey and Christian refugees from Iraq.

The ornate structure that forms the front of the church courtyard is San Antoine Apartmanı, an edifice in the neo-Renaissance style erected in the years 1911-13. It consists of two five-storey towers linked by a central arcade on two levels, the ogive arches of the porticoes and windows giving it the appearance of a Venetian palazzo.

The site of San Antoine Apartmanı was occupied for a time by the Concordia (Omonia) Theater, where comic operas, operettas, variety shows and plays in French, Italian and Greek were performed. The Concordia was also a *café chantant*, where customers could invite female performers to their tables and make assignations with the waitresses. It was here that Fehim Pasha (he of the chocolate cakes)

San Antoino di Padova, San Antuan Kilisesi [the Franciscan church of St. Anthony of Padua] traces its origins back to the original church of St. Francis built in Galata in 1626.

began a scandalous affair with Margareth Morgan, the 17 year-old star of the Morgan family acrobatic troupe that was performing there. However, Margareth's hopes of marrying into wealth and aristocracy were dashed when the Pasha was exiled to Bursa, and she returned to the bosom of her family. Said Duhani tells us that the Concordia and Palais de Cristal across the street (about which more later) operated illegal gambling dens in their back rooms. The police raided these dens frequently but were not able to put a stop to the gambling because the proprietors, being foreigners, were under the protection of foreign embassies.

The monumental building just beyond the church is the former residence of Abbas Halim Pasha, the Khedive of Egypt. This was built in 1910 by the architect Hovsep Aznavour; it was originally in six storeys, but two more floors were added subsequently. After the end of the Ottoman Empire it was divided up into apartments and came to be known as Mısır [Egypt] Apartmanı; more recently it has become an office building, with a restaurant on its top floor. The site was previously occupied by a variety theater called the Trocadero, where many of the best known stars of the day appeared.

Just past Mısır Apartmanı is Acara Sokak, formerly Ada Sokak, which is only a block long. Between about 1890 and the mid 1920s, the last building on the left was the fabled Yankee House, the classiest and most expensive brothel in Beyoğlu. The site was later occupied in turn by Melodi Cabaret and the fondly remembered Boem Taverna. On the right side of the street, the Olimpia Cabaret, which closed only recently, was the last of the strip clubs that proliferated in Beyoğlu during the 1970s. In recent years this street has become home to a number of trendy cafes, restaurants and concert venues.

The next block is occupied by a seven-storey building that houses cultural center of Yapı Kredi. The center has a bookshop and art gallery on the ground floor, an exhibition hall on the second floor, and the offices of the Yapı Kredi Publishing House on the upper floors. This site was formerly occupied by Olivio Han (not to be confused with the present Olivio Han across the street), two buildings separated by a courtyard and home to a variety of shops and businesses, including the Üç Fil [Three Elephants], which sold material and thread. Giovanni Scognamillo recalls a newspaper shop, run by two Jewish sisters, where during World War II his father used to regularly buy the German Nazi propaganda magazine *Signal* and the Italian fascist propaganda magazine *Tempo*.

The Galatasaray Police Station, built in 1849 and demolished in 1940, stood on part of the area now occupied by the Yapı Kredi building.

During Ottoman times, the policing of Beyoğlu was a complicated business. The Turkish police had little or no authority over the foreign nationals who constituted such a large part of the population, and the embassies had their own law courts and sometimes even their own prisons. At best, the Turkish police were sometimes allowed to deport foreign criminals who did not have influence with their embassies. And the Ottoman subjects over whom the police did have authority spoke such a variety of languages that the police chief could not function without a team of interpreters. Indeed the chief dragoman often had more power and influence than the police chief himself.

During the Allied occupation of Istanbul that situation became even more complicated, because each of the occupying powers had its own force of military police. While in theory the foreign police had no authority over Ottoman subjects, the British military police in particular (Beyoğlu was in the British sector) often behaved as if they did (In his 1936 novel *La Niege a Galata*, set during the occupation, Louis Francis describes how the British police required butchers to protect their wares with screens, and imposed a fine of 25 liras for every fly that was seen to land on their meat). The situation was further complicated by the large influx of refugees, many of whom were technically stateless, and by the ongoing struggle between the British authorities and the Turkish nationalist underground resistance, with whom the Turkish police were often in close and enthusiastic collaboration.

In the 1922 *Pathfinder Survey of Constantinople*, Charles Trowbridge Riggs describes a visit to the prison behind the police station. The prisoners, mostly those either awaiting trial or whose trials were in progress, were kept together in small, bare rooms that had little light or air.

> There is no bath attached to this prison; when persons are in it more than a month, they are sent to a neighboring public bath, under guard at the order of the doctor. The toilets were in fair condition, though the general odor of the place was not good. About two thousand prisoners pass through this jail a year. At the time of our visit, of the 59 prisoners, 25 were Turks, 13 Greeks, 10 Armenians, 4 Russians, 2 Jews and 5 scattering. The warden, however, informed us that in general the largest element of the population was Greek, corresponding to the preponderatingly Greek character of the population of Pera, and that the smallest number in proportion to inhabitants was from the Jews. By far the greater number here found were charged with larceny, while those under arrest for assault and for murder were approximately 8 or 9 each. In nearly half the cases, the prisoners on being asked why they were there, said it was a case of mistaken identity or of undeserved arrest, they not being guilty at all.

Sermet Muhtar Alus describes the police station as it was in the early years of the Republic: 'The building had a character all its own, and there was always a tumultuous chaos both within and without. It had a singularly dilapidated aspect, which it preserved until it was demolished. The roof was falling in, the plaster was peeling and broken windows had been boarded up or covered with wrapping paper.'

Until the late 1950s there was another building beyond Yapı Kredi building. This was a triangular building called Galatasaray Hanı that thrust deep into the square, almost level with the ornamental gates of Galatasaray Lisesi [Galatasaray Lycée] and that housed Makras Shoemaker's, Teofanides, which sold luxury foods, and Hristos wig shop. All of these establishments closed down after they were looted during the 1955 riots.

We have now come to Galatasaray Meydanı, the square that marks the halfway point of Istiklal Caddesi, where the tram stops on the way from Tünel to Taksim. At this point we will turn around and begin strolling back along the west side of the avenue from Galatasaray to Tünel.

The first building on the right on the west side of Istiklal Caddesi was once the Hotel Metropol, and a little further along was the famous Due Fratelli, purveyor of fine imported wines, which for many years stocked the cellars of Pera's upper crust. The first turning on the right is Tütüncü Çıkmazı, 'the Cul-de-Sac of the Tobacconist.' Not far beyond was Brasserie de Londres, the first beer-hall in Pera, opened about 1890 by one Herr Bruchs. Herr Bruchs hired a group of waiters from the town of Karpenisi in the Epirus Mountains of Greece, all of whom, for the rest of their careers, continued to wear their native costume, including the *foustanella*, a kilt-like skirt (and all of whom had to learn German and French in order to communicate with the customers). Later, six of these waiters opened their own establishments in the district, all of which we will encounter in our strolls. In the early years of the Turkish Republic, Brasserie de Londres became Londra Bar, which featured jazz orchestras in the evenings. During the 1930s Londra Bar experienced something of an identity crisis, offering performances of traditional Anatolian *saz* music as well as of American jazz. During the 1950s and 1960s it became more of a cabaret, offering performances by stars and former stars of Yeşilçam (Turkey's 'Hollywood' until the 1970s, located in and around Yeşilçam Sokak, which we will visit in the course of a later stroll), and in the 1970s it changed hands and identity to become Şanzelize [Champs Élysées], a sleazy belly-dance bar. For years, the entrance to Şanzelize was marked by a large, mirrored 'disco-ball' which became a landmark of sorts, until an ordinance passed in 2001 decreed that all signs on the Avenue be uniform, brass lettering on a wooden background (this ordinance was only enforced for about a year.) More recently, the former Brasserie de Londres has become a bar frequented by young aficionados of a type of Turkish pop music.

A short way beyond this is Aznavur Pasajı, so called because the passageway leads under a building once owned by the Aznavours, a prominent Armenian family. The building, dating from the early 20th century, is distinguished by the elaborate ironwork decoration of its façade, one of the outstanding examples of the art nouveau style in Istanbul. Aznavur Pasajı was once home to Café Commerce, whose billiard room was a meeting place for a faction of the Young Turk movement. Another smaller ornamental gate at the rear, opening onto Meşrutiyet Caddesi, was demolished in 1980. The entire *pasaj* was renovated in 1993, and now houses small shops selling cheap jewelry, 'accessories' and home decorations.

A little past Aznavur Pasajı was Kizizana Beer-hall, opened by the Pollak family in 1898, which called itself 'the first automat beer-hall in the East', offering beer, cognac, *ouzo*, *mastika*, coffee, cocoa, tea and punch from coin-operated dispensers (another automat beer-hall, Otomatik Birahanesi, later opened near Taksim Meydanı). Kizizana also had a separate ladies-only salon.

The next turning on the right leads through a tiny two-storied building called Danışman Geçidi into Hacopulo Pasajı, a picturesque alley reminiscent of Pera of times past. The alley is paved in cobblestone and the remains of an old gas-lamp is still standing, surrounded by some of the oldest buildings in the quarter. The passageway, which opened on April 15, 1871, was founded by a Greek tailor named Hacopoulo, whose shop and other commercial establishments were in the arcade, and with luxury apartments on the upper floors. The poet Namık Kemal founded a newspaper called *İbret* that was published in the shop at what was formerly number

13, and because of this the arcade was a meeting place for members of the Young Turk movement. The pharmacy of Dacat Güler, father of the famous Turkish photographer Ara Güler, was also located here, as was the Sabuncakis florist shop.

An alleyway to the left connects Hacopulo Pasajı with the next two passageways leading off from Istiklal, Emir Nevruz Pasajı and Olivio Pasajı. The alley ends in a stairway leading to Panayia İsodion Rum Ortodoks Kilisesi [the Greek Orthodox church of Eisodeia tis Theotokou, the Presentation of the Virgin], also known as Our Lady of Pera, dedicated in 1807 and rebuilt in its present form in 1855, with extensive restoration in 1893. It is a large five-aisled basilica, with a splendid iconostasis, or chancel screen. On the right side of the iconostasis there is an icon of the

Hacopulo Pasajı
[Hacopulo Passage].

Virgin and Christ-Child dating from the tenth century.

The area around and behind this church, between the Grand Rue and what is now Meşrutiyet Caddesi, was occupied from the late 15th century to the late 19th century by the Pera Fish Market.

A stairway in front of the church goes down to the inner end of Emir Nevruz Pasajı, where we turn right into an alley that leads to the inner end of Olivio Pasajı. This brings us to the former Rejans, the old Russian restaurant, one of the landmarks of Beyoğlu. Rejans was founded in 1934 by White Russian refugees, and its menu include many Russian specialties such as 'borscht', 'piroshky', 'boef strogonoff' and 'chicken kievsky,' washed down with lemon vodka. A restaurant called Turquoise was originally opened at this site in 1924 by Mihail Mihailovitch, who later became part-owner of Rejans. Rejans finally closed its doors in 2011 after it was evicted by the owners of the building, who wanted to establish their own restaurant there.

The German Post Office was also located nearby. Said Duhani tells us that during the reign of Abdülhamid II, the German Post Office rented private mailboxes, and that these were very much in demand from those who hoped this might help them avoid having their letters read by Fehim Pasha's secret police (though he adds that it is doubtful it did).

Returning to Istiklal, just beyond Olivio Pasajı we come to Elhamra Hanı. This stands on the site of the French Theater, which opened in 1827 and was destroyed in the fire of 1830. It was rebuilt on a grander scale by a Levantine named Giustiniani; a ballroom with a 200 square-meter dance-floor and a foyer made entirely of glass was added in 1861 and it became Palais de Cristal, which closed in 1906, to be replaced by the Ottoman-Austrian Furniture and Carpet Company, while the building itself was demolished in 1920. It was replaced in 1922 by the present structure, a monumental edifice in the neoclassical style designed by the Turkish architect Ekrem Hakkı Ayverdi. Elhamra Sineması opened here the following year, and for a time it was considered the most comfortable and elegant cinema in Beyoğlu, with Atatürk himself attending regularly. Over the years it changed management and name several times, for a while becoming the home of Istanbul Opereti and of several theatrical and comedy troupes. In the 1970s it once again became Elhamra Sineması, only this time serving as a rather disreputable soft-core porn theater. The theater burned down on the night of February 15, 1999, in a fire that threatened many neighboring buildings and was put out with the assistance of the fire brigades of four neighboring municipalities. The former entrance to the theater is now occupied by a bar, and there are rumors that the theater is being restored and will be turned into a nightclub with a capacity of 1500.

We now cross Kallavi Sokak, formerly Rue Glavani (which Said Duhani refers to as 'that dank, dark street'), a through street leading to Meşrutiyet Caddesi, and a cul-de-sac called Kallavi Çıkmazı. One of the first modern European restaurants in Pera, Chez Georges, opened here in 1860. The first privately owned art gallery in Istanbul, Maya Sanat Galerisi [Maya Art Gallery], opened on this street in 1951, and for five years served as a meeting place for Turkish artists and writers. In more recent times this street was home to the fondly remembered Kallavi *meyhane*, run by our dear friend Aziz Köksal, who died in the first hour of 2005.

On the corner of Kallavi Sokak and Istiklal Caddesi once stood Oliondor [Au Lion D'Or or The Golden Lion] a gentlemen's clothing and shoe store that was in business, under different names, from 1870 to 1991. Next to this was the musical instrument shop of Alexandre Commendinger, at whose house on Polonya Sokak Franz Liszt was a guest. Alexandre's son Ernst took over the shop when he retired, and earned the title of 'piano-maker to the Sultan' after selling the palace a player piano that is said to have been the source of much gaiety and entertainment in the harem. Beyond this, on the corner of a cul-de-sac called Saka Salim Çıkmazı, was Kutulas Brasserie, opened by one of the waiters from Brasserie de Londres.

We then come to Odakule, a modern high-rise building with an arcade leading through to Meşrutiyet Caddesi. From the 1850s to the 1920s this was the site of the large Bon Marche store, owned

Oliondor gentlemen's clothing and shoe store.

by the Bartoli brothers. Said Duhani tells us that 'there was nothing that could not be found at Bon Marche', and remembers the lead soldiers, and the clockwork model ships with bronze cannons that fired gunpowder, 'which I could not take my eyes off until I was twenty.' Bon Marche was replaced by a store owned by the Carlmann family. Giovanni Scognamillo remembers that the Carlman store sold what seemed to be a limitless array of luxury goods.

In 1926, Mihail Mihailovitch, who later became a partner in the Rejans restaurant, rented the top floor of the building, to which he moved the Turquoise, which now included a bar, a patisserie, a restaurant with 250 tables (served by lovely Russian waitresses) and a ballroom where jazz orchestras performed nightly from 11:00 pm to 4:00 am. King Alfonso XIII spent an evening here shortly after being exiled from Spain in 1931. From 1930 until it closed, the Turquoise hosted the annual Miss Turkey beauty pageant. This building was demolished to make way for the present building, which was completed in 1976.

At the next corner we come to a cul-de-sac called Perukar Çıkmazı, 'the Dead-End of the Wig-Maker.' At the end of the cul-de-sac we see Surp Yerrortutyun Ermeni Katolik Kilisesi [Armenian Catholic church of Surp Yerrortutyun, Holy Trinity]. The first church here was a wooden structure built by the Armenian Catholic community in 1699. The church was destroyed by fire in 1762 and rebuilt as a masonry structure in 1774. During the years 1802-54 the building was used by the Latin Patriarchate vicary and it was used for a time as a Roman Catholic chapel by the Austrian community. When Napoleon III visited Istanbul in 1855 he persuaded Sultan Abdülaziz to give the church back to the Armenian Catholic community, who had been given the status of a separate *millet* by Mahmud II in 1830. The church is still used by the Armenian Catholics.

We now come to a cul-de-sac called Deva Çıkmazı, where the building at No. 2 is the headquarters of İtalyan İşçi Yardımlaşma Derneği [Italian Workers Association]. This association was founded on May 11, 1863 by Giuseppe Garibaldi and Giuseppe Mazzini, the leaders of the Risorgimento movement to unify Italy under a republican form of government. The purpose of the foundation was to care for the widows, orphans and poor among the Italian community in Istanbul, as well as to promote Italian culture in the city through concerts, theatrical performances, and balls. During Garibaldi's second stay in Istanbul in 1863 he and his followers also founded Societa Operaia Italiana.

Giovanni Scognamillo recalls the 'countless tea dances and musical evenings that were held here. Usually the entertainment would begin, in a somewhat nationalist mood, with waltzes and tangos, and then there would be a fox-trot and perhaps a rumba. Suddenly, a crowded table would break into song, and others would join in. These were Italian folk songs or popular songs, but nevertheless, the evening often ended with a *sirtaki*, the community being somewhat ethnically mixed.'

Giovanni Scognamillo also remembers that on Deva Çıkmazı there was His Master's Voice store, where there were booths in which one could listen to the 78 rpm records.

We then pass two more cul-de-sacs, Korsan Çıkmazı, "the Dead End of the Pirate," and Terkoz Çıkmazı. On the next corner, where the modern building housing Turkcell offices now stands, was "Brasserie Suisse", which was opened by Nikoli Lalas, one of the waiters at Brasserie de Londres (this beer hall was also known alternately as Nikoli and Lala). Nikoli was the sole representative in Istanbul of the famous Munich *Paulanesbrau Salvatorbrauerei*. Most of the customers were Swiss and German, and the most famous of them was the director of the Anatolian railway, Herr Heguenin (Nikoli Lalas also managed the buffet at Haydarpaşa Railway Station). Its two-storey building was illuminated by gas lamps and offered a variety of Bavarian beers and French wines. Akylas Millas tells us that 'the select clientele had the opportunity to indulge in all the foreign and national newspapers: *Journal de Constantinople, Echo de Smyrne, Portfolio Maltese, Courrier d'Athens, Mönitor Ottoman*. They could also flick through periodicals such as *L'Annuaire Oriental, Didot Bottin* and the *London Directory*.'

Just beyond Brasserie Suisse, where the Paşabahçe glassware shop is now, was Alman Pazarı [German Market], which later became Bazar dü Levan, run by one Monsieur Paluka. Said Duhani tells us that this shop sold 'piles of goods of every conceivable price and quality. But especially the wall clocks and cuckoo clocks that greeted customers with their syncopated ticking. The richest displays were of exotic animals, monkeys, birds brought from the islands and other winged species. The most faithful purchaser of these rare animals was Sultan Abdülhamid. Monsieur Paluka struggled to keep his collection of animals as extensive as possible in order to please his most famous customer.'

We now come to Balyoz Sokak, formerly Venedik Sokak, or Rue de Venice, a street that leads through to Meşrutiyet Caddesi. A little way down the street on the left was an establishment called the Thuringien, run by one Wilhelm Kuchs. As well as beer, the Thuringien served a wide variety of German sausages, Westphalian ham and sauerkraut. The regulars at the Thuringien were quite

Bazar dü Levan.

a rowdy crowd, and Herr Kuchs kept a stout cudgel behind the counter, with which he did not hesitate to administer beatings to those who got out of line or couldn't or wouldn't pay their bills. It was said that his dazed or unconscious victims were often to be seen stretched out in the street outside his establishment. One day, however, Herr Kuchs had the misfortune to administer a beating to one of Fehim Pasha's secret policemen, after which an agreement was reached between the Pasha and the German Ambassador (the same Ambassador who was later instrumental in having the Pasha exiled), and Herr Kuchs was deported.

The next building beyond Balyoz Sokak was the Hotel des Ambassadeurs, which when it opened in 1850 was one of Pera's first luxury hotels. This later became the Hotel Byzance, which for a time, after he abdicated his throne, was the home of King Milan I of Serbia. The ground floor of this building was later occupied by the Italian Post Office. Next to this post office was the famous Brasserie Viennois (also known as Yani I Birahanesi, opened by Yannis Kakavopoulos, another of the waiters from Brasserie de Londres, who also ran the buffet at the Sirkeci Train Station). The Viennois, which had a large garden in back, served Löwenbrau, Spatenbrau,

Dreker, Nektar and Yakodina beer (accompanied in winter by the famous Bosphorus oysters that are now unfortunately extinct), and was frequented mostly by Austrians, Hungarians and Germans. During the 1930s these premises were occupied by the popular Turan Bar, which was said to have the most beautiful *consommatrices* in the district and where the Fehmi Ege orchestra played nightly, and in the 1950s by a nightclub called Vagon Blö [Wagon Blue], where a South American group called Los Colorados used to perform. Vagon Blö was the scene of a sensational murder in 1956 when the then Beyoğlu police chief's chauffeur, Hayrettin Sinem, shot one Ahmet Faruk over a debt of five liras. Hayrettin Sinem was sentenced to 7 years, 9 months and 10 days in prison and ordered to pay 2,000 liras to the victim's family.

The next street on the right, recently renamed Orhan Adli Apaydın Sokak, was formerly known as Piremeci Sokak. The word *piremeci* is a corruption of *peremeci,* which refers to the operators of a type of *kayık,* described as gondola-like, called the *pereme,* which was used since Byzantine times to carry goods and passengers back and forth across the Golden Horn. The verb *pereme* in Greek means 'to cross to the other side', and comes from the same root as *pera,* 'the other side'. The block beyond this is occupied by a handsome six-storey building known as Suriye Hanı, formerly called Cité de Syrie. This was originally a complex of three contiguous structures; then in 1908 the *han* was rebuilt as a single interconnected building with a covered passage, Suriye Pasajı, on its ground floor. Among the enterprises housed in the passage was *Apogevmatini,* a Greek-language newspaper established in 1925. From 1875 to 1965 it housed *Stamboul,* the longest running French language newspaper in Istanbul. The *pasaj* was also home to one of Beyoğlu's first cinemas, Ciné Centrale [Santral Sineması], which has been described as small and airless, with uncomfortable wooden benches, and also, before the present structure was built, to a shop run by a man named Smirnoff, who sold foods imported from Russia, caviar and salted fish and such, and also bottled and sold his own vodka. Among the establishments that now occupy the *pasaj* is the Retro second-hand clothing store, which occupies almost the entire basement and advertises itself as 'the second largest second-hand clothing store in the world.'

The next street to the right is Gönül Sokak, formerly Timoni Sokak. A little way down the street on the left there was, until fairly recently, an establishment known as the China Bar [Çin Barı], perhaps one of the longest lived of the *pavyons* with which Beyoğlu abounded for much of the twentieth century (the *pavyon* is similar to in nature, and in a sense the successor to, the *baloz* that we encountered in one of our strolls through Galata. They feature musical entertainment, *consommatrices,* and occasionally variety shows or erotic dancers, and tend to charge shockingly high prices that only cotton farmers or sheep merchants can afford. There are very few *pavyons* left in Beyoğlu today, and these are mostly small, seedy and very run-down places on or near Tarlabaşı Bulvarı [Tarlabaşı Boulevard]. The China Bar would have considered itself much classier than these places). Further down on the left is the Nil Pasajı, which leads through to Asmalimescit Sokak, and above which during the 1950s was located a Hungarian restaurant called Csárdás [Çardaş].

The first building past Gönül Sokak was once the Hotel de la Paix et de France, the ground floor of which was occupied by the Brasserie Strasbourg (also known as Yani II Birahanesi, opened by yet another of the waiters from Brasserie de Londres), whose clientele was mostly French. Next to this was the Dimitrakopoulos grocery and wine store. (Dimitrakopulos wine is still produced, and can be found in some stores, though we will refrain from commenting on its quality.)

We now come to a passageway called Şark Pasajı, originally known as the Oriental Passage. The Oriental Passage opened in the 1840s, and after a restoration it reopened in 2003. Among the establishments in the original arcade was the Pera Gallery, Beyoğlu's first art gallery, which opened in 1901 under the direction of the architect Alexandre Vallaury. The Austrian post-office was also located in the passage, as well as a branch of the French post-office. It is now occupied by a branch of Darty chain of electronics and appliance stores.

On the left side of the entrance to the passageway we see the famous Markiz Pastanesi, which reopened in 2003 after the restoration of Şark Pasajı. This was originally Café Lebon, which opened after the completion of the Oriental Passage in the 1840s. After it was bought by Avedis Ohanyan Çakır in 1940 it reopened as the

The entrance of Şark Pasajı [The Oriental Passage] opened in the 1840s.

Markiz Pastanesi, which became the most famous café in Beyoğlu, frequented by businessmen, politicians, journalists, writers, artists and their ladies. (Monsieur Lebon moved his patisserie across the street, where it still exists today, as we saw towards the beginning of this stroll.) The two art nouveau tile panels depicting Spring and Autumn in the form of beautiful young women were designed by Alexandre Vallaury and are signed Arnoux. There were originally supposed to be four panels, but the ones representing Summer and Winter were destroyed during shipment from Paris; they were replaced by two cut-glass scenes designed by Mazhar Resmor. Markiz closed in the late 1970s and remained closed until the first decade of this century, when it reopened briefly before closing again. The premises are now occupied by a fast food establishment catering to office workers.

It is in front of the old Lebon that we once again encounter Vassilis Zacharias, later to be known as Sir Basil Zaharoff, who we last saw among the pimps and *tulumbacı* of Galata. Apparently he used to stroll up and down in front of Lebon, trolling for customers, and it was here that he met Count Orloff, who paid him the very generous sum of 100 gold pounds for his services (we have no record of what these services consisted of). It was after this that

Vassilis started pretending he was Russian, and went to seek his fortune in London, where he immediately got in trouble with the law for 'irregular imports from Constantinople'.

We then cross Asmalımescit Sokak, the lower part of which we will return to a bit later on our itinerary. At the end of the next block, directly across the street from the Swedish Consulate, we see Narmanlı Yurdu, distinguished by its portico of engaged Doric columns and the round-arched portal leading to its interior courtyard. This is one of the oldest buildings along Istiklal Caddesi, probably dating from the late 18ᵗʰ century. During the early 1830s, when the present Russian Consulate was being built farther along the avenue, Narmanlı Yurdu housed the Russian Legation, with the annex on Sofyalı Sokak serving as a hospital. The Armenian newspaper *Jamanak*, the oldest daily paper in Turkey, was for years published here. During the first half-century of the Turkish Republic a number of prominent figures lived here, including the author Ahmet Hamdi Tanpınar and the painters Bedri Rahmi Eyüboğlu and Aliye Berger-Boronai. Aliye's apartment, whose balcony was at the left corner of the *piano nobile*, was the meeting-place for all of the artists, writers, journalists and Bohemian intellectuals and eccentrics of Beyoğlu. Trotsky stayed here for a time when he arrived in Istanbul in 1929. The last Russian occupants, the Neft Trade Union and the Intourist office, left the building in 1933 when it was sold to Avni and Sıtkı Narmanlı. There was once a pool in the courtyard, where a small building housing a notary stands now. The left and right of the entrance passage once housed stables.

After crossing Müeyyet Sokak (down which, on the right, we can see the former home of Count Orloff, which is now Beyoğlu's other Masonic lodge), having come to the southern end of Istiklal Caddesi, we turn right on General Yazgan Sokak, which brings us to the rear gateway of Tünel Hanı, with Sofyalı Sokak to our right. This area is now dense with café-bars, most of which have opened since 2008. The first of these was Badehane Bar, which was opened in 2000 by Bade Uygun, and was for some years the only such place in the area. Of the many colorful characters to be encountered there at that time, perhaps the best remembered is Erdem Uçkan, the impoverished and often homeless painter who used to hawk his paint-

A picturesque passageway called Tünel Geçidi, flanked by cafés, restaurants, and an old bookshop.

ings from table to table for the price of a drink. Erdem died in December of 2009.

We will return to this point after a short excursion, which will take us a farther along General Yazgan Sokak to the next corner on the right, where we turn in to Yemenici Abdüllatif Sokak.

There on the right is a large five-storey building dating from the early twentieth century, we come to Hahambaşılık, or the Chief Rabbinate. This is the headquarters of the chief rabbi of Turkey, a post established by Mehmed II after his conquest of Constantinople in 1453, when he grouped the various minorities of the Ottoman Empire into *millets*, or 'nations'. The chief rabbi was head of all the Jews in the empire, while the Ecumenical Patriarch was in charge of all the Orthodox Greeks, and the Armenian Patriarch headed the members of the Gregorian Church. The building also serves as the headquarters of the community council, and is thus both the spiritual and political center of Turkish Jewry. The office of the chief rabbi is the most spacious room in the building; the other rooms are used by members of the court and the secretariat or serve as the library and archives, with the walls hung with portraits of famous rabbis and representations of important events in the history of Turkish Jewry.

The large building facing Hahambaşılık is the former headquarters of the banker Abraham Camondo, who in the mid-19th century was the wealthiest and most influential member of the Jewish community in Istanbul.

We now retrace our steps to the rear gateway of Tünel Hanı. Where we turn left on Sofyalı Sokak. At the beginning of the street on the left is Eren Kitabevi, the best bookshop in the city for books about Turkey, mostly in Turkish. Next to it, under the same ownership, is Ottomania, where one can buy old prints and maps.

We now continue along Sofyalı Sokak, a narrow street flanked by cafés and restaurants. By far the oldest of the restaurants is Refik. The owner, Refik Arslan, came to Istanbul at the age of 15 from his native Çamlı Hemşin in the Black Sea region, and began work as a dishwasher at the Fischer Restaurant (which we mentioned at the beginning of this stroll) in Tünel Meydanı. Later he worked as a waiter, assistant chef and then chef at Hristaki's tavern on Postacılar Sokak. Then, in partnership with Rudolph Fischer, he opened Nil Lokantası on Asmalımescit Sokak, across from the Nil Pasajı, on the premises formerly occupied by the Vienna Restaurant, and finally opened his present restaurant in 1954. Over the years it has served as a hangout for many well-known Turkish writers, poets and painters.

A short way down the street on the left is Babylon, one of the principal venues for musical events in downtown Beyoğlu, bringing in performers from all over the world. Babylon's opening in 1999 was the beginning of a profound change in the neighborhood, and also in the night life of Beyoğlu in general. Across the street, until recently, was the very bohemian Little Wing Café, run by Esra Uygun, where local musicians often had impromptu late night jam sessions with the internationally known musicians who had earlier performed at Babylon.

At the end of Sofyalı Sokak we turn left on Asmalımescit Sokak. This street long had a mixed reputation, combining the bourgeois and the bohemian, the respectable and the risqué. Much of the street's mystique stems from Fikret Adil's 1933 novel, *Asmalımescit 74*. The novel tells the story of a young man whose curiosity is aroused by the comings and goings of a number of foreign men and women at number 74. His curiosity is deepened when he sees two women kissing each other passionately in the doorway, and he is drawn into a bohemian demi-monde of painters, poets and writers, where he observes the tumultuous love affair between Lily and Georgette, and enjoys a number of dalliances himself. *Asmalımescit 74* is believed to be a *roman à clef*. It is also believed that the author was actually describing number 47, which according to the new numbering system would be number 25. This building is now under restoration.

Fikret Adil wrote that 'a *souteneour* from Marseille, a *lazarone* from Naples or a gangster from Chicago would not feel out of place on Asmalımescit,' but Giovanni Scognamillo, describing his childhood here in the 1930s, paints a very different picture of the street. For him it was a world of staid, respectable, church-going, bourgeois Levantine families.

Next to number 25 is Asmalı Apartmanı, number 23, the building that housed the offices of the *Levant Herald*, the city's first and longest running English language newspaper, founded in 1856 by the Irish author and journalist James Carlisle McCoan and publishing continuously until World War I. The ground floor of the building next to this was occupied by the famous Nil Lokantası, which we mentioned earlier. Nil was replaced in 1970 by Yakup II, whose owner, Yakup Arslan, had previously run another restaurant called Yakup near Tünel Meydanı. In the 1980s and 90s, Yakup II was a favorite hangout for many well-known Turkish writers and poets.

In recent years, a number of new restaurants and cafés have opened on the street, which has become quite fashionable. Directly across the street from Yakup II, is Asmalı Cavit, which was opened in 2004 by our friend Cavit Saatçi, former head waiter at Yakup II (who once worked on the Love Boat in Miami, and was also former chief wine steward on the Norwegian Cruise Line). Also of note is Boncuk, which relocated here from Nevizade Sokak (which we will visit on a later stroll).

At the lower end we cross a side street which on the left is called Minare Sokak, the Street of the Minaret, and on the right Oteller Sokak, formerly Mezarlık Sokak, the Street of the Cemetery. The first of these streets takes its name from the minaret of the masjit that once stood there, Asmalı Mescit, the Vine-Covered Masjit, from which the main street takes its name. The second street takes its name from Petits Champs des Morts, the Little Field of the Dead, a cemetery on the slope of the hill leading down to the Golden Horn.

A few steps farther along Asmalımescit Sokak ends at Meşrutiyet Caddesi. Across the avenue on our left we see the former consulate of the United States of America. This is Palazzo Corpi, built in the years 1873-82 for Ignazio Corpi, a Genoese ship-owner by the Italian architect Giacomo Leoni. Thomas J. Carolan Jr. tells us that:

"Most of the building materials were imported from Italy – doors and window frames of rosewood from Piemonte, and marble flooring and facings from Carrara. The ground-floor reception hall was remarkable for the beauty of frescoes representing mythological scenes, while frescoes over the grand stairway and Great Hall upstairs represented Bacchic and other classical subjects. To the magnificent frescoes were added finely etched glasswork, inlaid parquet floors, elegant fireplaces another exquisite artistic/ architectural features too numerous to mention. All the frescoes were executed by Italian artists brought to Constantinople by the architect Leoni. Sadly, during a "renovation" in 1937, the walls and ceilings on the ground floor were plastered and/or painted over. Left untouched on the ceiling of the upstairs Great Hall, but vulnerable to annual accumulations of Istanbul grime, were depictions of Diana, Neptune, eight Muses, various Graces, Bacchantes and other mythological figures."

Ignazio Corpi died soon after the building was completed. The building was inherited by his nephews who rented it to the American government in 1882. It served as the U.S. Embassy from 1906 to 1937 and as U.S Consulate General until 2003, when it moved to a new building at İstinye on the European shore of the Bosphorus.

Palazzo Corpi was purchased by the American Ambassador John G. A. Leishman in 1907 for 28,000 Ottoman gold liras. He assumed that he would be reimbursed, but the government refused to do so. According to Harry Dwight, on Leishman's return to Washington he threw a large party to which he invited many influential congressmen and senators. During a poker game that lasted well into the night, Leishman lost a significant amount of money to 'a certain potent gentleman'. He then suggested that they play for the embassy. If he lost, he would pay for it, and if he won the government would pay for it. Leishman won and 'the debt of honor was accordingly paid by Congress, the Constantinople Embassy becoming the first we acquired in Europe'.

At the end of the block on the right is the former Hotel Kroeger. During the Allied occupation of Istanbul that followed World War I, the Hotel Kroeger served as the headquarters of the British military police and military intelligence. Stories are told of the rooms in the basement of the hotel where heroes of the Turkish nationalist resistance were interrogated and tortured. The villain of these stories is Captain J.G. Bennett, head of British military intelligence at the time, and later to become known as a mathematician, scientist, writer on mysticism, follower of Gourdjieff and Ouspenski, and founder of an experimental school.

In 1923 the Hotel Kroeger was divided in two. The building on the corner became the Hotel Kohut, and now houses the Chamber of Industry, and the other building housed in turn the YMCA, the Istanbul Conservatory and an evening art school for women, and is now Öğretmen Evi, a lodging house for teachers.

The building across the avenue from Palazzo Corpi once housed the Union Française, a social center for Istanbul's French-speaking community. The building, whose façade is designed in the neo-classical style, was built by the architect Alexandre Vallaury. The building was damaged by fire in 1938 and 1970, after which it was sold to Esbank and restored.

On our right we see the famous Pera Palas Hotel, built in the years 1893-5 by the French architect Alexandre Vallaury. It was built in response to the need for a luxurious hotel to serve travelers arriving aboard the famed Orient Express, which made its first through run from Paris to Istanbul in 1888. It was taken over by the Allied forces during their occupation of Istanbul in the years 1918-22, when the British General Hamilton used it as his headquarters. Agatha Christie was a frequent guest at Pera Palas. In 1979, the celebrity Hollywood medium Tara Rand claimed that Christie's spirit had informed her that the secret behind her disappearance for 11 days in England in 1926 was in a dairy whose key was hidden under the floorboards of room 411 of Pera Palas. On March 7, 1979, reporters from all over the world squeezed into the room as Tara Rand gave instructions over the telephone. A rusty

Pera Palas Hotel, built in the years 1893-5 by the French architect Alexandre Vallaury.

key, 8 centimeters long, was found under the floorboards in exactly the spot she described. In 1986, another key was found under the floorboards of room 511, directly above room 411.

Eric Ambler used Pera Palas as a setting for his thriller, *The Mask of Demetrios*, as did Graham Greene in *Stamboul Train* and *Travels with My Aunt*, Ian Fleming in *From Russia With Love*, Alfred Hitchcock in his film, *The Lady Vanishes* and Ernest Hemingway in *The Snows of Kilimanjaro*. The hotel was the setting for a real-life thriller on 11 March 1941, when terrorists aiming to kill the British ambassador to Bulgaria, Randall, set off a bomb in the hotel lobby, killing six people and wounding nineteen. But they missed their target, for Randall, on arriving, had gone straight to the bar for a drink rather than waiting in the lobby.

Atatürk stayed at the Royal Suite, Room 101, when he came to Istanbul, and the suite is now preserved as a museum. King Zog of Albania also stayed in 101 after his country was invaded by Italy in 1941. Other heads of state who have stayed here include Shah Reza Pahlevi of Iran, King Edward VIII of Great Britain, King Ferdinand of Bulgaria, King Karol of Rumania, King Peter of Serbia, President Giscard d'Estaing of France, President Tito of Yugoslavia, President Fahri Korutürk of Turkey, and Prime Minister Adnan Menderes of Turkey.

The public rooms are very grand, particularly the Louis XVI dining room and the neo-Ottoman bar room, the scene of so many intrigues, both real and fictional, the most notable of the spies who drank there being Kim Philby and Mata Hari, who should perhaps have cocktails named after them. A complete restoration of the hotel was completed on September 1, 2010.

Just beyond Pera Palas, in the corner of Tepebaşı Parkı, was the famous Garden Bar, which opened there in 1911, and which during the 1920s in particular was the place to go in Pera, with variety shows performed by Russian ballerinas, jazz orchestras and dancing until morning (chilled vodka and shouts of *nostrovye*, champagne corks popping and, according to some, cocaine being consumed openly). The Garden Bar closed in 1935, and was demolished in the 1940s. Fikret Adil describes the scene just after it was demolished.

> All that remained of the Garden Bar was the dance-floor and piles of rubble. A few drunks were wandering around rummaging through the ruins. What were they looking for? I approached one of them and asked. After looking me over to make sure I wasn't a potential rival, he said, 'A great deal of money was spent here, sir. Some of it might have fallen through cracks and holes in the floor. That's what we're looking for.' I left them to it and walked away. But at home, I began searching through the ruins of my own memory, trying to retrieve my Garden Bar nights.

We continue past Pera Palas on Meşrutiyet Caddesi, which at the next corner becomes a crescent-shaped avenue open on the left (south) side to a sweeping view across the Golden Horn to the majestic skyline of the old city. This is the quarter known as Tepebaşı, 'Top of the Hill.' This once rivaled Grand Rue de Pera as the most fashionable street in Pera, with a crescent row of hotels, restaurants and cafés on one side of the street, and on the other side a public park (this area having been filled in with the stone and earth excavated during the construction of Tünel underground railway) and a theater. In summer months the park was often a venue for circuses and other spectacles. Akylas Millas tells us that an issue of the *Nea Epitheorosis* announced that 'the renowned Spanish sprinter Mr. Ortegos is to compete in the park of Petits Champs on Sunday afternoon against an English lady on horseback and four cyclists.' Millas goes on to tell us that 'the money that was to be raised from Mr. Ortegos' performance was to go to charity.' On the day of the contest the park was 'decked in flags and brilliantly lit' whilst 'a large crowd of curious observers had gathered.' For the interested historian it should be noted that Mr. Ortegos did manage to outrun the English lady rider but not, however, one of the cyclists, who, 'in the midst of wild applause,' was pronounced the victor of the contest.'

The theater, known as Tepebaşı Kışlık [Winter] Tiyatrosu (to distinguish it from the open-air 'summer' theaters that had been held in the park since it was filled in the 1870s), was built c. 1880 by the Armenian architect Hovsep Aznavour, with a seating capacity of 438 (a theater, known both as *Theatre des Petites Champs* and *Theatre Français*, is thought to have existed here as early as 1860, and to have been destroyed in the fire of 1870). Sarah Bernhardt is reported to have performed at this theater in 1904. The theater changed its name and character a number of times, in 1908 becoming Cinema Pathé, Istanbul's first public cinema, and in 1911, after being remodeled, becoming Amfi Tiyatrosu, and then, in turn, Belediye Tiyatrosu and Şehir Tiyatrosu. Said Duhani tells us that the theater was often rented out for balls and other social functions. The theater was closed in 1970 and destroyed by fire two years later. The last play to be performed there, in December of 1969, was a Turkish adaption of Daphne du Maurier's *September Tide*. In 1984 the park was closed to make way for an underground parking garage, while a hideous exhibition hall was erected on the site of the theater. There are plans to demolish the exhibition hall and replace it with a cultural center.

Near the southern end of the crescent we see Casa d'Italia, a handsome edifice in the neo-Renaissance style built in 1871 by the Italian architect A. Breseni. During the early years of the twentieth century this housed the Italian Embassy; for the past half century it has served as İtalyan Kültür Merkezi [Italian Cultural Center]. From the mid 1920s until the mid 1940s it was also the headquarters of the local branch of the Fascist party, which organized regular

Tepebaşı once rivaled Grand Rue de Pera as the most fashionable street in Pera, with a crescent row of hotels, restaurants and cafés on one side of the street, and on the other side a public park.

Tepebaşı Kışlık Tiyatrosu [Tepebaşı Winter Theater] and its garden.

meetings, dances and showings of propaganda films. During this time, a hall was built on what had been the building's garden, a grand staircase was added, and there was extensive remodeling and redecoration. According to Giovanni Scognamillo, the Fascist party received considerable support among those of Italian descent in Beyoğlu, and fair number even enlisted to take part in the invasion of Ethiopia. According to Said Duhani, considerable trouble was taken after World War II to remove the many fascist symbols with which both the interior and exterior of the building had been emblazoned.

The next building was originally the Hotel Français and later the Continental Hotel, with Dandria Pasajı running through it, connecting to what is now Terkoz Çıkmazı and Istiklal Caddesi. A little further along was Fresko-Pinto building, now incorporated into the larger modern building that houses Turkcell offices. This building also had an arcade, Fresko-Pinto Pasajı, that led through to Istiklal Caddesi by way of what is now Deva Çıkmazı. This arcade was home to Café de la Paix, with its extensive billiard parlor.

At the middle of the crescent we see the former Hotel Bristol, now Pera Müzesi [the Pera Museum]. Hotel Bristol was built by the Greek architect Manoussos and opened in 1896. Ernest Hemingway stayed here in 1919, when he came to Istanbul on assignment for the *Toronto Star*. The building originally had five stories, two more having been added subsequently. It is designed in the neo-classical style, with two pairs of enormous Corinthian column framing a balcony whose pediment is supported by a pair of caryatids.

The Hotel Bristol was acquired in 2002 by Suna and İnan Kıraç Foundation, which restored and remodeled the building and reopened it on 3 June 2005 as Pera Müzesi. The permanent collection includes donations from the Kıraç family as well as from Sevgi and Erdoğan Gönül. Özalp Birol, the general manager of the foundation's art projects, stated at the opening that 'the families wanted to share their cultural and artistic collections with the people, and that's the main reason for the museum.'

The ground floor of the museum has an attractive cocktail lounge, Pera Café, as well as a shop selling books and other objects associated with the museum's collections. The first floor contains the museum's collection of Kütahya tiles and ceramics, as well as a display of old Anatolian weights and measures. The second floor is devoted to Sevgi and Erdoğan Gönül collection of imperial orientalist paintings, dating from the eighteenth century to the early twentieth century. The most famous of these is 'The Tortoise Trainer,' by Osman Hamdi Bey, founder of İstanbul Arkeoloji Müzesi. The top three floors are devoted to changing exhibitions.

Near the northern end of the crescent, at the corner of Kallavi Sokak, we see Büyük Londra Oteli. Originally the Glavanni family home, this was founded in 1891 as the Hotel Belle Vue, and is the oldest hotel in Istanbul. Its lobby is furnished in the style of late Ottoman Pera, its side windows hung with the cages of several resident parrots.

At the end of the crescent the short Beşir Fuat Sokak leads off to the left from Meşrutiyet Caddesi to join the highway leading up from Atatürk Köprüsü. Much of the area to the immediate right was occupied by the fish market from the late 15th century until the last decades of the 19th century, when it moved to its present location. Meşrutiyet Caddesi now follows on its left side the precinct wall of the old British Embassy, whose present entryway is at the far end of Beşir Fuat Sokak.

English diplomatic relations with Turkey began in the last quarter of the sixteenth century, culminating in the agreement between Queen Elizabeth I and Sultan Murad III that led to the founding of the Levant Company by English merchants in 1580. The company was founded by William Harbone, the first English ambassador to the Sublime Porte. Harbone was succeeded by Edward Barton, who became agent for the Levant Company in 1588 and ambassador about 1591. The English legation first settled in Pera near the embassies of the French and the Venetians, taking a 'faire house within a large field and pleasant gardens encompassed within a wall.' The first British embassy building on the present site was erected in 1800 by Lord Elgin, the ambassador, but this was destroyed in the 1830 fire and eventually replaced by the present edifice.

The present building, known as Pera House, was originally designed by Sir Charles Barry, architect of the Houses of Parliament in London, but it was completed in 1845 by Thomas Smith along somewhat different lines. Pera House was commissioned by Sir Stratford Canning, Lord Stratford de Redcliffe, whom Tennyson called 'the voice of England in the East.'

Pera House is a palatial building in the style of the Italian Renaissance, with a large courtyard in the front and in the rear a spacious and very beautiful English garden. The most notable features of the interior are its lovely Palm Court, just inside the entrance, and the grand ballroom on the *piano nobile*. The opening of Pera House was celebrated by a gala Christmas ball that Canning gave on December 25, 1855, one of the guests being Florence Nightingale, much weakened by an illness she had contracted while directing the military hospital at Scutari [Üsküdar] for the British soldiers who had been wounded or taken ill during the Crimean War. When she saw the many linen napkins on the dinner tables she asked Canning if she could have them to bind up the wounds of her patients at her hospital.

Lady Hornby, in her memoirs, writes that 'the palace was very beautiful, its spacious white stone corridors richly and warmly carpeted ... an air of perfectness was very striking.'

The embassy chapel, dedicated to St. Helena, is in the northeast corner of the courtyard. The chapel was founded during the reign of Queen Elizabeth I (r. 1558-1603), who sent a priest to Istanbul along with her ambassador William Harbone. A paving stone in the chapel is dedicated to 'The Rev. Thomas King, Pastor of Constantinople, 1618.' The present church was built in 1882, after the earlier wooden chapel had been destroyed by fire. A plaque in the chapel records this rebuilding: 'This chapel was erected in 1882 from the plans of W. L. Lynn of Belfast under the auspices of His Excellency, the Earl of Dufferin, her Brittanic Majesty's Ambassador to the Sublime Porte.' The chapel was recently the subject of controversy when rumors surfaced that the Foreign Office was planning to sell it to an entrepreneur who intended to turn it into a nightclub, and the local Anglican community was outraged. The chapel was rededicated by the Bishop of Gibraltar in December 2009. In 2013, a luxury café called Chapelle, operated by the next-door Rixos Hotel, began to operate in the chapel's courtyard. Concerts of classical music are occasionally held in the chapel itself.

A little further along to the right is the rear entrance to Hacopulo Pasajı. In the entryway is now to be found Hazzo Pulo restaurant, which opened in the late 1990s. Until the mid 1970s this was the site of the Ananiyas wine shop, opened at the beginning of the

The opening of Pera House was celebrated by a gala Christmas ball on December 25, 1855.

twentieth century by yet another of the famous, *foustanella*-wearing waiters from Brasserie de Londres.

We now come to the intersection where Meşrutiyet Caddesi makes a sharp turn to the right towards Galatasaray Meydanı, and Hamalbaşı Sokak. leads down to the left. On the corner to the left was once the main entrance to the British Consulate, a large gateway flanked by two gatehouses.

These gatehouses were destroyed on November 20, 2003 when, at 11:00 am, a white panel truck packed with 700 kilos of explosives crashed through the gates and exploded just inside the compound, blowing the outer wall onto the street. A 3-meter-deep crater was left where the bomb exploded. The explosion destroyed 6 buildings and damaged another 38. Storefronts were ripped open for blocks and windows were blown out hundreds of meters away. About five minutes earlier, a similar truck-bomb had exploded outside the HSBC Bank in Levent. 33 people were killed in the two bombings, including the British consul-general Roger Short, and 450 others were injured.

In his memoirs, Bensiyon Pinto, Honorary President of the Turkish-Jewish Community, recalls standing outside the gates of the British Consulate on another fateful day, September 6, 1955. He had been visiting a friend nearby when they saw crowds running in the streets and heard shouts of 'Run, run, they're looting the shops!'

> On the corner across from the British Consulate there was a store that sold Philco household appliances. People were throwing brand-new refrigerators out the second-storey window... I started running towards home along Istiklal Caddesi. They'd smashed the shop windows. There were rolls and rolls of silk cloth on the street. As I ran I was aware that I was stepping on furs and on hats of all colors, but I didn't dare stop. Young men with Turkish flags wrapped around their chests were continuing to smash shop windows with long sticks.

At home, as he was trying to reassure his father, they heard a group of men enter their street shouting, 'Burn them down! Burn them all down!' At this point the local imam came out and stopped the crowd, telling them that there were no non-Muslims living on that street.

It is now known that these riots, referred to in Turkey as 'the events of 6-7 September' and in Greece as 'Ta Septembriana', were orchestrated by the military's Tactical Mobilization Group, Operation Gladio's Turkish wing, in cooperation with several grass-roots organizations controlled by the ruling Democrat Party. Thousands of laborers and factory workers who had been recruited beforehand were brought to Istanbul from several Anatolian cities on trains, trucks, buses and even in private taxis. Many had been promised payments of between 3 and 5 dollars, and some later complained that they never received this money.

Tensions between Greece and Turkey over events in Cyprus had been running high. At a little past midnight on September 6, reports began to circulate that the Turkish Consulate in Thessaloniki, in the house where Atatürk was born, had been bombed. (During the trial a few years later of the then Prime Minister Adnan Menderes, it was revealed that the bomb had been planted by a member of the consulate staff who was working for the Turkish intelligence services.) The next morning the news, along with doctored photos exaggerating the damage, was on the front page of the newspapers.

The first reports of looting in the district (the rioting was not confined to Beyoğlu but occurred throughout the city) came from

Pangaltı at about five in the afternoon. Soon larger crowds began gathering in Taksim Meydanı, making their way down Istiklal Caddesi towards Kuledibi and Galata. In his account of the riots, Spyros Veronis says that there were three waves of looters. The first wave, equipped with crowbars, axes and acetylene torches focused on forcing open shop shutters and church gates, the second wave focused on looting shops and churches and the third on attacking homes. The rampage continued for nine hours until, in the early hours of September 7, the army intervened and martial law was declared. Though Greeks were the main target, nearly forty percent of the businesses and homes attacked belonged to Armenians and Jews. Some Turks, particularly Greek-speaking Muslim refugees from Macedonia and Crete, also fell victim to the crowds. And the Karaköy branch of that most Turkish and Muslim of establishments, Ali Muhiddin Hacı Bekir confectionary, was looted and burned as well.

Thousands of businesses and homes were attacked, churches were looted and burned and several cemeteries were desecrated. 37 people were killed, and there were hundreds of reports of rapes and beatings, and even of forced circumcision, particularly of priests.

John Foster Dulles, U.S Secretary of State under President Eisenhower, who was visiting Turkey at the time, urged the government to blame the riots on communists. In an interview he gave years later, retired General Sabri Yirmibeşoğlu, one of the organizers of the riots, said proudly that 'it was a superb special warfare operation that achieved its goals.'

We now follow Meşrutiyet Caddesi on the sharp right turn that it makes here. Before the fire of 1830 this was the site of a large slaughter house that attracted packs of vicious dogs that menaced and occasionally attacked passersby. About halfway along this block we pass the site of Sponeck Beer-hall, which served Czech beers and also had a small grocery store on the premises selling luxury foods imported from Europe. The upstairs salon is where, in 1897, a Polish Jew named Sigmund Weinberg (whose shop we passed earlier on the lower end of Istiklal Caddesi) held the first public screening of a film in Istanbul. The film was *A Train Entering the Station*, and because of Sultan Abdülhamid II's ban on electricity it was projected by gas lamp. Sigmund Weinberg, who also brought the phonograph to Istanbul, later opened Istanbul's first public cinema (Cinema Pathé in Tepebaşı Kışlık Tiyatrosu), became director of the Ottoman Army Film Center and produced the first feature film to be made in Turkey. He is considered by many to be the father of the Turkish film industry.

Sponeck later became Pandeli Beer-hall, a lively place with music, favored by students, that closed in the late 1950s.

We have now reached Galatasaray Meydanı, where this long stroll finally comes to an end.

© Beyoğlu Belediyesi Emlak ve İstimlak Müdürlüğü

CHAPTER 7
From Galatasaray To Taksim

Our next stroll will take us up and down Istiklal Caddesi between Galatasaray Meydanı and Taksim, going up the right (east) side of the avenue and coming on the other side, then returning to Galatasaray on streets to the west of Istiklal.

Almost everything we will see in the course of this stroll dates from after the catastrophic fire that broke out on Feridiye Sokak (which leads west from Taksim down to Dolapdere) on the afternoon of Sunday June 5, 1870, when the wealthier residents had already moved to their summer homes on the Bosphorus and nearly everyone, including the Europeans, was at home taking their afternoon nap. The strong *poyraz* [north-east wind] that was blowing that day quickly spread the fire through Tarlabaşı and the area below Grand Champs des Morts (then known as Yeni Mahalle, or the New Neighborhood), finally stopping at the gates of Galatasaray Lisesi, behind which many of the residents had taken refuge.

The area quickly rebounded, however, and in 1872 *Journal de Constantinople* reported that 'we are celebrating carnival again even as smoke still rises from the ruins of Pera.' The shortage of housing led to a boom in often substandard construction, and in 1876 the municipality launched a campaign to demolish a large number of 'shoddily built and ugly buildings.'

During the decades that followed, this upper stretch of Grand Rue was lined with the mansions of wealthy Levantines, Armenian Catholics, Syrian and Lebanese Christians and Greeks, interspersed by small farms. Many of these mansions were surrounded by large gardens, and the area retained a partly rural air. The period between 1890 and 1910 (when Edouard Blaque was serving his second term as mayor) saw a boom in the construction of large, stone, European style apartment buildings and by 1911, with the introduction of

A street near Galatasaray in the early 20th century.

electricity and electric street lighting it became a modern urban district.

During this time the extortion, gambling and prostitution rackets were largely controlled by a man known variously as Abu Abdullah or Abdullah the Arab (even though he was a Kurd) and his 'gang of twelve', and Arif the Circassian, who also served as Fehim Pasha's hit-man. Abdullah, who also worked closely with the notorious Fehim Pasha, was even said to have established what amounted to a private prison in Feridiye.

As larger numbers of the Ottoman elite began to move to the area, Muslim holidays began to be celebrated in addition to Carnival and Easter, and special entertainments were offered in the evening during the month of Ramadan, including performances of traditional Turkish music in many of the theaters where operettas were usually performed.

The European character of this district was eroded further after the establishment of the Turkish Republic, when foreign nationals lost their privileged status and when, with the development of areas such as Talimhane and Gümüşsuyu, there was an influx of a new Turkish Republican elite. This process of change was accelerated by the Turkification campaigns of the 1930s, after which Turkish replaced French as the principal language of what was now no longer Pera but Beyoğlu. The imposition of Varlık Vergisi [wealth tax or capital tax] in 1942 bankrupted the remaining non-Muslim population. The Armenian, Jewish and Greek communities were hard hit, and Beyoğlu's Levantine community all but vanished. Law 4304 on capital property was ostensibly aimed at war profiteers, but was in fact aimed at religious minorities. Committees selected those who were to be subject to the tax according to their surnames, with the result that 87 percent were non-Muslims. Payment was to be made within 15 days, and those who failed to pay were subject to arrest and the seizure of their property. Thousands of those who were arrested were sent to a forced labor camp in Aşkale in the province of Erzurum. This was followed in the late 1940s by an influx of a newly wealthy Turkish elite often referred to as war profiteers. The riots of 1955 and the deportation in 1964 of much of the remaining Greek population put an end to Greek Pera. (In 1964, in response to attacks on Turkish communities in Cyprus, the Prime Minister abrogated the Lausanne Treaty provision under which Greek citizens who were established in Istanbul prior to 1918 were granted the right to reside in the city. Between 17,000 and 18,000 Greeks were expelled, most on a few hours notice. They were allowed to take with them only $22 and one suitcase of clothing. The Turkish newspaper Cumhuriyet reported that 30,000 Turkish citizens of Greek descent also left at this time, most as a result of semi-official and unofficial harassment.)

This period also saw the end of the Greek and Italian gangsters who operated in Beyoğlu during and after the Allied occupation. They were replaced largely by Albanian, Arab and Laz gangsters. Former police chief Yaşar Danacıoğlu remembers the turf wars between Cafer the Albanian's gang and Nasri the Arab's gang.

The flight of the remaining bourgeois and their replacement by Anatolian migrants in the 1960s and the political violence of the 1970s began a process of decay, and even into the late 1990s Beyoğlu was seen by many as a crime-infested slum. What night life remained was dominated by sleazy *pavyons* and strip clubs. In these years the district was largely controlled by the Of Mafia, a gang from the Black Sea town of Of, one of many criminal gangs that evolved from the right-wing militant groups of the 1970s. The Of gang controlled gambling, prostitution and drugs and also ran an extensive protection racket.

In the late 1980s signs of the district's rebirth began to appear with the opening of a handful of new cafes, bars and restaurants and the restoration of a handful of buildings. This rebirth gathered pace in the late 1990s and took off after 2005, when the character of the district once again began to change profoundly. Hundreds of buildings were restored, rents and property prices soared, the number of cafes, bars and restaurants rose to the thousands and art galleries and boutiques began to appear in what had only recently been derelict back streets.

The Of Mafia lost its hold on Beyoğlu, only to be replaced by a number of Kurdish gangs. We are told that the Diyarbakır gang now controls gambling, drugs and prostitution, a group from the Baykanlı district of Siirt province has a monopoly on parking lots and taxi stands, and a gang from Mardin controls street peddlers and the stuffed mussel industry.

The middle of the first decade of this century saw a dramatic increase in pick pocketing, bag snatching and late night muggings. Much of this was the work of a highly organized gang run by Fırat Delibaş, a native of Diyarbakır province who was seen by many as a Robin Hood figure because he brought electricity and plumbing to several poor and remote villages. He recruited boys directly from these villages, housed them in several buildings in Tarlabaşı, and organized them into disciplined and efficient teams. The Delibaş gang was broken up in 2006 after a series of raids involving hundreds of policemen and months of surveillance. This operation and a dramatic increase in the number of police (both uniformed and plain clothes) placed on the streets after an army officer was murdered by glue-sniffers in Taksim led to a significant decrease in crime.

The nationwide ban on smoking in public indoor spaces that was imposed in 2009 had the unintended consequence of increasing the amount of outdoor seating at cafés, bars and restaurants, and to the continued use of this seating, with the aid of gas and electric heaters, even in the coldest months of winter. This and the spread of bars and cafés into back streets had another unintended consequence; streets that it had been wise to avoid after dark became safe. However, in the summer of 2010 the Beyoğlu Municipality abruptly and without explanation banned outdoor seating and sent workers in trucks, accompanied by police, to confiscate outdoor tables and chairs, despite having collected substantial rents from these establishments for the use of the space.

Galatasaray Meydanı, which takes its name from Galatasaray Lisesi, whose ornate gateway at the northeast corner of the intersection leads to the extensive grounds of the school. Although the present lycée building dates only to 1908, Galatasaray traces its origins back to the early Ottoman period in Istanbul. It was founded by Bayezid II (r. 1481-1512) as a school for the imperial pages, ancillary to the one in Topkapı Sarayı. After a somewhat chequered career, it was reorganized in 1868 under Sultan Abdülaziz as a modern lycée on the French model, with the instruction partly in Turkish, partly in French, to become 'a window of westernization

Galatasaray Meydanı [Galatasaray Square] takes its name from Galatasaray Lisesi [Galatasaray Lycée].

onto the empire and a breeding ground for members of the upper echelons of the Ottoman government.' After Istanbul University, Galatasaray is the oldest Turkish institution of learning in the city, and it has produced a large number of the statesmen and intellectuals who have shaped modern Turkey. The school now has a division of higher education, Galatasaray University, whose campus is at Beşiktaş on the European shore of the Bosphorus.

On May 27, 1995 a group of about 30 people, mostly women, staged a sit-in outside the gates of Galatasaray Lisesi to protest the disappearance of relatives who had been taken into custody by security forces. They began gathering here every Saturday and soon became known as the Saturday Mothers. They suspended these demonstrations in 1999, and resumed them in 2009. Since then Galatasaray Meydanı has become something of a Speakers' Corner, with almost daily demonstrations by a very wide variety of political and interest groups.

The side street leading downhill from the east side of Galatasaray Meydanı past the retaining wall of Galatasaray Lisesi is Yeni Çarşı Caddesi. Below the lycée the name changes from Yeniçarşı Caddesi to Boğazkesen Caddesi. The latter name is based on an historic incident that took place during the siege of Constantinople in the spring of 1453, when, under the cover of night, Mehmed II had the ships of his fleet pulled up the hill from the Bosphorus (in Turkish, Boğaz, or Throat) along this route and then down the other slope into the Golden Horn before dawn, thus bypassing the huge chain that had protected the Byzantine port. Thus the name Boğazkesen, or Cut-Throat, for Mehmed had literally cut his way up from the Boğaz, or Bosphorus.

A short way down Yeni Çarşı Caddesi we find Homer Kitabevi, specializing in works on history, archaeology, architecture, art and travel, particularly those dealing with Turkey.

The narrow street leading off to right in a dog-leg from the top of Yeni Çarşı Caddesi is Tosbağa Sokak. The building on the left at the beginning of the street is Güler Apartmanı, where the renowned Turkish-Armenian photographer Ara Güler has his studio and archives, which can be visited by appointment. He has also given his name to Ara Kafe beside Güler Apartmanı. Ara, whom Cartier-Bresson referred to as 'my co-pilot above the

Golden Horn,' began his career as a photo-journalist in 1950, and his work has now won him recognition throughout the world. His 1994 book, *A Photographic Sketch on Lost Istanbul (1950-1990)*, is a haunting picture of the old Istanbul, including Beyoğlu, that is rapidly being destroyed forever by the relentless march of time. Just beyond the lycée, the first side street to the right is Kartal Sokak, the Street of the Eagle. Once a deserted back alley, it is now home to a number of cafés, bars and restaurants, the oldest of which, about halfway along on the left, is Urban Cafe. These premises were once occupied by the Greek-owned Trianon Patisserie, where tea and cakes were served by waitresses in lace aprons and where a respectable young woman could sit alone without being accosted. Trianon was a hangout for literary figures such as Sait Faik and Tomris Uyar (though it is said that Sait Faik never stayed long, eager as he was to begin the evening's drinking).

After Trianon was smashed up during the 1955 riots and the owners fled to Athens, the premises were occupied by a *pavyon* called Rivayet, where it is said the famous singer Zeki Müren was shot in the leg by a jealous lover. Later these premises served in turn as a warehouse, a yoghurt factory and a coffee house. The Urban Cafe opened in 1995.

The building whose wall occupies much of the right side of the street served as a prison during the first decade of the Turkish Republic and now forms part of Galatasaray Lisesi.

At the end of the street, on the right, sunk just below street level, are premises that have been home over the years to a succession of restaurants and *meyhanes*. In the 1960s, when it was Adalar Restaurant, the Greek singer and guitarist Todori Negroponte used to perform here, and in recent years it has been occupied by the popular Çukur Meyhane [the Sunken Meyhane], presided over by the very charming, thoughtful and efficient Aret Silahlı.

Turning right on Turnacıbaşı Sokak (formerly Su Terazi Sokak), which is the main route between Galatasaray and the neighborhoods of Çukurcuma, Firuzağa and Cihangir, and consequently thronged with pedestrian traffic day and night, we see on the left side of the street a huge neoclassical edifice. This is Zografyon Lisesi [Zographeion Lyceum], designed by the Greek architect Pericles Fotiadis, paid for with donations made by prominent members of the Istanbul Greek community and named after the most generous of these donors, the Paris-based banker Christos Zographos, who contributed 10,000 gold liras. The Zographion replaced a Greek school for boys opened in 1846 by the church of the Panaghia, which was destroyed by fire in 1870. The school was inaugurated in 1893 and its first alumni were graduated in 1899. The school now has a much reduced enrollment, due to the exodus of the Greeks from Istanbul in the past half century. Among its many illustrious graduates is His All Holiness Bartolemeos, the present Patriarch of the Greek Orthodox Church.

On the right side of the street at the end of the block, where it takes a sharp turn to the left, we see Galatasaray Hamamı. This is a public bath founded in 1715 for the use of the students and faculty at the Galatasaray school. Reşad Ekrem Koçu tells us that in his time the *hamam* was favored by revelers who would come in the early hours after a night of drinking. It was well restored in 1965 and is still in use.

The film-maker and artist Kutluğ Ataman often tells the story of how once, as a boarding student at Galatasaray Lisesi in the 1970s, he and his friends climbed over the wall next to the *hamam* as they were sneaking out to enjoy an evening on the town. As he was climbing down he lost his footing and instinctively grabbed for the tangle of wires with which the walls of Beyoğlu were festooned in those years. The wires came loose, and the neighborhood was immediately plunged into darkness. Then a deep, booming voice from within the *hamam* was heard to shout, 'Hey, keep your hands to yourself!'

We follow Turnacıbaşı Sokak as it turns to the left, and a short way down on the right we pass Beyoğlu İtalyan Lisesi [Beyoğlu Italian Lycée], originally the Italian School for Girls, which was founded in 1876 by Mother Luiga Cenegrati of the Sisters of the Immaculate Conception and moved to the present building, whose construction was funded largely by the banker Abraham Solomon Camondo (who with the unification of Italy renounced his Austrian citizenship and took Italian citizenship), in 1882. The school was closed briefly during the Italo-Turkish War and during WWI. Its graduates include several noted classical musicians and businesswomen, and one winner of the Miss Turkey beauty pageant. In 2004 the school's name was changed to Özel Galileo Galilei İtalyan Lisesi.

Across the street, at the corner of Baş Ağa Çeşmesi Sokak, is a baroque street-fountain. The fountain itself is now covered over, and only the dedicatory inscription is still visible. This inscription states that it was founded in 1732 by one Ali Ağa, a commander of the janissary detachment at Galatasaray School.

Just next to the Italian lycée we see the Greek Consulate, housed in a mid-nineteenth-century building, the Palais D'Ionie, which served as the Istanbul residence of Patriarch Cyril II of Jerusalem from 1845 until he was deposed in 1872. The building was later bought by one Yorgos Konstantinidis, who held a literary salon there for Greek writers, out of which emerged the Greek Syllogus Literary Society [Ellenikos Filologikos Silogos Konstantinopoleos].

Beyond the consulate we see the art nouveau facade of Rassam Apartmanı, and across the street, at the corner of Ayhan Işık Sokak, Vakıf Han, built by the architect Ahmet Kemaleddin Bey and completed in 1913, which has been used as a location for two popular Turkish television series and a Coca-Cola advertisement, and also appears in a street scene in the 2011 film adaption of John Le Carré's *Tinker, Tailor, Soldier, Spy*. A short way along on the right we come to the Ağa Hamamı, built in 1454, from which the continuation of Turnacıbaşı Sokak, as it bends around to the right towards Firuzağa, takes its name.

In the latter half of the 19th century, salons began appearing in the area offering rooms with bathtubs for those who preferred to bathe in private and in the European style (most apartments of this period did not have bathrooms, and almost everyone bathed in *hamams*).

We now retrace our steps to Istiklal Caddesi. Just before we reach the avenue we see on the left a building now occupied by a fish restaurant, and which from the early 1960s to the late 1990s housed Ye-Ye Cafe, which featured portraits of the four Beatles on its facade.

A few buildings to the left on Istiklal Caddesi, we see an ornately decorated building dating from the beginning of the twentieth century. The building is currently known as Örs İş Merkezi [Örs Business Center]. Originally this was the home of

The building currently known as Örs İş Merkezi (Örs Business Center) was originally the home of the Esayans, a prominent Armenian family noted for their philanthropy.

the Esayans, a prominent Armenian family noted for their philanthropy. The ground floor of the building housed one of the branches of the famous Baker's department store, a British firm founded by George Percival Baker, who came to Istanbul in 1847 to work as the gardener at the British summer embassy in Tarabya. When the new embassy was built he was put in charge of establishing the gardens there, and during this time he imported a consignment of linen from his brother James in England, which he sold with ease to the employees at the embassy. He continued this practice until 1862, when he was able to leave his position as gardener and open a shop just below Tünel, eventually opening two more shops, one in Sirkeci and the other here, as well as engaging in other enterprises, including a coal mine in Zonguldak and plantations on the island of Eubea in Greece. The Maison Baker remained in operation until the early 1960s. The building also housed the British Pharmacy, established by Noel Canzuch, a British national, in 1859. Because of the large scale of its drug manufacturing business, it became one of the pioneering pharmacies of the Ottoman Empire. Said

Duhani fondly remembers the affable Gianetti brothers, who ran the pharmacy in his time, and who never lost patience with his constant demands for chemicals for his dark-room. In 1932 the pharmacy was purchased by Muhittin Hüsnü, who adopted the surname Kansuk and continued operating it as the British Kansuk Pharmacy until 1965. In 1960, Muhittin Kansuk and Dr. İsmet Sözen founded a drug manufacturing company called Kansuk Laboratuarı, which still operates, producing among other things the popular Kansuk throat pastilles.

A few doors down from Kansuk were the offices of the French Wagons-Lits company, which in 1933 was the scene of an incident that reflected the profound change that was occurring in Beyoğlu's social fabric. On February 22 of that year a Turkish employee was fined and suspended from his job for speaking Turkish rather than French. A few days later, after the incident was reported in the newspapers, a crowd of students, organized by the Turkish intellectual Peyami Safa and the mathematician Cahit Arf, gathered outside the offices to protest. The demonstration got out of hand and the protesters entered the offices, smashed the windows and tossed out desks and filing cabinets.

According to Said Duhani, the building on the right hand corner of Turnacıbaşı Sokak was for many years the residence of the Serbian Ambassador to the Ottoman Empire. The site of the next building along Istiklal Caddesi, a modern building whose ground floor is a branch of Akbank, was once occupied by the two-storey Theatre Varieté, built in 1875 by the architect Barborini. In 1877 it became a cabaret called El Dorado, and in 1897 once again became a theater, briefly called the Verdi Theater and then the Odeon. Early in the twentieth century it became Éclair Sineması, where Sigmund Weinberg (who we encountered on a previous stroll when he introduced the public of Beyoğlu to film at the Sponeck) presented the first "talkie" movies in Turkey. In the early years of the Turkish Republic it became Şık Sineması, which Giovani Scognamillo tells us was in its time the most elegant and luxurious of the Beyoğlu cinemas. He adds that over time it became more and more dilapidated, but that in its last years he saw classic films there such as Julien Duvivier's *Pepe le Moco* (1936), *Rasputin and* the *Empress* (1935), starring John, Ethel and Lionel Barrymore, and Alessandro Biasetti's *La Corona di Ferro* (1941).

An interesting story associated with Şık Sineması is that of Mehmet Erol Ağakay, a refugee from Chania, Crete, who at the age of 19, in the early 1920s, was working as a ticket-taker there. One day the artist who prepared the posters for the cinema's billboards fell ill and was unable to work. Ağakay, who happened to be an aspiring artist, immediately stepped in and began painting the posters for the film that would be showing the following week. He went on to become the leading designer and printer of film posters in Turkey until the mid 1970s.

Scognamillo also remembers, vaguely, that next to Şık Sineması, on the site now occupied by a modern building housing offices of the Government of Istanbul Province and a branch of İşbank, there was in his time a two-storey beer-hall surrounded by a garden. (He wonders which old Pera family once lived there, adding, 'I consulted Duhani, but couldn't find it.')

We now come to a building entered through an ornate passageway known as Atlas Pasajı. The building was erected in 1870 by Agop Koçeoğlu, an Armenian Catholic banker during the successive reigns of sultans Abdülmecid and Abdülaziz. According to Paolo Girardelli, Agop Efendi had the building designed with reference to the Roman Renaissance style of the Palazzo Farnese in Rome. Sultan Abdülaziz had a private suite in the building during the years 1870-6. Later on Koçeoğlu, also known as Koçeyan, signed the building over to Surp Ohan Vosgeperan Ermeni Kilisesi [the Armenian Catholic church of Surp Ohan Vosgeperan]. In the early 1930s the building was bought by the brothers Aziz and Ahmet Borovalı, and was known for a time as Borovalı Han. Since 1948 the building has housed the Atlas Sineması, which in its early years hosted performances by visiting dance companies, including the Modern Ballet Theater, and foreign drama troupes, including Jean Cocteau's troupe and the German Operetta Society. Josephine Baker performed at the Atlas during her second visit to Istanbul in 1959. It is also the home of Küçük Sahne Sadri Alışık Tiyatrosu (named after Mehmet Sadrettin (Sadri) Alışık, one of the best loved actors of Turkish film, remembered chiefly for his comic roles but whose dramatic roles, particularly as down-and-out, hard-drinking

Atlas Pasajı [Atlas Passage] was erected in 1870 by Agop Koçeoğlu, an Armenian Catholic banker during the successive reigns of Sultans Abdülmecid and Abdülaziz.

characters, revealed his true range. He began performing on the stage at a young age and launched his film career in 1946, going on to appear in nearly 200 films and a popular television series and winning a number of awards. He also had a career as a singer, recording a number of 45 rpm records and performing at *gazinos*, published a volume of poetry and had some success as a painter. He died in 1995 at the age of 69).

Küçük Sahne Tiyatrosu was founded in 1951 by Muhsin Ertuğrul, and the first play to be performed there was an adaption, in Turkish, of John Steinbeck's *Of Mice and Men*. The entryway to the cinema is via a monumental neo-classical hall flanked by marble colonnades. At the far end of the hall on the left was the site of

Kulis [Backstage] Bar, which was opened in 1948 by Galip San, the director of the theater (previously the premises had been occupied by a *pavyon* called Buket). Kulis was perhaps the first American bar, that is, a bar rather than *meyhane, pavyon, brasserie* or café, to open in Beyoğlu. The first manager was a Russian named Alexander who was famous for his *piroshki*. The actor Mücap Ofluoğlu, the oldest living former patron of the bar, remembers that 'Alexander would drink from one dawn to the next without stop, and with each passing hour his face would run through various shades of red until he passed out on the spotlessly shiny surface of the bar.'

Alexander was replaced by a refined gentleman remembered as George I, who on his death in 1957 was replaced by George II, who is remembered chiefly for prohibiting the sale and consumption of *rakı* on the premises, presumably to preserve its distinction as a bar rather than a *meyhane* (and also because he believed *rakı* to be a poisonous substance, having seen what it had done to Alexander). This prohibition was lifted after two years when his patrons rebelled. Among the famous actors, writers and painters who frequented Kulis in its early years were Aliye Berger, Füreya, Edip Hakkı, Özdemir Asaf, Cahit Irgat, Gülriz Sururi, Engin Cezzar, Dürnev Tunaseli, Erol Günaydın, Bilge Zobu, Turgut Boralı, İsmet Ay, Hamit Belli, Ümit Yaşar, Ümit Deniz, Sadri Alışık, Sait Faik, Çetin Altan and Yaşar Kemal. The American writer James Baldwin also spent many evenings here during his time in Istanbul.

Kulis closed in the late 1960s, and was reopened in 1973 by Mehmet Ali Değirmenci, closed again in 1978, the site serving for a time as a branch of the Dutch Bank, and was reopened as Eski Kulis (Old Kulis) in 1985 by Cevdet Güntürk. Eski Kulis remained open until 2009. For a time the site served as part of the headquarters for Istanbul as European Capital of Culture 2010. As of this writing the premises are home to a tattoo parlor.

Beyond the entrance, the area that is now a shopping arcade was formerly used as a stable for breeding and raising thoroughbred horses, and later as a circus. It was redesigned in the 1950s, and today is home to discount clothing and jewelry stores. During the 1990s it was the center of the 'grunge' fashion that became popular among some segments of Istanbul's youth. A rear entrance opens onto Baş Ağa Çeşmesi Sokak, which provides a shortcut down to Turnacıbaşı Sokak.

A few steps further along bring us to Anadolu Han, erected in the late nineteenth century by Ragıb Pasha, court chamberlain in the reign of Abdülhamid II (r. 1876-1909). Sarıcazade Ragıb Pasha, of the famous Sarıca family (who moved to the city from the island of Eubea in the fifteenth century), was the longest serving and most trusted of Abdülhamid II's advisors, and indeed the only of his chamberlains to serve continuously throughout his reign. G. Barclay, charge d'affairs at the British Embassy in 1907, describes him as being 'one of those with the most influence over the Sultan' and to have 'amassed a large fortune through his connections at the Palace' (and adds that he was 'sympathetic to British interests'). In her memoirs, Abdülhamid II's daughter Ayşe Sultan writes that 'My father was very fond of Ragıb Pasha and his brother Arif Bey. He placed a great deal of trust in Ragıb Pasha'. Not without his detractors, he was known as a sophisticated and fun-loving gentleman who believed sincerely in the reform and modernization of the empire. He spoke fluent Greek and French, and maintained close social ties to the leading Greek and Levantine families of Beyoğlu and Moda. He and his brother Arif Pasha, who after studying medicine in Athens became Abdülhamid II's personal physician, envisioned moving the cultural focus of Istanbul away from the old city to districts such as Beyoğlu and Moda by building western-style urban housing for the modernized elite of a reformed empire. Ragıb Pasha also had a good head for business, successfully competing with foreign firms for a stake in the coal mines of Zonguldak and establishing a *rakı* factory, the first to be owned by a Muslim, in Umurca in Thrace. His Umurca rakı became popular throughout the Empire, and earned him the enmity of the more religious factions within the Ottoman state. When Abdülhamid II abdicated, Ragıb Pasha was sent into exile on the island of Mytilene. He was allowed to return after a few years on grounds of ill health, and died in Istanbul in 1920 of stomach cancer. During the last years of the Ottoman Empire and the early years of the Turkish Republic, members of his family continued building apartment houses, particularly in the districts of Gümüşsuyu and Harbiye. One of his descendants was among the framers of the 1960 constitution, and in recent years others of his descendants were in the news when they took the government to court, claiming that the large tract of land on which Abide-i Hürriyet Meydanı in Çağlayan had been built in fact belonged to them and had been appropriated illegally.

Ragıb Pasha built three large hans in Beyoğlu, Anadolu, Rumeli and Afrika *hans*, named after the three continents over which the Ottoman Empire was spread. Said Duhani jokes that had Abdülhamid not been forced to abdicate, 'we would in time have had America and Australia *hans* as well.'

Until recently there was an arcade, known as Anadolu Pasajı, leading through the ground floor of the building. For many years, the length of this arcade was occupied by Brasserie de L'Orient, known familiarly as Balabani and established by Nikos Balabanis, yet another of the enterprising Epirote waiters from Herr Bruchs' Brasserie de Londres, which we encountered on a previous stroll. Brasserie de L'Orient, with its high ceilings, caged songbirds, little pools and cascades surrounded by greenery and a huge aquarium in which red fish swam to and fro, was famous particularly for its Arnavutköy oysters, and most of the clientele were gentlemen who would have considered themselves Ottomans. In 1934 the establishment changed hands and became Şark Kafe, known familiarly as Anadolu Birahanesi, which remained a hangout for writers and painters until the late 1950s. Sait Faik spent his last evening in Beyoğlu drinking here just two days before his death on Burgaz Adası on May 11, 1954.

In Said Duhani's time, Belfast Shirtmaker's, owned by the Etronguilos brothers, and where the Sultan bought many of his shirts, was to the right of the entrance to the *pasaj*, and to the left was Lazaro Franco's shop, which sold the fabric from which the suits of the best-dressed gentlemen of Pera were made.

Anadolu Pasajı was also home from 1984 to 2005 to the famous Hacı Salih Lokantası. Hacı Salih Efendi, who began his career as a busboy at Hacı Abdullah Lokantası (which we will see later in this stroll), opened his first restaurant nearby on Bursa Sokak in 1944. Hacı Salih Lokantası closed in 2005 when Anadolu Han changed hands, and reopened on Mis Sokak in the summer of 2011.

Just inside the entrance to Anadolu Pasajı there was for years a tiny shop that sold unwrapped, handmade Zambo Çikolata.

Zambo Çikolata [Zambo Chocolate company] was founded in 1950 by İsmail Özgey, and the chocolate was originally made in a small room in Karaköy. The shop is gone, but Zambo later became a national brand. The entire ground floor of Anadolu Han is now occupied by Flo shoestore. The elimination of Anadolu Pasajı was protested by many, but proceeded with the support of Beyoğlu's current mayor, Ahmet Misbah Demircan.

We then come to Fuat Uzkınay Sokak, named after a pioneer of Turkish film, who as a physics student at Galatasaray Lisesi grew fascinated by film and became Sigmund Weinberg's assistant. In 1914 he made the first documentary film to be produced in Turkey, about the demolition of a Russian war monument in Yeşilköy, and in 1918 made the first Turkish feature film, *The Marriage of Himmet*.

The street was formerly Hava Sokak (named after the Syrian Christian Hava family, whose mansion was on the other side of Istiklal Caddesi and who once owned a lettuce field where the street is now.) At the end of this street we come to Gazeteci Erol Dernek Sokak (formerly Alyon Sokak after the famous Galata banker Jacques Alleon) which was for many years part of the world of Yeşilçam, as the Turkish film industry was known in its heyday. While most of the film studios were on the lower end of nearby Yeşilçam Sokak (which we will visit later), many of the production companies had their offices on or near Alyon Sokak. This was also the site of the famous Figüranlar Kahvesi, or Extras Coffeehouse, where professional extras and bit-part actors would spend their days hoping to be called in. A similar institution exists today in the parking lot behind Atatürk Kültür Merkezi [the Atatürk Cultural Center] in Taksim, in a teahouse where professional extras wait for the busses that ferry them to the film and television studios on the fringes of the city.

Returning to Istiklal we come, after a very short block, to Ayhan Işık Sokak, named after another much loved film actor, often referred to as the 'uncrowned king', who played in over 200 films, usually as the romantic lead, released two best-selling records and had some success as a painter. He died in 1979 at the age of 50.

The street was formerly known as Kuloğlu Sokak, 'the Street of the Slave's Son.' The first building on this block formerly housed the famous Della Suda Pharmacy. This was the first commercial pharmacy in Pera, opened in 1847 by François Della Suda, who served as a pharmacist in the Ottoman army and rose to the rank of general, taking the name Faik Dellasuda Pasha. Later it became the famous Niçoise Patisserie (Nisuaz Pastanesi), where beautiful and elegant Russian waitresses fluttered among the customers with their silver trays, and which from the 1920s to 1950 was the scene of regular gatherings of the Turkish literary world (Salâh Birsel referred to it as the Nisuaz Literature Faculty). The Niçoise served as a restaurant as well as a patisserie. One could eat *piroshky* and *borscht* rather than cake, and drink vodka rather than coffee or tea. The building burned down and was subsequently restored; it now houses a branch of Garanti Bankası. At the bottom of the street are two of the best known 'fortune telling cafes' of Istanbul, Melekler Kahvesi [Angels' Coffeehouse], whose basement rooms are restricted to female customers, and the Kadınlar Kahvesi [Women's Coffeehouse], both of which have a permanent staff of fortune tellers who read coffee grounds and Tarot cards.

At mid-block we see a very narrow building in the neoclassical style. This is the former Alkazar Sineması, which was first opened by the İpekçi brothers in 1920 as the Cine-Salon Electra, taking the name Alkazar in 1925. Giovanni Scognamillo tells us that in his mother's time it was quite elegant, with the hall decorated in rococo style with ornamental plasterwork on the ceilings and walls, and that as well as showing films and concerts it also hosted *thés dansants*. In his own time it had fallen into disrepair, and showed mostly cowboy, horror and adventure films. By the early 1970s it had fallen even further into disrepair and became home to colonies of mice, and tended to show mostly soft-core porn films. The building ceased to be a cinema in the mid 1970s, when the lower floor was transformed into a beer-hall and billiard parlor. In 1994 it was reopened by Onat Kutlar as an art cinema, showing mostly independent films. (Onat Kutlar was seriously injured soon afterwards in the bombing of the Marmara Hotel, and died within a month.) The new Alkazar Sineması went bankrupt and closed in 2010, and there are rumors that the building will be turned into a museum.

Two doors along from the Alkazar is the famous Saray Muhallebicisi [Saray Pudding Shop]. The forerunner of Saray was opened in 1860 in Fındıklı by Kerem Çavuş and his brothers. Kerem's grandson Hüseyin Topbaş (said to be the inventor of 'chicken breast pudding') opened the first Saray Muhallebicisi in Kasımpaşa in 1935, and moved it to what was then still Luxembourg Apartmanı, directly across the avenue, in 1949. It moved to its present location in 2008. With its extensive menu of puddings, sweets and cakes, it is the most reputable establishment of its kind in Beyoğlu, though, as one local wit says, the staff seem to have sworn an oath never to smile. It is now owned by Kadir Topbaş, the current mayor of Istanbul.

We now come to Sadri Alışık Sokak, formerly Ahududu Sokak and before that Bursa Sokak. Said Duhani remembers that in his time, on the corner, there was what he described as a picturesque coffee house whose owner refused to use coffee grinders, and hired two muscular men who worked ceaselessly, bathed in sweat, pounding coffee beans with a giant mortar. Beyond this, on what was then Bursa Sokak, there was Paris Saddle Shop, run by the Dumas brothers, Epiros Coffee House, frequented almost exclusively by Greek tradesmen, a fez-maker and a money changer's. By the late 1960s Bursa Sokak had become so infamous as a center of crime and prostitution, with numerous brothels and bars staffed with *consomatrices,* such as the Picadilly Cocktail Lounge, that the then mayor of Istanbul, Dr. Fahri Atabey, on hearing that natives of Bursa were offended to have such a street associated with the name of their city, changed the name to Ahududu Sokak. The lower end of the street, past the police station on the right, is still a center of prostitution, almost exclusively male prostitution, with a number of very seedy-looking bars and Aquarius Men's Bath House and Gym, which is open 24 hours a day and exudes desperation.

Returning to Istiklal Caddesi, we traverse a short block ending in Bahçeli Hamam Sokak, a very short side street that makes a right-angle turn behind the block to join Sadri Alışık Sokak. This street took its name from Bahçeli Hamam, 'the Bath-House with a Garden,' which stood on the block between Ahududu Sokak and Bahçeli Hamam Sokak. The *hamam* was built at the beginning of the 17th century by Davud Ağa, successor to the great Sinan as head of the imperial architects. At the beginning of the twentieth century the *hamam* was purchased by the court chamberlain Ragıb Pasha, and it continued in use as a public bath up until 1925. For many years it was occupied by Akademi Istanbul, which incorporated the *hamam* within its structure. The *hamam* is now occupied by the somewhat rough-looking Hamam Bar.

A little farther along the block is Camondo Apartmanı. This late Ottoman building is named for the Camondo family, Sephardic Jews who settled in Istanbul in the late eighteenth century. The brothers Abraham and Isaac Camondo founded a bank that became one of the most important of its day, financing the Ottoman government's military expenditures during the Crimean War. As a reward for his services to the state, Abraham Camondo was decorated by Sultan Abdülmecid. He was also rewarded for his services to Italy, and received the title of count from King Victor Emmanuel I. He moved

Camondo Apartmanı [Camondo Apartment], a late Ottoman building named for the Camondo family, Sephardic Jews who settled in Istanbul in the late eighteenth century.

to Paris in 1866 and died there in 1873, but by the terms of his will his remains were returned to Istanbul and buried in the Jewish cemetery above Hasköy on the north shore of the Golden Horn. Next door is Ali Muhiddin Hacı Bekir, a branch of the famous confectionary in the Eminönü quarter of the old city. Eminönü confectionary was founded in 1777 by Hacı Bekir, chef confectioner in the reign of Abdülhamid I (r. 1774-89); he is renowned for his creation of *lokum*, which was first sold in his shop. After his death at an advanced age, the shop was taken over by his son Ali Muhiddin, who was the first confectioner in Istanbul to used refined sugar (previously confectioners had used honey and *pekmez*).

Just next door is the building that housed the Vakko department store from 1963 to 2007. Vakko was established by Vitali Hakko, who made his fortune during what is known in Turkey as 'the hat revolution,' when the fez was banned and men, and indeed women as well, were encouraged to wear hats, opening a hat shop in the Grand Bazaar in the early 1930s. He later founded and served as the first director of the Beyoğlu Beautification Society. In its early years, Vakko was the largest and most popular department store in Turkey. Vitali Hakko died in 2007 at the age of 94 (funeral services were held at Neve Şalom Sinagogu and he was buried in the Jewish cemetery in Ulus) and shortly afterwards Vakko's main store was moved to the Nişantaşı district. The building is now occupied by a branch of the Mango chain of clothing stores.

One of the buildings that the Vakko building replaced was a two-storey building that housed the famous Petrograd Café, which opened in 1920. Jak Deleon tells us that it was run for years by a Russian named Alexander and his daughters Lydia and Elena (Lydia later married a man named Milinsky who ran a flower shop in the Balık Pazarı). The Petrograd was famous for its cognac punch, which was enjoyed in the evenings by writers (Ahmet Hamdi Tanpınar and Sait Faik among them) artists and actors as well as by the leading members of the Russian émigré community. The Petrograd was the first establishment of its kind in Beyoğlu to remain open twenty-four hours a day, a boon for those who missed the last ferry to Kadıköy or the islands. It is rumored that during the 1920s there was an upstairs room where favored customers could consume cocaine.

During the Turkification campaign of 1934 the name was changed to Ankara Pastanesi. In his *Ah Beyoğlu, Vah Beyoğlu*, Salâh Birsel describes it as it was in its later years.

> In the 1940s the Petrograd Café was called the Ankara Pastanesi. But all of the writers referred to it simply as the Petrograd... The waitress at the Petrograd in the 1940s was a beautiful blonde Russian woman in her thirties. She never spoke when she served the coffee and tea. She never gave any of the customers a chance to chat her up. On the right when you entered there was a refrigerated display case that took up the entire right wall. The tables were to the left. This area was separated from the avenue by a large plate-glass window.

The next street on the right is Büyükparmakkapı Sokak. Said Duhani tells us that one Hoci Efendi, retired director of the Istanbul Tramway Authority, used to live in the building on the corner (above the shop that is one of the last places to sell the once famous handmade Pera chocolate), and that he had a miniature tram line in the front window that caught the eye of passersby.

The building on the opposite corner is now mostly occupied by Akademi Istanbul, which was founded in 1911 by American missionaries as the American School of Languages and Art with the aim of encouraging the inclusion of Turkish women in social and business spheres. After the founding of the Turkish Republic it was recognized by the new Ministry of Education, and continued to develop over the years, taking the name Akademi Istanbul in 1995. The Akademi provides education in the fine arts and contributes to the cultural life of Beyoğlu.

At the turn of the twentieth century, Büyükparmakkapı and the surrounding area constituted a respectable neighborhood inhabited by *haute bourgeois* Levantine, Ottoman and Greek families. However the departure of these families in the first decades of the century led to its decline, and by the late 1940s it had become a disreputable area of cheap boarding houses, cheap cookhouses and sleazy bars and *pavyons*.

Vefa Zat describes a typical Büyükparmakkapı *pavyon* of this period. After being admitted by a large and intimidating bouncer, you find yourself in a dim, dank room illuminated by red lamps. The room is dominated by a disgusting and unbearable smell of nicotine and cheap perfume. There are tables, bare of anything but ashtrays, and dilapidated stools. The tables are scattered randomly about the room. Along one wall there are booths, some with swinging doors and some without. The tables and stools in these booths are also in poor shape. The booths are arranged so that those sitting in them have a comfortable view of the stage. The stage is usually directly opposite the entrance, and there is usually a dance-floor in front of the stage. The *consomatrices* who work in these places usually sit together in a corner until customers arrive.

In the 1990s Büyükparmakkapı Sokak began to change identity yet again with the opening of a number of bars that catered primarily to university students and other young people. The best-known of these were Hayal Kahvesi, Jazz Stop and Mojo. For a time the street was also home to a UFO museum. Despite this change of identity, the street retained a bad reputation, with rumors of drug-dealing and late night street fights. Today it has perhaps the densest concentration of bars, restaurants and cafés of any street in Beyoğlu. Many buildings have a bar or café on each floor, as well as roof-top bars. Although it is associated now more with crowds and noise than with any kind of crime, there have been two sensational murders on the street in recent years, one of a Georgian woman who was killed by her jealous, bartender lover and another of a young man who was stabbed on his way home late at night, apparently by an undercover policeman from another district, and apparently for no reason other than having cast a hostile or suspicious glance.

On the night of April 5, 2000, the denizens of Büyükpamakkapı witnessed the presence once again of British policemen on the streets of Beyoğlu. Representatives of the West Yorkshire police, together with hundreds of local police, were on hand to control the rowdy crowds of Leeds United fans, in Istanbul for the Leeds United-Galatasaray UEFA semi-final match, who had filled the local bars. Despite the best efforts of the police, two Leeds fans were stabbed to death and four others injured in an altercation with Galatasaray fans.

A short way up on the left is Pandora Kitabevi, one of the best-known bookstores in the city, which has a large selection of books in English. An annex of Pandora across the street was the site in the 1990s of Beyoğlu's first reggae bar, run by Osman Ozman, a native of Sudan who was an important figure in the revival of Beyoğlu's nightlife beginning in the late 1980s.

The first street on the right is Hasnun Galip Sokak (named after an early member of the Galatasaray Sports Club, a star of the field hockey and ice hockey teams, who served in the Balkan Wars and was killed in action at Gallipoli in 1915). The first stretch of this street has long been known for its second-hand bookstores, several of which are still in operation. A little way along on the right is Umut Ocakbaşı, a *kebab* restaurant that has been popular since the 1970s, though it lost much of its charm when it expanded to occupy five floors and the rooftop of the building next door in 2004. The original premises were previously occupied by a coffee house owned by the famous footballer Suat Mamat.

On the left we see the former headquarters of the Galatasaray Sports Club, which has teams in quite a wide variety of sports, and which was founded in 1905 as a football club by students of Galatasaray Lisesi. This building served as its headquarters from 1925 to 2004, and still houses administrative offices and a private café. At the far end of the street there have for some years been a number of bars that offer live Anatolian folk music.

Returning to Büyükparmakkapı Sokak, we see a short way up on the left Afrika Han, built ca. 1905 by the court chamberlain Ragıb Pasha. When it was built the apartments in this building were considered the most luxurious in Beyoğlu, but later, with the flight of the bourgeois from the district, they were divided into cheap studio apartments and single rooms for bachelors. Afrika Han was the last residence of Hayalet (the Ghost) Oğuz Alpaçin, a minor writer and major eccentric who died prematurely in the late 1970s, and who has since become enshrined as one of the archetypical characters of the bohemian Beyoğlu of his time. Except for the shops on the ground floor and a couple of cafes on upper floors, the *han* has been empty for some years, but there are rumors that it is to be restored and turned into a hotel. A passage, known as Afrika Pasajı, runs through to Küçükparmakkapı Sokak. Part of the ground floor is occupied by a branch of the famous Nizam Pide Salonu, which we will see on a later stroll.

Just past Afrika Han on the left is Beyoğlu's first vegetarian restaurant, which opened in 1995, and across the street on the right is one of the last of the beer halls that proliferated in Beyoğlu in the 1970s.

At the end of Büyükparmakkapı Sokak we come to Tel Sokak, formerly Telgraf Sokak, or Rue Telegraphe, which was filled in at the same time as Tepebaşı Parkı with the earth and rock excavated during the building of the underground funicular at Tünel. Said Duhani tells us of the many distinguished diplomats, statesmen and businessmen who lived on this street and of the literary salons and musical evenings they held (at one of which the Baron Von Reinlein, formerly pianist to the King of Bavaria, used to perform regularly). He adds that Willy Sperco, the Levantine writer, lived at number 19 and that Pierre Loti and Claude Farrere were regulars at Alfred Caporal's salon as well as frequent visitors to the house of the Düz family, whose veranda overlooked the street.

The first building on the left has been the headquarters of the Beyoğlu Spor Kulübü [Beyoğlu Sports Club] since 1926. This club, which began as the Hermes Football Club in the 1880s and changed its name to the Pera Sports Club in 1914, took its current name in 1923. During a tour of France, part of the team decided to remain in Marseilles to establish the Union Sportif Hellenique. Soon afterwards another segment of the team moved to Athens to establish the Athletiki Enosis Konstaninopoleos (AEK), which went on to become one of Greece's major football teams. Beyoğlu Spor Kulübü building formerly housed Pera Greek Ladies' Charitable Sorority. Previous to this, it was occupied by the German Protestant Charitable Society, and for a brief period was home to Alman Hastanesi [German Hospital], after it moved from Sakız Sokak and before settling in its present location. The basement of the building, which was occupied by the popular Jazz Stop bar from 1992 to 2012, was home to Haldun Dormen's first theater, Cep Tiyatrosu, in the mid 1950s.

The next building on the left has served as a homeless shelter since 2003. The site of the next building beyond this, Taksim Ticaret Lisesi [Taksim Commercial Vocational School], was once occupied by the mansion [konak] of a branch of the famous Baltazzi family (Genoese by way of the island of Chios), which was later bought by the notoriously corrupt Selim Melhame Pasha, a Maronite Christian of Lebanese origin who became Abdülhamid II's Minister of Mines, Forestry and Agriculture. After Abdülhamid II was forced to abdicate and Selim Pasha managed to abscond to Italy with a large fortune in embezzled government funds, the building served briefly as the Danish Embassy. Afterwards it served in turn as a tobacco warehouse and an office building. The present building was built in 1932 and served as a primary school until 1993, when it assumed its present function.

If we were to turn left on Tel Sokak, we would come in a few steps to Çukurlu Çeşme Sokak. Just before us, on the corner of Taksim Kuyu Sokak, we would see the spot where Naum Pasha's konak once stood. Naum Pasha (whose uncles Michael and Joseph owned the famous Naum Tiyatrosu, of which we will learn more later), a Roman Catholic of the Tütüncü family with roots in Aleppo, graduated from Galatasaray Lisesi, served as confidential secretary at the Ottoman Embassy in St. Petersburg, as Governor of Lebanon and finally as the Ottoman Ambassador to Paris, to drop dead during a visit to Istanbul, as we learned earlier, moments after drawing the ace of spades during a game of bridge. The current building dates from the turn of the twentieth century.

Naum Pasha's son was none other than Said Duhani, who has been one of our companions on these strolls. Said spent his youth in Paris during the *Belle Epoque*, enjoying all that the city had to offer and with plenty of money to spend, receiving no formal education to speak of and learning only two things well; the art of living and the French language. After his father's death he returned to Istanbul with his wife, a glamorous French actress, settled into a flat on the first floor of Naum Paşa Apartmanı and spent the 1920s living the carefree life of a sophisticated boulevardier. However, tragedy struck in the early 30s when his bright and promising son Sadi inexplicably took his own life. Soon afterwards his wife returned to Paris, and he rented out their flat and spent the remainder of his years living a monkish life in Spartan rooms in the attic, working a few hours a day at Türkiye Turing ve Otomobil Kulübü [Turkish Touring and Automobile Club] and later sitting at Lebon with his copies of *Le Figaro* and *Le Canard Enchainé*. He is the author of two excellent books on late 19th century Beyoğlu (*Vieilles Gens,*

Vieilles Demeures – Topographie Social de Beyoğlu au XIXéme siècle and *Quand Beyoğlu s'Appelait Pera*) published in French and in Turkish translation by the Türkiye Turing ve Otomobil Kulübü. He is believed to have written another book about the infamous Abanoz Sokak, titled *Une Rue Denominé Abanoz Où Tout N'est Pas Noir* [A Street Called Abanoz Where All Is Not Black],* but unfortunately it was never published and no copy is known to exist. Said Naum Duhani died in Alman Hastanesi in 1970 and was buried in Feriköy Katolik Mezarlığı [Feriköy Catholic Cemetery].

Said Duhani tells us that in his time there was a Greek carpenter on the opposite corner who had learned his trade from Mihalis Raftakis, who had served as apprentice to none other than Sultan Abdülhamid II. Abdülhamid was a skilled carpenter and worked for years with two assistants, Mihalis Raftakis and Stamatis Vulgaris, both of whom later went into business on their own.

A little further down the street on the right is Taksim Atatürk Lisesi. This school was founded in the late 19th century as the St. Jean Baptiste Catholic Primary School, became Taksim Middle School in 1937 and Taksim Erkek Lisesi [Taksim Boys' Lycée] in 1940. In 1984 the school began accepting girls and took its present name.

Returning to Çukurlu Çeşme Sokak, we see on our right the massive St. Pulchérie Fransız Lisesi [St. Pulchérie Lycée]. This building was built in 1890 by Italian Jesuits as a boys' lycée. It was later taken over by French Lazarist priests, who established their own boys' school. St. Pulchérie was founded as a girls' school in 1846 by nuns of the Sisters of Charity. It was originally housed in the French Hospital, and moved to Bursa Sokak (Ayhan Işık Sokak) in 1884. The school was closed during World War I, and when the French nuns returned in 1919 they found their building in ruins, and moved to the then empty building that had housed the Lazarist school. St. Pulchérie was recognized by the new Turkish Ministry of Education in 1927, became a lycée in 1998 and began accepting boys in 2000.

The modern grey building across the street houses the Istanbul branch of the Human Rights Association, which has been the scene of numerous police raids and street battles and one bomb attack.

* Abanoz: Ebony.

Maç Sokak, the street to the right at the end of Çukurlu Çeşme Sokak, leads down past a long abandoned Greek primary school and what was once a flower farm where the flowers sold at Çiçek Pasajı were once grown (the hideous hospital building on this site was built in 1969), to Ağa Hamam Caddesi. Billurcu Sokak, to the left, leads up to the intersection of Meşelik Sokak and Sıraselviler Caddesi. Plans were recently announced to demolish and rebuild the hospital. The municipal authorities persistently deny rumors that the hospital will be replaced by a luxury hotel and shopping center.

We now return, finally, to Istiklal Caddesi. On the short block between Büyükparmakkapı and Küçükparmakkapı we see the site of Russo-American Cinema, which operated here from 1913 to 1937. Originally known as Amerikan Sinema because it showed mostly American films, it became known as Russo-American Cinema when it became a gathering place for Russian refugees who had fled the Bolshevik Revolution.

The first building on the next block once housed a small cinema that opened in 1933 as Ciné Étoile and became Yıldız Sineması in 1940. Giovanni Scognamillo tells us that in his time Yıldız showed mostly English films starring the likes of Stewart Granger, Margareth Lockwood and James Mason, as well as films produced by the American RKO studios. He also remembers the two prostitutes, one very fat and wall-eyed and the other skin and bones, who used to stand near the entrance summer and winter. Yıldız Sineması closed in 1955.

A few doors up, in premises now occupied by an electronics store and on the site of what was once Noradunciyan Efendi Apartmanı, was Lale Sineması, which was opened in 1939 by Cemil Filmer, who once worked as Fuat Uzkınay's cameraman and went on to become a major film producer and studio owner. During World War II he was once threatened in his office by agents from the German Consulate for showing anti-fascist films. They told him that when their tanks arrived, they would drag him from his office and hang him from a lamppost on the avenue. He replied that if German tanks came to Turkey they would not find him in his office because he would be fighting in the resistance. The gala opening, which featured a showing of *Lumieres de Paris* starring Tino Rossi, caused quite a stir in Beyoğlu. Giovanni Scognamillo tells us that in his time Lale showed mostly films produced by the Paramount and Warner Brothers studios. Lale was also famous for the enormous illuminated and brightly painted figures, of actors or scenes from the films being shown, that were placed outside the entrance. The last building before Meşelik Sokak, a modern six-storey structure with a glass façade, houses İşbank Art Gallery.

We now turn into Meşelik Sokak (formerly Rum Kabristan Sokak, or the Street of the Greek Cemetery; the street and the area to the right, as well as much of the precincts of the church and of Zapyon Okulu [Zappeion School], was once a Greek Orthodox cemetery), where on the left side we enter the courtyard of Aya Triada Rum Ortodoks Kilisesi [Greek Orthodox Church of Haghia Triada, the Holy Trinity], distinguished by its high dome and twin bell towers.

The first church on this site was a much smaller wooden structure erected in 1865. The present structure, by far the largest Greek Orthodox church built in Istanbul after the Turkish conquest, was designed in the neo-Byzantine style by the Greek architect P. Kampanaki and completed in 1882. This was the first church in Istanbul to be built with a dome after the conquest, the permission to construct a dome coming from the reforms that were instituted by Mahmud II (r. 1808-39) and Abdülmecid (r. 1839-61). The great size of the church reflects the large number of Greeks in Istanbul at the time it was built, when they made up twenty-one percent of the population, about 180,000 of some 850,000 of whom fifty-three percent were Muslims.

Şarl Berger remembers that in the 1960s an orangutan named Yaşar lived in the church garden. Yaşar, who always wore a jacket and a fedora, became a mascot for local taxi drivers, who fed him and provided him with the bottled water of which he was so fond.

Farther along Meşelik Sokak the street passes between two of the largest schools built in the late Ottoman period by the Christian minorities in Istanbul.

On the left is Özel Zapyon Rum İlköğretim Okulu [Zapyon Greek School for Girls], named for its founder, the philanthropist Konstantinos Zappas, who built in the years 1883-5. The school has classes in the primary, junior-high and high-school levels. The student body is now very small because of the exodus of the Greeks from Istanbul in the past half century. The school was closed for some years during the 1920s.

Across the street on the right is Esayan Ermeni Okulu [Esayan Armenian School], founded in 1895 by the brothers Mıgırdiç and Hovhannes Esayan. It was originally primary and middle-school, but a high-school was added in 1930. Behind the school is Surp Harutyun Ermeni Kilisesi [the Armenian Gregorian church of Surp Harutyun], originally a wooden structure that was replaced by the present building in 1895, another benefaction of the Esayan brothers.

We retrace our steps along Meşelik Sokak to Istiklal Caddesi, where on the corner to the right was the entrance of the famous Hacı Baba Lokantası. This was the oldest restaurant on Istiklal Caddesi, founded in 1921, the terrace of the restaurant overlooked the courtyard of Aya Triada Kilisesi [Haghia Triada church]. The restaurant closed in 2013. The site of the restaurant was previously occupied by the massive Evgenidios Aşevi [Evgenidios Refectory], built towards the end of the 19th century, where the poor of the parish were fed. The rest of the block, as far as the famous Eptalofos Kahvesi [Eptalofos Café] whose terrace overlooking Taksim Meydanı is now occupied by Burger King, was owned by Balıklı Rum Hastanesi [the Greek Hospital at Balıklı].

We have now reached Taksim Meydanı, where we cross Istiklal Caddesi and start strolling back to Galatasaray along the west side of the avenue.

On the first block, between Taksim Sokak and Zambak Sokak we see the old French Consulate, a long one-storey building. This was first built in 1719 as the French Consulate, not to be confused with the old French Embassy much farther down the avenue. It was also known as the Plague Hospital, for in 1760 it was used to house and treat victims of the plague that struck Istanbul that year. The building took on its present form when it was rebuilt in stone in 1898 by the French architect M. Carré. It has housed the French Consulate since 1920, and also serves as Fransız Kültür Merkezi [French Cultural Center], with exhibition halls, a library and language courses.

Around the corner on Zambak Sokak is Surp Ohan Vosgeperan

Ermeni Kilisesi [the Armenian Catholic church of Surp Ohan Vosgeperan, St. John Chrysostom]. The original church was a wooden structure erected in 1837. The present structure was built by the Armenian architects Andon and Garabet Tülbentçiyan in 1860-3. The major patron of the church was the Armenian Catholic banker Agop Koçeoğlu.

The next block along Istiklal beyond the French Consulate is bounded by Zambak Sokak and Bekar Sokak The first building beyond Zambak Sokak is Akbank Sanat, a cultural center established by Akbank. At mid-block is AFM Sinemaları building. An earlier building on this on this site was an Ottoman government meteorological station, founded in 1868 under the direction of Aristidi Kumbari Efendi (the meteorological station was actually in the building's back garden). After the meteorological station was closed in the 1920s, the building housed Kosmograf Sineması which changed its name in turn to the Nuvo and later Halk Sineması. After the 1930s this became Mulen Ruj Nightclub, advertised by a large neon windmill jutting out over the street. Mücap Ofluoğlu recalls that in its first years it was an expensive, chic and well-run place where famous singers and musicians performed. One would proceed down a carpeted corridor to the cloakroom, from which a waiter in evening dress would lead one to a table (with a linen table-cloth and the best tableware). 'I remember very well, I was brought to Mulen Ruj when I was about ten, and I was intoxicated by the smell of rakı, that anise smell of which I was to become so fond.' Later Mulen Ruj shared duty as a theater, featuring mostly operettas, and a nightclub, and eventually became a cinema. Giovanni Scognamillo remembers that the entrance was long and narrow and that the cinema had wicker chairs. The present building, Fitaş Pasajı, was built in 1960 and housed two cinemas, Fitaş upstairs and the Dünya downstairs. The pasaj was later converted into AFM Sinemaları.

The next street on the right is Bekar Sokak, which is home to one of the last remaining 'pavyons' of Beyoğlu, the Jackie Club. Next to this is Süper Birahanesi [Süper Beer-hall], one of the few remaining places of its type in the district. Across the street is Pia Café-bar, one of the pioneers of Beyoğlu's revival in the early 1990s. Further down the street is Beyoğlu Ocakbaşı, which has been popular since 1970, and across the street from this is İstasyon Güzel Sanatlar Akademisi [İstasyon Fine Arts Academy].

The next block on Istiklal Caddesi was the site of the first Greek Consulate in Istanbul, before it moved to its present location on Turnacıbaşı Sokak Said Duhani tells us that the second floor of the building was later occupied by Florya Bar, which was impeccably run by a certain Tayfur Bey, who served wine and drinks imported from Paris and encouraged couples onto the dance floor by dancing to the lively tunes played by the orchestra, which was admirably led by Ziya Bey, who would occasionally perform a trumpet solo of the *Charge de Malakoff.*

The next side street to the right is Mis Sokak, which since the 1990s has become very popular and is densely packed with bars, cafes and restaurants (though the street has suffered from the ban on outdoor seating). The first building on Istiklal just beyond Mis Sokak was home between 1943 and 1963 to Gen Kitap Sarayı [Gen Book Palace], one of Beyoğlu's most important bookstores. In its time the Gen served as a cultural center, publishing house and art gallery as well as bookstore. The company went bankrupt in 1963. Shortly afterwards the building was demolished to make way for the present modern structure, Vakıf Gökçek Han. In the middle of the block we see Kız Teknik Öğretim ve Olgunlaşma Enstitüsü, an advanced technical institute for girls, founded in 1945 by Refia Övüç with the aim of providing young Turkish women with a profession. The institute has departments in fashion design, textile technology, clothing production, traditional hand-crafts, jewelry-making and marketing research. The last building on the block, at the corner of İmam Adnan Sokak, is Ragıb Paşa Apartmanı. This was built early in the 20th century for the court chamberlain Ragıb Pasha by the architect A. J. Karakaş, who produced one of the most beautiful examples of the art nouveau style in Istanbul.

The next block on the right side is bounded at its far end by Sakızağacı Sokak. The second building along this block is Cité de Roumelie [Rumeli Pasajı], a monumental edifice in the neoclassical style erected in 1894 by the court chamberlain Ragıb Pasha. The complex included three residential buildings with a total of fifty-eight apartments above the ground floor, where there was a shopping arcade known as Rumeli Pasajı.

Built early in the 20th century for the court chamberlain Ragıb Pasha by the architect A. J. Karakaş.

Said Duhani mentions that there was a pudding shop in Rumeli Pasajı (with two entrances, one from the street and the other from the passageway), where a man associated with a triple murder was himself murdered. He goes on to tell us the story of the triple murder.

A young woman named Camelia, her mother Despoina, their cook Kirkor and the family dog were found stabbed to death in their home on Taksim Sokak. The police initially concluded that the murderer was their cook Agop, who took his own life during the course of the investigation. Suspicion later fell on a barber named Yanko but the police decided there was insufficient evidence to prosecute him. There was a great deal of speculation in the press (the foreign press, that is, the local press having been subject in those years to strict censorship). Among the rumors was that one of the Sultan's sons-in-law had been in love with Camelia, and that she had been done away with in the higher interest of the state and for the happiness of the dynastic family. Others said that the murderer was the man who had been killed in the pudding shop. Some even said that it was the man who had killed a prostitute on Timoni Sokak, and who had been identified by Maksimov, Chief Dragoman of the Russian Embassy (Maksimov had frequently tried to protect this woman, his neighbor, who had been the target of abuse and harassment by Fehim Pasha's secret police. This is the same Maximov who conducted negotiations during the seizure of the Ottoman Bank).

By far the oldest tenant of Cité de Roumelie is Rebul Eczanesi [Rebul Pharmacy], now at the corner but originally occupying premises that extended to the passageway. This pharmacy was founded by Jean Cesar Reboul, who served as president of the Association of Ottoman Pharmacists, was honored by the French Academy, and in 1936 began producing the still popular Rebul Lavender cologne, made with lavender imported from a particular producer in Grasse in Provence. Reboul happened to pass through Istanbul in 1895 after visiting his father, an engineer who was building the Trabzon to Hopa road, became enchanted with the city, and decided to settle here, opening Grande Pharmacie Parisienne in the newly completed Cité. In 1920 Reboul was approached by a young pharmacy student named Kemal Müderissoğlu, who told him that he had fallen in love with his establishment and wanted to perform his internship there. However, Kemal did not speak French, and was told that knowledge of French was a requisite for anyone who worked on Grand Rue de Pera. Kemal studied French for a year, after which he was accepted as an intern, and then hired as a pharmacist when he received his diploma in 1923. The childless Reboul and the orphan Kemal soon developed a father-son relationship, and Reboul turned the pharmacy over to him when he retired in 1938. The pharmacy is now run by one of Kemal's grandsons, and the pharmacists who work there are still required to know French. The Rumeli Pasajı was also once the site of the famous Hacı Abdullah Lokantası, whose present location we will pass in a few moments.

Beyond Cité de Roumelie we come to Ağa Camii, the only mosque on Istiklal Caddesi. The first mosque on this site was founded in 1594–5 by Hüseyin Ağa, commandant of the Galatasaray School. The mosque, which is built of cut stone, was reconstructed in 1834 and again in 1934 (at the request of Atatürk), when it took on its present form. In the center of the courtyard at the rear there is a beautiful şadırvan, or ablution fountain, with the reservoir surrounded by a circlet of marble columns and the water taps set into marble screens between the monoliths. The şadırvan was originally part of Sinan Paşa Camii in Kasımpaşa, but when that mosque was demolished the ablution fountain was moved to Ağa Camii. The mosque sustained serious damage to its foundations, walls and roof from the vibrations caused by the construction of the new Demirören Alışveriş Merkezi [Demirören Shopping Center], and remained closed from 2011 to 2014. Demirören family promised to pay for the restoration, but the 1,000,000 TL they set aside for this soon proved insufficient and work stopped altogether for five months, until the family finally agreed to put up more money. The mosque was finally reopened for worship on February 14, 2014 by Deputy Prime Minister Bülent Arınç, who recited a poem by Nâzım Hikmet at the ceremony. Architect Kornan Gümüş has criticized the work as a reconstruction rather than a restoration, and claims that nothing of the original mosque remains.

We now make a short diversion down Sakızağacı Sokak. A little way down on the left we pass the site of the famous Ağa restaurant, which operated here from 1920 until it was engulfed by the new Demirören Alışveriş Merkezi in 2008. Just past this, in a building which may soon be demolished because its foundations were damaged during the construction of the shopping center, is Hacı Abdullah Lokantası, where visitors to Istanbul have been eating for well over a century. The restaurant first opened in Karaköy in 1888, with a license granted personally by Sultan Abdülhamid II, and operated for many years in the Rumeli Pasajı before moving here. On September 5, 1955, Prime Minister Adnan Menderes and President Celal Bayar had lunch at Hacı Abdullah with a number of local officials to iron out the details of the riots that would devastate the city over the following days. The restaurant was one of the few establishments in Beyoğlu unscathed by the riots.

On the left side of the street at the end of the block we see Armenian Catholic Patriarchate and Surp Asdvadzadzin Ermeni Katolik Kilisesi [patriarchal church of Surp Asdvadzadzin, the Immaculate Conception]. The original building was of wood. In 1864 this building was demolished and new church and patriarchate were built in masonry by the architect Andon Tülbentçiyan. The patriarchate was burned down in the 1870 fire that destroyed eight to ten thousand houses in Beyoğlu, but except for the bell tower the church was unharmed. The damaged buildings were rebuilt in 1800-1801.

The whole of the next block is occupied by the new and controversial Demirören Alışveriş Merkezi. This site was once occupied by a mansion, surrounded by a large garden, belonging to Monsieur Emile Devaux, director of the Ottoman Bank. This was replaced in the late nineteenth century by the Grand Hotel de Luxembourg, which until the opening of Pera Palas was the hotel of choice for travelers arriving from Europe on the Orient Express and by ship. Tchaikovsky stayed here during his visit to the city, and described it as 'delightfully furnished.' In 1897 the hotel closed and was converted into an apartment building, known over the years as either Devaux Apartmanı or the Luxembourg Apartmanı.

Grand Café de Luxembourg, run by Victor Bossi, continued to operate on the ground floor, with a billiard parlor on the floor above. In 1897 a man remembered only as Matalon rented suites next to the billiard parlor and converted them into the small and rather shabby Luxembourg cinema.

Later Café de Luxembourg passed into the hands of the Macedonian Tsangopoulos family. Nikos Tsangopoulos (credited by some with having taught Atatürk to play billiards) tells us that, 'I came to Istanbul from *manastır* when I was twelve. My uncle, who was running the Luxembourg Café then, sent me to school. I studied during the day and worked in the billiard parlor in the evening. My uncle died when I was twenty and he left the billiard parlor to me. I imported six more billiard tables from France. Most of the customers were wealthy young men.'

Later Nikos took over the Luxembourg cinema, expanding it by incorporating the billiard parlor (he continued to operate another very popular billiard parlor near the cinema's rear exit on Sakızağacı

Sokak) and part of the café. Both the cinema and the café took the name Glorya in the 1930s. The cinema took the name Saray, and in the 1940s the café was replaced by Saray Muhallebicisi (now directly across the avenue). Giovanni Scognamillo recalls that in the 1940s Saray tended to show French poetic-realist films by the likes of Jean Renoir, Marcel Carne and Julien Duvivier, and that in the 1950s it began showing films by the British Rank studios. The Saray also served as a concert hall, and among the musicians who performed here were Josephine Baker, Louis Armstrong, Dave Brubeck, the Modern Jazz Quartet, the French singers Charles Trenet, Tino Rossi and Maurice Chevalier, and the king of the tango, Eduardo Bianco. İstanbul Devlet Senfoni Orkestrası [Istanbul State Symphony Orchestra] gave its first public performance at the Saray, under the direction of Cemal Reşit Rey, on the 13th of December 1945.

Leonid Senkopopowski tells us that in the 1930s, 'the smell of perfume at the entrance to Saray was intoxicating. Every week when the film was changed there would be a gala evening. Waltz and tango music would waft from a gramophone. The ladies were

Saray Sineması [Saray Cinema] that also served as a concert hall in the 1940s.

all as pretty as pictures and the gentlemen were dressed to the nines. The guests would be served liquors during the intermission. The governor of Istanbul would come to every gala.'

Éclair Sineması (later to be renamed Şark and then Lüks) opened in another part of the building in 1909. Said Duhani tells us that in its early years Éclair was run by a gentleman named Vassilaki Papadopoulos, who he describes as a 'top-notch manager and quite the ladies' man.' Mr. Papadopoulos was also known for his generosity. He often invited prominent citizens to sit in the theater boxes free of charge, and during intermission would present the ladies accompanying them with chocolates from the Tokatlıyan or sweets from Hacı Bekir. Unfortunately his generosity and extravagance led to his ruin, and the cinema was taken over by Aleko and Filotas Tsangopoulos.

The building was damaged by fire in the early 1950s, after which it was purchased by the Public Insurance Board and restored as an office building, which was known henceforth as Sin-Em Han. Sin-Em Han was bought by the Demirören Holding and Construction company in 1980 and vacated in 1986, remaining vacant until 2008, when it was demolished to make way for the present shopping center.

The construction company illegally doubled the construction area, destroying several buildings to the rear, including two that were listed as first degree historical buildings, and added several storeys both above and below ground. The excavation of the underground floors caused extensive damage to nearby buildings, including Ağa Camii.

The new building, billed during its planning stages as a reconstruction, makes what might be termed post-modern references to the previous building. Architecture critic Ömer Kanıpak calls it 'yet another example of risible design in Istanbul... dipped in historical sauce.' Mehveş Evin, columnist for the *Milliyet* newspaper, described it as 'an overgrown pumpkin.' The architect credited with the design, Han Tümertekin, insists that he withdrew from the project early on in disagreement with the construction company.

Ahmet Misbah Demircan, Beyoğlu's current mayor, and supporter and defender of this and other similar projects, has said: 'This building was dirty and rundown for years. Were the people who are complaining now happy about the state it was in?' He added that the facade would darken within a few years and no one would notice the difference.

We now make a short diversion down Yeşilçam Sokak (formerly Yeşil Sokak and before that the Rue Devaux). Most of the left side of the street was once part of the Cercle d'Orient's back garden, where the members' carriages awaited them. After Abraham Pasha, the owner of the Cercle d'Orient building, went bankrupt at the beginning of the twentieth century, the building and its garden were bought for 108,000 £ by Manuk Manukyan, who then sold it to the impresarios Arditi and Soltiel.

Ruşen Eşref Ünaydın remembers that the rear of the garden was occupied for a time by Strangali's Greek Athletic Gymnasium and Practice Field. In 1909 Arditi began using this area for performances of his Cirque Nouveau, which featured mostly equestrian acrobatics. In the same year the Skating Palace, a roller skating rink (occasionally falsely described as an ice-skating rink) that featured performances of figure roller skating, speed roller skating competitions and roller hockey matches, was built in the rear right corner of the garden. For a time the hockey matches and speed skating competitions were extremely popular as spectator sports among the young men of Beyoğlu, and on Saturdays in particular the place would be packed with excited and somewhat rowdy crowds. The Skating Palace also served as a venue for balls, the best remembered of which were those organized regularly by the famous dance instructor Monsieur Psalty (a poster for one of his balls promises 'skating from 9pm to 11pm, and dancing from 11 pm until morning'). The memory of the Skating Palace is preserved in the name of the building next to Emek Sineması, İsketing Apartmanı.

The Skating Palace was replaced by Yeni Tiyatro [the New Theater] in 1918. Vedat Tek describes this as 'a hole-in-the-wall where operetta companies from Vienna used to perform. The beautiful operetta star Jordie Milovitch, who stole so many hearts in her day, used to perform at this miserable theater.' We know that the illusionist Dr. Radwan also performed here.

In 1924 İhsan İpekçi built and opened the Melek Sineması, with a capacity of 875 and baroque wall and ceiling ornaments, which remained a favorite in the district for many years. Salâh Birsel tells us that in its heyday, finding tickets for the Melek's galas was a matter of concern for anyone in the swing of Beyoğlu's social life. Giovanni Scognamillo remembers that in his time the Melek showed films produced by the 20th Century Fox, MGM and Columbia studios, and favored musicals such as *Broadway Melody* and *Strike up the Band*. The cinema broke all local box office records with *Gone with the Wind*.

In 1926 the first Miss Turkey Beauty Pageant was held at the Melek. The winner was Araksi Çetinyan, who worked as an usher at the cinema.

In 1945, after Arditi and Soltiel were bankrupted by the Wealth Tax, the Cercle d'Orient complex was bought by the Istanbul Municipality. The municipality tried repeatedly to sell the property, but could not find a buyer until the Emekli Sandığı [Civil Service Pension Fund] eventually purchased it in 1957 for 26.5 million Turkish liras. The new owners established a company called Emek Film to run the cinema, and changed the name to Emek Sineması. In 1969 the cinema was taken over by Turgut Demirağ, and after 1975 it was run by İsmet Kurtuluş and Süheyla Kurtuluş. In 2009 the Emek Sineması was closed and an announcement was made that the Cercle d'Orient complex would be turned into yet another modern shopping mall. In May of 2010 the Istanbul 9th Administrative Court ruled against the demolition of the theater and other buildings included in the plan, but the plan proceeded nevertheless.

In 2010 a coalition called the Emek Sinemasını Yıktırmayalım Platformu [Platform Against the Destruction of the Emek Cinema] was formed to organize protests and a petition drive and in December 2012 the Istanbul Foundation for Culture and Arts (İKSV) announce that it was working on concrete plans to save the cinema. İKSV was given assurances by the then Culture Minister Ertuğrul Günay, Beyoğlu Mayor Ahmet Misbah Demircan and the architects of the project that the cinema would not be demolished, but would simply be 'moved to an upper floor'. On March 30, 2013 a group of about thirty protesters briefly occupied the building, and on April 7 a larger demonstration, attended by a number of well-known Turkish and foreign directors and film critics including

Costa Gavras, was met with a violent response from the police, who used tear gas and water cannons to disperse the crowd. The building was finally demolished on May 20, 2013. Also destroyed were nearly a dozen other buildings, including several theaters, İsketing Apartmanı and several buildings that served as studios during the golden age of Turkish cinema.

In 1924 İpekçi's also opened the Opera Sineması (later to become İpek Sineması), whose entrance was originally next to that of the Melek but in later years was through the Cercle d'Orient on Istiklal Caddesi. In its first years it was considered the grandest of Beyoğlu's cinemas, with carpeted floors and ushers who wore frock coats and white gloves. In 1932 Atatürk came here to see a British-made film about the Dardanelles campaign, and is said to have been very impressed by the theater.

Giovanni Scognamillo remembers that the walls were covered with murals of idealized Ottoman life (Bosphorus mansions with *kayıks* moored in front, and veiled women gathered in lush gardens) by the artist Kalmukoğlu (Kalmukov). He also remembers that the stage was flanked by two large paintings of angels in the liberty style (these angels are sometimes remembered to have been in the Melek, and are even said to have inspired that cinema's name).*

İpek Sineması later became Şehir Tiyatroları Komedi Sahnesi [City Theaters Comedy Stage], and when this closed the premises were used for some years as a machine shop, until they were damaged by fire, since which time they have remained vacant.

Yet another cinema, Sinepop, exists a little further down on the right side of the street, just before it takes a sharp turn to the left. According to local folklore, these premises were once occupied by a beer hall that was popular among German soldiers during World War I, and that later it became 'a cinema run by two Frenchmen'. However, we have found no documented evidence of the existence of either. We do know that Ar Sineması opened here in 1943 (Aydın Boysan remembers attending a concert by the piano virtuoso Walter Gieseking here in that year, when food and fuel were scarce and strictly rationed, and having to walk home through the snow to Laleli afterwards), that it was renamed Yeni Ar in 1956 and that

* Melek: Angel.

it became Sinepop in 1973. In its first years Sinepop was known for showing what Giovanni Scognamillo refers to as 'educational' German sex films. Sinepop now shows mostly popular Hollywood films, and has been a participant in the annual Istanbul Film Festival since 1991.

The name Yeşilçam is synonymous with the heyday of the Turkish film industry from the late 1940s to the mid 1970s. As early as the 1930s, many of the companies that imported films were based on this street. When the tax on domestically produced films was drastically reduced in 1948, the Turkish film industry boomed, and many of the new production companies opened their offices here. During the 1950s and 60s, many of the production companies established their studios on the lower end of the street and, as we saw earlier, moved their offices to the other side of Istiklal Caddesi, to the area around Alyon Sokak (now Gazeteci Erol Dernek Sokak). The Turkish film industry suffered from the advent of television in the 1970s, and many of the production companies that survived were reduced to producing low-quality, soft-core porn films. By the early 1980s, all of the studios on Yeşilçam Sokak had closed, and the lower end of the street remained abandoned for years.

In the 1990s Yeşilçam Sokak came to be referred to by some as 'Metal Sokak' because youthful aficionados of heavy metal rock music began gathering here to drink beer in the doorways of abandoned buildings. Later, several 'heavy metal' bars opened on the street. These bars were raided and temporarily closed during periodic outbreaks of public hysteria about Satanic cults and were finally closed altogether after a 16 year-old girl died of a drug overdose in 2006. For a time after this there were sidewalk bars, staffed by transvestites and transsexuals, where beer barrels were used as tables and customers sat on small stools.

In 2008, Engin Yaşar (owner of the Kafe Pi chain of bars) and Nursel Onarır (owner of the Ferdane on Mis Sokak) purchased the entire lower end of the street and converted the abandoned buildings into a series of bars that they named Küçük Beyoğlu [Little Beyoğlu]. Küçük Beyoğlu quickly became very popular, particularly among students and alumni of private lycées and universities, but has suffered from the ban on outdoor seating.

The long and monumental building along the first stretch of the next block on Istiklal is the Cercle d'Orient. The building was commissioned in 1882 by Abraham Pasha, representative of the Egyptian Khedive İsmail Pasha and built by the architect Alexandre Vallaury. This housed the most prestigious of the social clubs in late Ottoman Pera, the Cercle d'Orient. Among the members of the club were leading members of the business and banking community, foreign ambassadors, and high-ranking members of the Ottoman government, including several grand viziers and two of the Young Turks who virtually ruled the empire in its last years, Talat Pasha and Enver Pasha.

The origins of the Cercle d'Orient are uncertain. Some claim that it was founded in 1882 by the Scottish-Levantine Chief Dragoman at the British Embassy, Sir Alfred Sandison. Sandison is sometimes wrongly described as the British Ambassador; his official title was Oriental Secretary of the British Legation. He is also said to have founded the Grand Orient Masonic Lodge, which existed in Europe since at least the beginning of the 18th century and the Istanbul branch of which is believed to have been in operation since before Sandison was born. According to others it grew out of the Cercle de Pera, said to have been founded by the Jewish-German railroad tycoon Baron Maurice de Hirsch, and according to still others it evolved from the Club des Chasseurs de Constantinople, said to have been founded by Abraham Pasha himself. Whatever the truth of its origins, the Cercle d'Orient is known to have been established in this building in 1884.

There is anecdotal evidence that the game of bridge originated at the Cercle d'Orient (though it may in fact have originated at the Khedival Club in Cairo). O.H. van Millingen recalls encountering 'a game called Biritch which became very popular at the club and dethroned the game of whist.' Baccarat and poker were also played at the club, and huge sums of money were won and lost. American Ambassador Henry Morgenthau mentions in his diary that 'the Baron von Wangenheim lost 25,000 francs at baccarat in a single night.'

The food served at the club was legendary. Sidney Whitman tells us that,

... it is only at the Cercle d'Orient, the club of the diplomatic world... that the cuisine has that Parisian foundation to which the epicure can look forward with pleasure... It is a great pleasure to be invited by one of the 'gros bonnets' of the diplomatic world whose dinners enjoy a well-deserved popularity. It was on such an occasion that, carried away by the excellence of the fare, I ventured to suggest to His Excellency that he might perhaps prevail upon His Majesty to bestow a decoration upon the cook.

The club's board was always directed by an ambassador, and membership was restricted to high-ranking diplomats and the most wealthy and notable of the foreign community. Abdülhamid II let it be known that the presence of any of his subjects in the club would be considered an act of open defiance, and the entrance was always under surveillance by Fehim Pasha's secret police. This rule, however, did not apply to viziers and a few other trusted higher officials, who the Sultan encouraged to join so that he could have eyes and ears inside the club. Indeed anyone with the title of vizier was expected to be granted membership without question or condition.

Said Duhani tells of us of a certain Necib Efendi who was denied membership because of his feud with the French Ambassador (after the French capture of Tunisia, Necib Efendi led a campaign against the Ambassador in the local newspapers), but who upon being appointed vizier strode arrogantly up the steps, confident in the knowledge that he could not be turned away. It was Necib Efendi who led the investigation into the assassination attempt on the Sultan at Yıldız Sarayı in 1905, and who discovered, to the horror and alarm of the members, that the doorman and several other employees had hidden two large and powerful bombs in a disused cistern beneath the club.

Turkish membership increased after the forced abdication of Abdülhamid II in 1908, and in the following years, particularly in the lead-up to World War I, there was increasing intrigue among the western diplomats. The outbreak of the War saw the departure of many of these diplomats. In his diary, American Ambassador Henry Morgenthau recounts the complex machinations involved in his relationship with the German Ambassador and several of the Young Turks, much of which were played out at the club.

The club saw a revival during the Allied occupation (it is said that Atatürk was a frequent visitor during the first six months of the occupation, before he left for Samsun), but after the embassies moved to Ankara the nature of the club changed profoundly. Turkish as well as French was spoken at board meetings, ladies were admitted as members in accordance with the ideals of the Republic, and instead of poker, baccarat and cigars there were tango evenings, poetry readings and concerts of classical music. In 1944 the name was changed to Büyük Kulüp [The Grand Club], and in 1975 this club moved to Kadıköy, where it still exists today as one of the last bastions of the Republican elite.

Said Duhani tells us that the ground floor of the building was occupied by the large and well-appointed shops such as Chavin, who imported the latest fashions from Paris, the famous tailors Mir and Cottereau, the luxury shirt-maker Tatalyan and the barber Stavraki, to whom even viziers entrusted their heads. Abraham Pasha had suites on the mezzanine floor (his principal residence was a large estate in Büyükdere), which after he went bankrupt were occupied by the Russian-run nightclubs Rose-Noir and Almara. Alexandra Roube-Jansky tells us that,

> The Rose Noir was livelier at night. Hirschfeld opened this place when he came to Istanbul with the other Russians in 1919... It was considered one of the most classy places and people of all nationalities used to come. Others took it as an example and opened places like Maksim, the Moscovite and the Parisienne... The hostesses were all from wealthy families that had been impoverished by the Bolshevik Revolution, and there were a few countesses and princesses among them. They didn't wander around with trays, they dressed elegantly and welcomed people as if into their own homes, showing them to their tables, asking what they would like and conveying their desires to the white jacketed waiters, all of whom were former Tsarist officers. They would dance with those they wished to dance with, generally choosing those who seemed to have fat wallets.

Later the shops on the ground floor were subdivided, and most of these were vacated in preparation for the building's conversion into a modern shopping mall. One of the notable holdouts is the İnci Pastanesi, famous for decades for its *profiterol*. İnci was founded in

1944 by Lukas Zigoridis, and since then was never been redecorated, indeed nothing about its style changed, even the staff seemed to be the same unageing people, giving one, on entering, the impression of having stepped back through the years. The management went to court to resist eviction, but to no avail. İnci closed on the 7th of December of 2012, and seventy days later, on the 14th of February 2013, reopened at Mis Sokak number 18, choosing Valentine's Day to emphasize the bond of love between the management and the public.

Part of the building was occupied by Artistik Sineması, which became Sümer Sineması in 1934 and Küçük Emek in 1958. In the 1970s this became the Rüya Sineması, featuring soft-core porn films, which remained in operation until developers began vacating the Cercle d'Orient complex in 2009.

In 1991 the Istanbul 1st Cultural and Natural Heritage Protection Board decreed that no changes could be made to the interior or exterior of the building and in 1993 proclaimed the building an Urban Conservation Area. In the same year, the owner of the building, Sosyal Güvenlik Kurumu [the Social Security Institution], reached agreement with Kamer Construction Company to restore the complex. According to the agreement, the complex would be leased to the firm for a period of twenty-five years on the build-operate-transfer model. Then in 2006 the Beyoğlu Municipality revealed its Yeşilçam Sokak. Sustainable Urban Development and Renewal Project in partnership with the SGK and the Ministry of Culture and Tourism, and on October 10, 2009 agreement was reached with Kamer Construction to begin work on the project. The entire complex, except for the façade of the Cercle d'Orient building, was demolished in the summer of 2013. The project organizers have made conflicting statements about the nature of the new complex that will replace it, saying at different times that it will be a hotel, a shopping mall, an entertainment center and even a museum.

The next building, known in Turkish as Şişmanoğlu Konağı and in Greek as Sismanoglio Megaro, was built in 1909 as the home of the Sismanoglou family. The brothers Constantine and Athanaseos Sismanoglou only occupied the building for a short time before moving to Paris and finally settling on the island of Corfu. In

1939 Constantine Sismanoglou donated the building to the Greek government on condition that it be used as a consulate, though for financial and political reasons it as many years before this condition could be fulfilled. From 1952 to 1968 the building was leased to the United States Information Service, and housed a library, a carpentry workshop and a television and radio studio (the ground floor was occupied by shops). In 2000 the Greek government launched a restoration project that was completed in 2003. Today the building serves as a cultural center, hosting exhibits and offering language courses. It also houses Veroia Kütüphanesi [Veroia Library] and consular residences.

The next building we come to is Halep Çarşısı, or Aleppo Market, erected in 1885 by M. Hacar of Aleppo. In its first years, a wooden structure at the rear of the passageway known variously as Halep Pasajı, Süreyya Pasajı and in more recent years Beyoğlu Pasajı was occupied by the Cirque de Pera, run by a Spaniard named Ramon Ramirez, and where the talented and fearless Tourniere family performed sensational feats of equestrian acrobatics (in summer the circus operated in the park at Tepebaşı, because the building's inadequate ventilation made the smell of horses unbearable).

With the help of the Spanish Ambassador, Ramirez organized the Wednesday Diplomatic Soirees that became a sensation in the district. These evenings, attended not just by diplomats and the crème of Pera society but also by everyone who was anyone in the government, included performances by the best magicians, acrobats and gymnasts, performing dogs ('The Magnificent Dogs', local street dogs trained by Leonidas Amiotis, who had gained renown even in Paris), the trapeze artist Charles le Follet, the illusionist Door le Blanc (le maitre de la magie), the wolf and hyena tamer Herr Mortemart and an African-American step-dancer. (This last artist, whose name is sadly forgotten, was invited by Abdülhamid II to join the Palace Artistic Performers. The Sultan is said to have derived endless amusement from watching him dance as he sang 'The Honeysuckle and the Bee'.)

The original structure was modified in 1889 to serve as a theater and an opera house, and burned down in 1904, to be rebuilt as Theatre Varieté, run by the Lamberger brothers. The opening night featured the Folies Bergers de Paris dancers as well as performances by acrobats and clowns. In the following years the theater hosted drama, opera and operetta troupes from Europe, particularly from France and Greece. Turkish drama troupes performed during the month of Ramadan. From 1907, off and on until 1960, the theater served as a cinema during the summer months (under a variety of names).

The theater was taken over by Muhsin Ertuğrul in 1918, and in 1923, during a performance of *Othello*, Turkish actresses appeared for the first time in a public performance on stage. In 1929 the name was changed to French Theater, hosting both foreign and Turkish drama troupes. In 1942 it became Ses Tiyatrosu [Ses Theater], where Ses Tiyatrosu ve Opereti [Ses Theater and Operette] performed under the direction of Avni Dilligil. The theater was taken over by Haldun Dormen in 1962, becoming Dormen Tiyatrosu. In 1972 the theater was converted into a cinema, Ses Sineması, which like many cinemas of that era featured low-quality, soft-core porn films. In 1989 the premises were taken over by Ferhan Şensoy and once again became a theater, featuring performances by the Ferhan Şensoy Drama Troupe (Ortaoyuncular).

In 1971, Ertuğrul Bora opened the legendary Papirus Bar on the second floor above the passageway. Papirus was a favorite hangout for intellectuals, writers and people from the worlds of the theater and of Yeşilçam. It is said that dozens of stillborn revolutions were plotted at Papirus, and some remember that the round table directly opposite the entrance was always occupied by a group of communists jokingly referred to as the Kızılçam group.* After part of the building was destroyed by fire in 1977, Papirus moved to Ayhan Işık Sokak and finally closed in the late 1990s.

In 1984 the entire building, except for the façade, was torn down and rebuilt (several buildings in the rear were also demolished, and the new building is considerably larger than the original). In 1989 the Beyoğlu and Pera cinemas, featuring mostly art films, opened in the basement of the new Halep Çarşısı. In 2001 a small theater, Maya Sahnesi, featuring experimental drama, music and performance art, opened on the second floor of the building.

The next two buildings occupy the site of what was once the

---

* Yeşilçam: Green Pine, Kızılçam: Red Pine.

mansion of a branch of the famous Mavrokordato family. The first of these is Luvr Apartmanı, formerly the Beler Hotel, the ground floor of which was once occupied by the Café l'Orient, opened in 1923 by Phillip Lenas not long after he emigrated from Albania. The name of the café was changed to Baylan during the Turkification campaign of 1934, and in the years after World War II it became a gathering place for many of the leading figures of the Turkish literary scene. The upper floors of the building housed the offices of İstanbul Kültür ve Sanat Vakfı [Istanbul Foundation for Culture and Art] from 1973 until they moved to the Deniz Palas building in Tepebaşı in 2009.

The building next to this was once home to Japon Pazarı [Japanese Market], run in its first years by a man named Nakamura. Giovanni Scognamillo remembers that as a child, he saw this store as an exotic world of wonders. The window to the right was completely filled with

The Tokatlıyan, which had 160 rooms, was one of the most prestigious hotels in Istanbul, with all of its fixtures, furniture and decorations imported from Western Europe, renowned for its restaurant and patisserie as well as for its elevator.

toys (soldiers, castles, cars, tanks, sailboats, ships, guns, cowboy hats, helmets, firemen's uniforms, dolls, miniature kitchens, etc.), and that to the left contained displays of kimonos, fans, umbrellas, a wide variety of Japanese and Chinese porcelain and glassware and carnival masks. The rest of the block was formerly occupied by the mansion of the Syrian Christian Hava family, who moved to Marseilles after the death of their daughter Margueritte in 1893.

We have now come to Balo Sokak (the first stretch of which was formerly Sağ Sokak, and the lower end of which was formerly Mektep Sokak). This street's past is similar to that of many streets in this part of Beyoğlu, originally home to Armenian, Greek and Levantine bourgeois families, joined by Turkish bourgeois families towards the end of the Ottoman Empire and the early years of the Republic, living in uneasy proximity to the infamous Abanoz Sokak. During the 1930s and 40s it was home of the Beyoğlu Police Station (after it moved from Galatasaray and before it moved to its present location on the corner of Tarlabaşı Bulvarı and Kalyoncu Kulluğu Sokak), which stood on the corner of Nevizade Sokak where the newly built the Inter-Royal Hotel now stands (in earlier times, this site was occupied by the home of Yusuf Franco-Cussa Pasha, who served as Governor of Lebanon and later as Minister of Posts and Foreign Affairs). After the flight of the bourgeois at the end of the 1950s, the street sank into decay and disrepute, becoming home to sleazy *pavyons*, and later, in the 1980s, when the street was a base for the Black Sea gangs who controlled Beyoğlu in those years, to illegal gambling dens and brothels. The notorious gangster godfather Dündar Kılıç is said to have held court regularly at a coffee house on Balo Sokak. Even in the late 1990s, when Beyoğlu was coming back to life, this street was to be avoided after dark.

In the first years of the twenty-first century, Balo Sokak began to change rapidly with the opening of a number of bars, of which there are now many, some of them occupying entire buildings, catering to a variety of musical tastes, lifestyles and sexual preferences. Today, particularly on weekend nights, it can be difficult to negotiate the street because of the crowds. Balo Sokak is now home to Beyoğlu's first Irish Pub, the overpriced and somewhat pretentious James Joyce. It was also home for some years to Osman Ozman's legendary and very colorful Nayah Bar (now on the corner of Mis Sokak and Kurabiye Sokak, and not nearly as colorful).

Until very recently, the lower end of the street still retained something of the air of the Beyoğlu of the 1970s. In January of 2011, two people were killed in a gunfight at one of the *pavyons* that were still operating there. This part of the street is now home to Doğançay Müzesi [the Doğançay Museum], featuring permanent exhibits of the works of Turkish artists Burhan Doğançay and Adil Doğançay. Across the street is Beyoğlu Akademililer Sanat Merkezi [Beyoğlu Academic Art Center] which offers classes and workshops and hosts exhibits.

Returning to Istiklal, the top floor of the single building between Balo Sokak and Solakzade Sokak (formerly Sol Sokak) is, in keeping with Beyoğlu's long tradition of dance schools, the home of what is now the district's oldest tango school, Baila Tango, originally founded in Munich in 1993 by Metin Yazır, a pioneer in the revival of tango in Istanbul. Baila Tango hosts regular tango evenings. The building is also home to Otantik Kafe [Otantik Café], long a popular place for Anatolian folk music and dancing. The ground floor was once occupied by the Themosticles Patisserie.

The next block is bounded by Solakzade Sokak and Sahne Sokak. The first building on the block is Tokatlıyan İş Hanı, formerly Hotel Tokatlıyan. The name stems from Mıgırdıç Tokalıyan, who in 1859 established a patisserie on this site that he called the Café-Restaurant de Paris. When this and the other establishments on the site were destroyed by a fire in 1892, Tokatlıyan made an agreement with the owner of the property, a foundation of the Armenian Gregorian Church, to build a hotel, which opened in 1895, originally as the Hotel Splendide, though soon afterwards to be renamed the Hotel M. Tokatlıyan. In 1919 the hotel was taken over his son-in-law, a Serb named Medovitch, who opened a branch of the Tokatlıyan in Tarabya. The Tokatlıyan, which had 160 rooms, was one of the most prestigious hotels in Istanbul, with all of its fixtures, furniture and decorations imported from Western Europe, renowned for its restaurant and patisserie as well as for its elevator. Like many other of the Pera hotels of its time, it was the scene of memorable balls, intrigues and momentous meetings, including one that marked the foundation of the Hilal-i Ahmer Cemiyeti [Ottoman Red Crescent Society]. In the late 1930s it became a focus of controversy and was boycotted by Jews when the Austrian manager hung a Nazi flag next to the Turkish flag in front of the entrance. Among the distinguished guests at the hotel was Leon Trotsky, who stayed at the Tokatlıyan in 1929, after he left Narmanlı Han and before he moved out to Prinkipo [Büyükada] on Princes' Isles (arriving through the back door late at night to avoid attracting the attention of the many local Russians who had sworn to kill him). Agatha Christie stayed here during one of her visits to Istanbul, and it appears in *Murder on the Orient Express* (Hercule Poirot stays at the Tokatlıyan before boarding the train). Josephine Baker also stayed here during her second visit to Istanbul in 1934. Other famous guests include Lawrence of Arabia and the literary critic Leo Spitzer. The hotel came under Turkish management in 1945, becoming the Hotel Konak (though everyone still referred to it as the Tokatlıyan). The hotel closed in 1961, and was converted into an office building, with shops on the ground floor. The upper floors have for some years been condemned as unsafe to enter.

Giovanni Scognamillo, who refers to the Tokatlıyan as 'one of the hearts of Beyoğlu, together with the Pera Palas and the now vanished the Park Hotel,' remembers that throughout the 1940s there was a certain elegantly dressed individual with a thin moustache who was always either sitting at one of the sidewalk tables or loitering near the entrance. He often wondered who this person was, and why his father pursed his lips and shook his head when he saw him. It was only years later that he learned the man was a procurer, whose business card announced him to be a *courtier de plaisir*.

Said Duhani tells us that in the days of horse-drawn trams, the terminus of the Şişli-Pera line was in front of the Tokatlıyan Hotel, and that it was only through a complicated series of maneuvers that the skilled drivers were able to turn the trams around on the narrow avenue.

A short way beyond Tokatlıyan İş Hanı we come to one of the entrances to the famous Çiçek Pasajı, or the Passage of Flowers, an L-shaped passageway lined with *meyhanes*, with another entrance on Sahne Sokak, the next side street off Istiklal Caddesi. This was originally known as Cité de Pera, designed by the Greek architect Kleanthes Zano and built in 1870 by the Greek businessman Hristaki Zographos Efendi as a luxury apartment house with elegant shops along the arcade on the street level, all designed in the Parisian manner (there were a total of 18 apartments and 24 shops). The apartments were among the first in the district to have luxuries such as running water and gas lighting. Some of the shops that occupied the arcade in its first thirty years were the Maison Parret, which sold the latest fashions from Paris, Vallaury Patisserie, Dulas the florist, Schumacher's bakery, Keserciyan the tailor, Christo's café and Acemyan the tobacconist. Among the first residents of the apartments was the famous dressmaker Madame Ephigenia Epenetos, who for many years dressed the ladies of the

Imperial Palace. In its first years the arcade was generally referred to as Hristaki Pasajı, and it was only after the property was bought by the Grand Vizier Küçük Said Pasha in 1908 and most of the shops were taken over by florists that it came to be known as Çiçek Pasajı (there is a persistent urban legend that this name derives from a time during the Allied occupation when Russian flower girls sought refuge here from the unwanted advances of French and British soldiers). An Italian restaurant known as Degustasyon opened in 1928 in the arcade to the right of the entrance on Istiklal, in what were formerly the premises of the Maison Parret. Giovanni Scognamillo remembers that this was a favorite place for the Italian-Levantine families of Beyoğlu to have a lunch of spaghetti or ravioli after church on Sundays. In his time, though the owners, the Morigi brothers, were Italian, the waiters were all Greek and the chef was a Turk from Bolu. In the 1950s, Degustasyon became a hangout for leading figures of the Turkish literary world as well as of the world of Yeşilçam. During the 1940s, the florists and other shops in the arcade were gradually replace by meyhanes and beer halls, the best remembered of which was Nektar Birahanesi.

By the early 1950s the passage was completely flanked by meyhanes, with tables in the form of marble slabs on beer-barrels set up in the alleyway. Part of the structure collapsed in 1978 and for a time the passage was abandoned. But then in 1988, after restoration, it was reopened for business, once again lined with meyhanes. Our own favorite is Sev-İç, Bayram'ın Yeri, at No. 8 on the right as you enter from Istiklal. The meyhanes of Çiçek Pasajı are now more respectable and less boisterous than they were in times past, though old-timers miss the presence of the peripatetic peddlers, musicians, street-singers, beggars, magicians, and the occasional fire-eater or sword-swallower, the procession of Beyoğlu's night-town including a line-up of its criminal class. The only one of the old entertainers who was allowed into the restored passage was Madame Anahit, an Armenian accordionist who over the years became an iconic figure both here and on nearby Nevizade Sokak (Anahit Yulanda Varan began her musical career at the age of 16 in Esayan Lisesi school orchestra, and started playing the accordion in meyhanes after the death of her first husband, a Greek musician, in order to support her two children. She was the subject of many newspaper and television interviews, and her life story was aired on Dutch television. She played minor roles in a number of Turkish films, and also appeared in several music video clips of well-known Turkish groups. Her lifelong fantasy was to dance in Çiçek Pasajı with her idol the actor Johnny Weismuller, of Tarzan fame, but sadly this never came true. However she did accompany the singer Joan Baez, who during a visit to Çiçek Pasajı graciously agreed to the crowd's request that she sing. Madame Anahit continued to play her accordion in *meyhanes* even when she was being treated for stomach cancer. She died in 2003 at the age of 86. She is also remembered by many as a lover of animals, and particularly of cats, of which she had many, and for her years of work with the Society for the Protection of Animals). Çiçek Pasajı was restored and redecorated again in 2005. The walls have been decorated with murals of some of the best remembered characters of its past, including Madame Anahit and the architect and writer Aydın Boysan, who still visits Sev-İç on Friday afternoons.

Cité de Pera stands on the site of the Naum Tiyatrosu, founded in 1840 by Mikail Naum Duhani. The first manager of the theater was Donizetti Pasha, older brother of the composer Gaetano Donizetti. Etienne Rey describes a visit to this theater in 1843. 'In the evening we went to the opening night of an Italian opera company that was staging *Norma*. The audience was large and select, the music good and the small theater hall wonderfully decorated.' (After the performance an official of the Sultan politely reminded them that should they walk the street at night without a lantern they would be arrested and obliged to spend the night in the police station.)

The original wooden structure burned down in 1846, and was rebuilt on a grander scale by an English architect named Thomas Smith, who also oversaw the building of the British Embassy. (We are told by Albert Richard Smith that the stage was 35 feet across at the proscenium, only five feet less than that of the Drury Lane Theater.) The reopening took place on November 4th 1848 with Guiseppe Verdi's *Macbeth*, directed by Guatelli and the orchestra conducted by Angelo Mariani. In 1868 Edward Prince of Wales (later King Edward VII) attended two performances at the Naum in the company of Sultan Abdülaziz.

When Sultan Abdülmecid attended the opera here, the length of the avenue would be covered in carpet for the procession of his six-horse carriage. The carpet on which the Sultan would walk from his carriage to the entrance to the Imperial box belonged to Said Duhani's maternal grandfather, Nasri Franco Pasha, and was kept in the family for many years as a memento. The theater was completely destroyed in the great fire of 1870, and, as Said Duhani tells us, his uncle not having the means at that time to rebuild it, it was replaced by Cité de Pera.

Continuing past Sahne Sokak, we pass the site where Azeriyan Konağı [Azarian mansion] once stood, the site of the former Hotel Central and just beyond this the site of the fondly remembered Patisserie Parisienne (Hatay Pastanesi after 1934), founded by the Lebanese Necib brothers.

At the corner where Meşrutiyet Caddesi joins Istiklal Caddesi at Galatasaray Meydanı, we see the old Galatasaray Postanesi, or Galatasaray Post Office. This handsome building, whose façade was constructed entirely of marble, was erected in 1875 as the residence of a wealthy Armenian named Theodor Sıvacıyan at a cost of 26,000 liras. The ground floor housed a pharmacy owned by a Greek named Apolonatos. In 1907 it was purchased by the Posta Telgraf Nezareti [Ministry of Posts and Telegraphs] for 13,500 liras. The ground floor was subsequently occupied by the Galatasaray Postanesi, the second floor was rented to the English Stern Telegraph company, the third floor to the German Telegraph Company and the fourth floor housed communications equipment.

Radio Istanbul operated from four rooms on the second floor for ten months during 1943, broadcasting daily from 18:00 to 23:00. Throughout World War II both the BBC and the German state radio broadcast from this building (making, one imagine, for some awkward encounters on the stairway).

The building was badly damaged by fire in 1977, and did not reopen as a post office until 1982, closing again in the mid 1990s due to urgent need for repairs. In 1998 a decision was made to restore the building and convert it into a museum. The restoration has been much criticized. As with many other restorations in Beyoğlu, all that remains of the original building is the façade, the rest of it having been completely demolished. There have been as yet unsubstantiated accusations that much of the original marble of the façade was replaced with inferior marble.

We now walk back a few steps and turn in to Sahne Sokak, which leads downhill through Galatasaray Balık Pazarı [Galatasaray Fish Market]. The French Consul Tameoigne, writing in 1810, tells us that 'In order to reach the Galatasaray you must first pass through the market of Pera, where the fish shops, grocers and butchers are.' After the reconstruction that followed the fire of 1870, a number of specialty charcuteries and shops selling luxury goods took their place among the fishmongers, greengrocers and purveyors of spices. Until recent times this market was known for shops that sold quality goods that could not be found elsewhere. Among the best remembered of these was Nea Agora, run by the Katanos brothers, which Giovanni Scognamillo describes as having been 'a supermarket long before there was any such thing as a supermarket.'

Until not long ago, this was the most colorful quarter in Beyoğlu, with the street and its tributary alleyways lined with the shops, stalls and barrows of fishmongers, greengrocers and other merchants and itinerant peddlers, along with curbside eating and drinking places and old-fashioned *meyhanes*. In recent times, many of the shops and *meyhanes* have been replaced by souvenir shops and touristic restaurants (at present there are only five actual fish shops left in the Balık Pazarı). Some of its charm was lost as well when it was re-paved and the high awning that covered it was removed. However, some of the charcuteries and specialty food stores remain, and from time to time we still enjoy watching the crowds pass from the curbside over beer and fried mussels or *kokoreç*.

After passing the side entrance of Çiçek Pasajı we see on the left Avrupa Pasajı which extends from Sahne Sokak to Meşrutiyet Caddesi. This was built by the architect Pulgher in 1870, modeled on a passage in Paris; it is also called Aynalı Pasaj, or the Mirrored Arcade, because of the mirrors that reflected the light of the gas lamps that once illuminated it in the evening. Originally many of the shops were florists, including the famous Sabuncakis shop, which still has a number of branches in Istanbul. The passage has recently been restored and is once again functioning as a shopping arcade. According to Said Duhani, this was previously the site of a café called 'Jardin de Fleurs.'

A few steps farther along we see on the left Aslıhan Çarşısı, originally the Passage Crespin, then Krepen Pasajı (during the

Turkification campaign of 1934 it was officially renamed Krizantem Pasajı, 'the Passage of Chrysanthemums,' though nearly everyone continued to refer to it as Krepen Pasajı). The passageway was built in the late 19th century and was originally lined with shops. Said Duhani tells us that two piano makers once had their shops here, Herr Commendiger (not to be confused with the other piano maker Commendiger who had his shop on Istiklal Caddesi) and Herr Lehner, as well as the shoemakers Amiralis, Bon and Dimitris Detzzos (Detzzos had been apprentice to a famous Paris shoemaker and was unparalleled at making shoes for 'diplomatic feet,' but unfortunately suffered from neurasthenia and ended up shooting himself in the heart, leaving a note in Greek that read 'I came, I saw, I left') and several tailors and cloth and thread merchants. *Meyhanes* began appearing here in the 1930s (reaching a total of seven by the late 1960s, three owned by Greeks and four by Turks), becoming over time what Tomris Uyar described as 'a haven for those who wished to end their lives expertly, deliberately and according to a specific code of self-destruction.'

The first *meyhane* to open here, in 1934, was the Krizantem. This was followed by the İmroz, opened in 1941 by Spiros Havoutsas and Thanasi Gialias. A young man named Yorgo Okumuş began working here as a busboy in 1952, eventually becoming partner and then owner, moving his establishment to Nevizade Sokak in 1982. Another of the *meyhanes* of the old Krepen Pasajı that still operates is Kadir'in Yeri, named for its present owner Kadir Karmak, who in 1953 began as a dishwasher in what was then Zaharopoulos Tavern, working his way up to the position of head waiter, becoming partner with the then owner Vilado Todorovitch in 1972, and then, as sole owner, moving his establishment to Nevizade Sokak in 1982. One of the last *meyhanes* to appear here was the Neşe, opened in 1965 by Bayram Aydındoğan, who began his working life in 1947 in Sev-İç in Çiçek Pasajı, and who returned to reopen Sev-İç when that *pasaj* was restored. A passageway that follows the same course as the old Krepen Pasajı has been opened through the modern building, and is occupied largely by second-hand bookstores.

A short way down Sahne Sokak beyond these passages we see on our right Ermeni Üç Horon, Kutsal Üçlü, Kilisesi [the Armenian Gregorian church of Üç Horon, the Holy Trinity]. This was first built in wood in 1807; then after being destroyed in a fire it was rebuilt in stone in 1838 by Garabet Balyan, chief architect of the imperial court. The church and its associated buildings then underwent a major restoration in 1907.

Just beyond this is the Mercan, now one of the oldest restaurants of its type on the street, opened in 1957 by Mehmet Hüsametin Tamkaynak.

The first turning on the left from Sahne Sokak is Dudu Odalar Sokak, an extension of the Galatasaray Balık Pazarı that leads out to Meşrutiyet Caddesi. On the left, just past Cumhuriyet İşkembe Salonu, where for decades drinkers have stopped by in the small hours for a bowl of the tripe soup that is believed to ward off hangovers, is Şütte Şarküteri [Şütte Delicatessen], established in 1918 by a German named Schütte and managed since 1969 by Jifko Elde (Jifko Elde and many of the staff are ethnic Poles from the village of Polonezköy). Şütte is one of the few shops in the city that sells pork products, and offers a wide variety of imported and domestic delicacies. A little further along on the left is Tunç Lakerdacı, where since 1957 Tunçer Ergunsü has been selling what many believe to be the world's best *lakerda* [pickled bonito]. The shop also offers smoked salmon (smoked on the premises) as well as a large variety of other smoked, dried, salted or pickled fish and a variety of caviars and other fish eggs. The last building on the right was once the Hotel St. Georges, where, Said Duhani tells us, 'Poles and Hungarians sheltered in great contentment.'

The first turning to the right from Sahne Sokak is Nevizade Sokak. During the latter part of the nineteenth century, the main activity on this street was the making of carriages, the repairing of carriage wheels and the shoeing of carriage horses. After the advent of the automobile, the street, never fashionable to begin with, went into steady decline.

In the 1940s two legendary *meyhanes* opened on the street. The first of these, on the left near the corner of Kameriye Sokak, was Lambo's, a hangout for literary figures such as Orhan Veli, Sait Faik, Mina Urgan, Peyami Safa and Cahit Irgat (Mücap Ofluoğlu describes it as 'a laboratory in which a generation of bohemian artists was schooled'). It was a tiny place (İlhan Berk describes it as 'perhaps the smallest *meyhane* in the world; no bigger than a tram car'), with room for only two people to sit on stools by the window, with the rest of the customers having to lean against the zinc counter. Lambo's offered little in the way of food, and the customers generally drank Marmara wine.

Lambo himself is described as a well-mannered, refined and educated man, an ethnic Greek from Russia who had been studying medicine in Moscow when he and his family fled the Bolshevik Revolution. Many have spoken of the famous notebook in which he recorded his customers' debts. Mücap Ofluoğlu recalls that once, when he asked that his bill be recorded in this notebook, Lambo turned to him and said, 'Mücap Bey, please don't place too heavy a load on these fragile shoulders.' There is a legend that this notebook was seized by the police when they were investigating a suspected communist plot, and that ever since then people have been searching for it as a memorial to an era of Turkish literature and art. The site of his *meyhane* was occupied for many years by a small grocery store (Şen Büfe), and recently a café-bar called Lambo (different in every sense from the original, quite large, occupying several floors, and catering to young urban professionals) opened in its place.

A little further along was Lefter's *meyhane*, also a favorite hangout for self-destructive writers, which was known for the quality and variety of its *mezes,* and where Lefter's brother Panayoti would play his *laterna.* This *meyhane* closed in 1964 when Lefter and his brother moved to Athens. Lefter's daughter Zöe, now a physics professor in Athens, tells the story of a certain Thanassi who used to annoy her father by hanging out in the kitchen and nibbling at dishes before they were served. One day, to teach Thanassi a lesson, Lefter caught and killed a rat and asked the chef to prepare it in the most attractive possible manner. When it was ready, the kitchen staff was instructed to tell Thanassi that he was under no circumstances to taste it. Of course Thanassi couldn't resist, and ate the whole thing. Then, when he was told what he'd eaten he fainted. They dressed him in a shroud and lay him out on a table surrounded by candles, and when he came to he thought he was at his own funeral.

Through the 1980s, as more *meyhanes* began to open on the street, it began to gain popularity (though it still had a decaying air, and was also the site of several rooming houses for young men

225

who had come the city seeking work), and by the mid 1990s had become 'the *meyhane* street'. At about this time a small place called Mini Meyhane (in which the denizens of the old Lambo's may have felt at home) opened at the far end of the street. An inexpensive place offering little in the way of food and with only a few low stools, it soon became popular with students. This popularity led to it becoming a 'concept', and dozens of similar places began opening on Nevizade and surrounding streets, gradually becoming larger, occupying multiple floors, and more expensive, with more elaborate menus.

In the late 1990s the owners of establishments on Nevizade Sokak and Kameriye Sokak formed an association, hiring security guards to keep out the riffraff (among them the very types who had made these *meyhanes* famous in the first place) and redecorated their establishments and the street itself to attract a more well-heeled clientele. The *meyhanes* here gradually became less distinguishable from each other, and the quality of the food and the service declined. At the beginning of 2012 the association announced that, with the support of the municipality, the street and its establishments would be refurbished and redesigned to attract package tourism. Some fear that this will rob the street of its charm and character, while others feel that it has no charm or character left to lose.

Returning to Sahne Sokak, we pass on our right one of the newest and least expensive establishments in the area, Rıhtım Bar, very popular with young people and particularly with the many foreign exchange students who now come to Istanbul each year. Directly opposite, on the left, is the oldest continuously operating *meyhane* in Beyoğlu, Cumhuriyet, which first opened as a tavern in about 1890 under joint Greek and Armenian ownership, and took its present name in the early years of the Republic.* During the 1940s and 50s it was considered slightly more respectable than the other *meyhanes* in the area. By the 1970s it had become slightly rougher, but had been restored to respectability by the late 1980s. Originally much smaller, Cumhuriyet expanded in the 1990s to occupy most of the ground floor and two upper floors, and can now seat 1,000 people.

---

* Cumhuriyet: Republic.

At the end of Sahne Sokak we come to Kamer Hatun Sokak (formerly an extension of Kalyoncu Kulluğu Caddesi), which leads to Tarlabaşı Bulvarı on the right and on the left to Hamalbaşı Caddesi, which intersects Meşrutiyet Caddesi just before it curves in to Galatasaray Meydanı. Should we turn left, we would pass, on our right, Nizam Pide Salonu, which has become something of an institution in Beyoğlu since it was established in the 1970s by Nizamettin Kızılkayalı, who comes from a long line of bakers and *pide* makers.

At the end of the street, on the left hand corner, is the former site of Pano, which was established in 1898 by Panayotis Papadopoulos, who sold his family property in Samatya to build this building, making it perhaps the first building in the district to be built as a tavern. Always remembered as a colorful place, the kind of tavern that would begin to fill up as soon as it opened in the morning, it grew steadily less reputable over the years. In the late 1960s, when it was taken over by an Armenian woman remembered only as Emel, the name was changed to Meral Şaraphanesi, though everyone still referred to it as Pano. By the time it closed when Emel died in the mid 1970s it had become distinctly seedy and was frequented only by the most down-and-out alcoholics. The establishment was reopened as a wine bar called Pano in 1997, and soon became popular with young professionals and Greek and Russian tourists. The new Pano moved to nearby Kameriye Sokak at the end of 2011.

A few doors up to the left on Hamalbaşı Caddesi is the site of Viktor Levi Şarapevi, which moved here in 1914 from its original location in Galata. The story goes that Viktor Levi, who came from a family of fishermen in Gallipoli, went into business importing sardines to Istanbul and later also began importing wine grapes from the island of Imbros, eventually deciding to make his own wine and open a wine house. Viktor Levi closed in 1985, and was reopened as a wine bar in 1999. It closed again in the spring of 2009, but a sign that has remained in the window since then promises that 'We'll be together again in September.'

The right hand corner of Kamer Hatun Sokak, directly across from Pano, where Belma Eczanesi [Belma Pharmacy] now operates, was the site for many years of Diamandi Şaraphanesi. İskender Özsoy describes Diamandi, which he says was 'a small place.'

The owner was always behind the counter, and would fill the bottles from the wine barrels himself. The *meze* at Diamandi was usually boiled eggs and boiled potatoes. The patrons would stand at tall tables covered in newspaper. The waiters would bring the *meze* and half-liter bottles of wine, and would never forget to ask to be paid right away. At Diamandi and the other wine houses of Beyoğlu, it was customary for the patrons to drink a small glass of liquor before leaving.

Said Duhani recalls that until World War I, in the basement of the same building (or rather an older building that stood on this site, the present building dates from the 1980s) Henry Yan and Luce Yol ran a cabaret called Catacoum that he found reminiscent of the nightclubs of Montmartre.

Halfway along the block to the right, on Hamalbaşı Caddesi, we see Aya Triada Kilisesi [the Greek Catholic church of Haghia Triada], built in 1863 along with an elementary school.

Ayia Triada now houses a congregation of Chaldean Catholics, an eastern Orthodox rite that reunited with the Roman Catholic Church in the seventeenth century.

Returning back along Kamer Hatun Sokak, we pass Asmaaltı Bar on the corner of Balık Sokak. This was originally opened as a

Taksim Meydanı [Taksim Square] and, at the back, Aya Triada [Haghia Triada].

Aya Triada Kilisesi [church of Haghia Triada], built in 1863, now houses the congregation of Chaldean Catholics.

meyhane in 1969 by one Panayotis Papadopoulos (no relation to the founder of Pano). Although it has changed ownership and character several times over the years, it remains a favorite spot to while away the hours while contemplating the fruits and vegetables at the greengrocer's across the street.

A little further along on our left we pass a narrow little street called Daracık Sokak (which means, literally, narrow little street), lined with crumbling buildings where the prostitutes (mostly but not exclusively transvestites) who prowl Tarlabaşı Bulvarı entertain their customers. There are also several small bars and *pavyons* on the street.

We now turn right on Topçekenler Sokak, formerly Silog Sokak. The vacant lot on the right about halfway down the street was the site of a large neoclassical building erected at the end of the nineteenth century by Hristakis Zographos to house the Greek Philological Syllogue of Constantinople. This building, which housed the archives, the great library and the museum of the syllogue, was appropriated by the Turkish government in 1925, after which it served as the Beyoğlu district courthouse until it was demolished in 1960.

At the end of the street we turn left onto Balo Sokak and then immediately right onto Halas Sokak, formerly Abanoz Sokak. In the last decades of the nineteenth century, this street was lined with boarding houses inhabited by the foreign actors, actresses, singers, dancers and other performers who worked in Beyoğlu's many places of entertainment. By the first decade of the twentieth century, these boarding houses were increasingly inhabited by *consommatrices*, and some of the houses are said to have begun renting rooms by the hour. At about this time, the first brothels began opening on neighboring streets (Blind Emin's on Küçükyazıcı Sokak. and Nikolaidis' on Toprak Lüle Sokak, which had a large garden with a pool).

By the beginning of World War I, Abanoz Sokak had become part of an officially sanctioned zone of licensed brothels including Karnavola Sokak (now Büyük Bayram Sokak), Toprak Lüle Sokak, Kilit Sokak, Lale Sokak and Küçükyazıcı Sokak (Küçükyazıcı Sokak, and parts of Kilit Sokak and Topraklüle Sokak disappeared when a block-wide swath was demolished in the early 1980s to widen Tarlabaşı Caddesi).

Pathfinder Survey of Constantinople describes conditions on the street as they were during the years of the Allied occupation:

> The houses on Abanoz Street are of better class than the others. The sanitary conditions are as good as can be expected under existing circumstances. There seems to be an attempt on the part of the keepers of these houses to keep the toilets clean. The rooms for the most part are clean and well-furnished. We hear indirectly that two houses on Abanoz Street sell drugs to any who have the money to buy. It is rumored that many American sailors use drugs. Wine and douziko (*rakı*), beer and sometimes champagne are on sale in several of the houses.

By the 1930s there were police boxes at the entrance to the street, and later walls were built blocking all but one entrance. The area saw some of its busiest days in April 1946 when the battleship U.S.S. Missouri was anchored off Dolmabahçe. The area was closed for two days before the ship's arrival so that the houses could be painted and cleaned. The municipality put buses into service to ferry the sailors from Dolmabahçe to Taksim, where they were met by 'guides' who brought them directly here.

The area was closed down for a few months in 1948, and when it reopened it was confined to Abanoz Sokak, on which there were now 45 licensed brothels with an average of ten women working in each. During the riots of September 1955, the mobs descended on this street as well, looting the houses and raping the women who worked in them.

The street was officially closed in 1964, though a number of brothels continued to operate illicitly. Then, in the early 1970s it became the main center of activity for transvestite and transsexual prostitutes, a number of whom, it is said, came from Western Europe and from Yugoslavia and the Soviet Union. This activity was largely dispersed in the late 1970s by police pressure and the political violence that was rife in the district then. The only remnant of this world is a single transvestite-transsexual brothel that still operates on Büyük Bayram Sokak. There is a legend that a woman there, a transsexual called Deniz Anne [Mother Deniz], has worked on the street for fifty years. This, incidentally, may be one of the last places one might hear 'Lubunca,' a slang used by Turkish transvestites and transsexuals that consists of four to five hundred words borrowed from Romany, Greek, Arabic, Armenian and French. Lubunca is said to date back to the 17th century, when it was used by dancing boys [köçek] and bath attendants [tellak].

At the end of the street we cross Sakızağacı Caddesi, continuing in the same direction along Süslü Saksı Sokak, which changes its name to Kurabiye Sokak and then to Ana Çeşmesi Sokak. Until not long ago a quiet back street, it has in recent years become crowded with bars, cafés and restaurants, particularly kebab and meat restaurants, though many have suffered from the ban on outdoor seating and some have been forced to close. At the end of the street, taking care on the last stretch not to be run over by Bakırköy and Topkapı dolmuşes that come barreling past we turn right on to Taksim Sokak, which brings us out to Istiklal Caddesi at the point where it reaches Taksim Meydanı.

Here we see on our left the attractive octagonal structure that has given its name to Taksim Meydanı and the surrounding quarter. This is Taksim Maksemi, or water-distribution centre, built by Mahmud I in 1732 to bring water to Beyoğlu from the reservoirs and aqueducts outside the city near the Black Sea coast. There are two dedicatory inscriptions on the structure, one by the admiral and Grand Vizier Cezayirli [the Algerian] Hasan Pasha and the other by the Grand Vizier Yusuf Pasha. The fountain extending from the side of the Taksim Maksemi was once the site of a street market, most of the vendors being sellers of secondhand books. For the past several decades this area has been used primarily as a staging point for riot police. These riot police have been the target of several suicide bombings that resulted in the death and injury of policemen and passersby. The flower sellers who were moved around the corner to Tarlabaşı Bulvarı several decades ago returned here in the winter of 2012 when construction began on a tunnel under part of the square.

The area beyond this once constituted the large cemetery known as the Grand Champs des Morts. It was first used as a cemetery for the victims of a plague epidemic in the sixteenth century and later became Pera's principal cemetery, divided according to religion and denomination. The Protestant cemetery was originally within what is now Taksim Gezi Parkı (it was moved a short distance when Topçu Kışlası, or the Artillery Barracks was built there in 1806), The Armenian Gregorian cemetery was behind this, where Divan Hotel is now, the Latin Catholic and Armenian Catholic cemeteries spread across most of what is now the square and down the slope descending to the right, the Greek Orthodox cemetery was on and beyond the grounds of Aya Triada Kilisesi (the church of Haghia Triada) and the Muslim cemetery was on the slope descending behind what is now Atatürk Kültür Merkezi.

Julia Pardoe describes the cemetery as it was in 1836:

> The first plot of ground, after passing the barrack, is the grave-yard of the Franks; and here you are greeted on all sides with inscriptions in Latin; injunctions to pray for the souls of the departed; flourishes of French sentiment; calembourgs graven into the everlasting stone, treating of roses and reine Marguerites; concise English records of births, deaths, ages, and diseases;

Italian elaborations of regret and despair; and all the common-places of an ordinary burial-ground.

Immediately in a line with the European cemetery, is the burial-ground of the Armenians. It is a thickly-peopled spot; and as you wander beneath the leafy boughs of the scented acacias, and thread your way among the tombs, you are struck by the peculiarity of their inscriptions. The noble Armenian character is graven deeply into the stone; name and date are duly set forth; but that which renders an Armenian slab peculiar and distinctive, is the chiseling upon the tomb the emblem of the trade or profession of the deceased. The Turkish cemetery stretches along the slope of the hill behind the barrack, and descends far into the valley. Its thickly-planted cypresses form a dense shade, beneath which the tall head-stones gleam out white and ghastly. The grove is intersected by footpaths, and here and there a green glade lets in the sunshine, to glitter upon many a gilded tomb. Plunge into the thick darkness of the more covered spots, and for a moment you will almost think that you stand amid the ruins of some devastated city. You are surrounded by what appears for an instant to be the myriad fragments of some mighty whole; but the gloom has deceived you –you are in the midst of a Necropolis– a City of the Dead.

By the middle of the nineteenth century, as the population of Pera grew and as the district then known as Yeni Mahalle was being developed, the cemetery had already begun to be used as a park, and teahouses had been built in those places offering the best views. Julia Pardoe tells us that:

> The whole of the Christian cemetery had assumed the appearance of a fair... Grave-stones steadied the poles which supported the swings - divans, comfortably overlaid with cushions, were but chintz-covered sepulchers – the kibaub merchants had dug hollows to cook their dainties under the shelter of the tombs, and the smoking booths were amply supplied with seats and counters from the same wide waste of death.
>
> Every hundred yards that we advanced, the scene became more striking. One long line of diminutive tents formed a tem-porary street of eating-houses; there were kibaubs, pillauf, fritters, pickled vegetables, soups, rolls stuffed with fine herbs, sausages, fried fish, bread of every quality, and cakes of all dimensions ... Here and there a flat tomb, fancifully covered with gold-embroidered handkerchiefs, was overspread with sweetmeats and preserved

Topçu Kışlası [Artillery Barracks], designed by Kirkor Balyan, which stood in what is now Taksim Gezi Parkı [Taksim Gezi Park] and which was completed in 1806.

fruits; while in the midst of these rival establishments, groups of men were seated in a circle, wherever a little shade could be obtained, smoking their long pipes in silence, with their diminutive coffee-cups resting on the ground beside them. The wooden kiosk overhanging the Bosphorus was crowded; and many a party was snugly niched among the acacias, with their backs resting against the tombs, and the sunshine flickering at their feet.

In the early 1860s the newly formed Municipality of Beyoğlu made the decision to turn the area into a park, and the Christian cemeteries were moved grave by grave over a period of six years (The Catholic and Protestant cemeteries were moved to Feriköy and the Greek Orthodox cemetery was moved to Mecidiyeköy). De Amicis describes this park as it was on a Sunday afternoon in summer about twenty years later.

During the week this neighborhood is buried in the most profound silence and solitude, but on Sunday afternoons it is crowded with people and equipages, all the gay world of Pera pouring out to scatter itself among the beer-gardens, cafés and pleasure-resorts....

It was in one of these cafés that we broke our fast – the café Belle Vue, a resort of the flower of Pera society, and well deserving its name, since from its numerous gardens, extending like a terrace over the summit of the hill, you have, spread out before you, the large Mussulman village of Findukli, the Bosphorus covered with ships, the coast of Asia dotted over with gardens and villages, Skutari [Üsküdar] with her gleaming white mosques – a luxuriance of color, green foliage, blue sea, and sky all bathed in light, which forms a scene of intoxicating beauty.

The first building after the maksem to be built in the area was the onion-domed Topçu Kışlası, designed by Kirkor Balyan, which stood in what is now Taksim Gezi Parkı and which was completed in 1806. It was partly destroyed during a military rebellion the following year and subsequently rebuilt.

In April 1909 an armed insurrection, instigated by the İttihad-ı Muhamedi [Mohammadan Union] and the publisher of the *Volkan* newspaper, a Cypriot Nahshibendi sheik named Dervish Vahdeti, was supported by troops stationed at Topçu Kışlası, and the nearby Taşkışla barracks. In the early hours of the insurrection, which aimed to overthrow the Constitutional Revolution of 1908, the troops murdered over twenty officers, in many instances by cutting their throats. Later when they stormed the Parliament they killed the Minister of Justice and the representative from Latakia, who they mistook for the editor and a columnist from the *Tanin* newspaper, which was perceived as the voice of the Committee for Union and Progress. The offices of this newspaper were also sacked and set on fire. Meanwhile thousands of theological students marched through the streets shouting "We want sharia!" and "Down with the Constitution!" Military units in the Balkans loyal to the Committee of Union and Progress assembled in Salonika and marched on Istanbul to defend the constitution.

H.G. Dwight, in his *Constantinople Old and New*, gives an account of the aftermath of the assault on the barracks by the Macedonian Blues on the morning of Sunday 24 April 1909. 'The fighting was brief but fierce, resulting in a large number of casualties, particularly among the troops defending the barracks. A number of passersby and inhabitants of nearby houses were killed or wounded. Among the civilians killed was Frederick Moore, a reporter for the *New York*

Graphic. Among the wounded were a Mr. Booth, also of the *New York Graphic*, and a Mr. Graves of the *London Times*.' The building was last used as a barracks during the Allied occupation, when it housed Senegalese troops. In the early years of the Republic the interior was gutted and the barracks was converted into a stadium, used mostly for football matches but also for sports as diverse as fencing, boxing, tennis and field hockey. The Turkish National Football Team played its first official match here against Romania in 1923. The building was demolished in 1940 by Mayor Lütfi Kırdar to make way for Taksim Gezi Parkı. There was originally a statue of İsmet İnönü on horseback at the entrance to the park, but this was destroyed when the Democrat Party came to power in 1950.

The back of the park was the site from 1900 to 1925 of Taksim Bahçesi, which in summer hosted regular balls and afternoon dances. It reopened in 1940 as Taksim Belediye Gazinosu, which had a bandstand and a pool filled with tropical fish. The Taksim Gazinosu closed in 1970.

In 2011 the Greater Istanbul Municipality announced plans to build a replica of Topçu Kışlası as part of a controversial plan to restructure Taksim Meydanı and its environs. No specific plans for the proposed usage of this reconstructed barracks were presented to the public, but official statements referred to a shopping center, a hotel, residences and perhaps some kind of cultural center. When construction was to begin in late May of 2013, despite a court injunction resulting from a suit filed by the Istanbul Chamber of architects, repeated police attacks on small groups of protesters led to what amounted to a nationwide uprising. For two weeks in June, as street battles raged elsewhere in the district and the city, thousands of enthusiastic protesters camped out in Taksim Gezi Parkı, entertained by musicians, dancers and speakers and with access to a library of donated books. On the evening of June 15 the police cleared the park in a show of force that included tear gas, flash bombs, water cannons and baton charges. Plans for the reconstruction of the barracks appear to have been shelved for the time being.

Taksim began to take on the shape and identity of a modern city square with the erection of Cumhuriyet Anıtı [Independence Monument], a statue group representing Atatürk and other leaders of the Turkish Nationalist movement, completed in 1928. The monument was the work of two Italian artists, with the architect Giulio Mongeri designing the structure and the sculptor Pietro Canonica creating the statues.

Talimhane, the area to the left of the Maksem as far as Cumhuriyet Caddesi, was used as a drilling and training field for the soldiers stationed at the barracks. This land was parceled and developed in the late 1920s, becoming very fashionable among the new Republican bourgeois. It began to lose its cachet in the late 1950s, and by the mid 1960s had largely ceased to be a residential neighborhood and was occupied almost entirely by dealers in automobile parts. Hotels began opening in this area in the late 1990s, and in 2003 the streets were repaved and closed to traffic. The area is now home to a large number of hotels as well as shops and restaurants catering to tourists.

The second floor of a colonnaded building in front of a block of flats that was demolished in the early 1980s was the site for many years of the famous Kristal Gazinosu, and before that Café du Croissant.

The far end of the square was once occupied by two buildings, the mansion, built in 1911, of M. Hansens, director of the electric company, and a Gendarmerie [Jandarma] post. The Gendarmerie post dated from about the middle of the nineteenth century, and its presence here demonstrates that at the time this area was considered to be outside the city limits (the Gendarmerie was and is a rural rather than an urban police force). These buildings were demolished in 1946 to make way for an opera house. The construction of the opera house was soon abandoned due to lack of funds, and did not resume until 1956, to be opened on April 12, 1969 as the Istanbul Culture Palace with a performance of Verdi's Aida. A fire that broke out on November 27, 1970 during a performance of a Turkish adaption of Arthur Miller's The Crucible destroyed much of the building and rendered it unusable. It was restored and finally reopened in 1978 as the Atatürk Kültür Merkezi, which closed again for renovations in 2005 and has yet to reopen.

The right far corner of the square was once the site of the prestigious Istanbul Club, but this and several other buildings were demolished in the early 1970s to make way for the Marmara Hotel.

During the 1970s Taksim Meydanı became the locus of mass demonstrations, particularly those marking International Workers' Day on May 1. May 1, 1977 saw the largest of these demonstrations to date, with an estimated 400,000 people marching on the square from different parts of the city. Shortly after 6:00 pm, during a moment of silence to honor those who had lost their lives in the struggle for workers' rights, several gunshots rang out. According to some witnesses these shots came from an upper window of the Marmara Hotel and according to others from the direction of Tarlabaşı Caddesi. Almost immediately soldiers and armored vehicles began entering the square from Istiklal Caddesi, Sıraselviler Caddesi and Taksim Gezi Parkı, detonating sound bombs and using high-pitched sirens that created panic in the crowd. There were also reports of shots being fired by men in a white car that raced into the square. The crowd was forced down the steep, narrow street of Kazancı Yokuşu, where many were trampled to death. The official death toll was 34, with hundreds injured.

In subsequent years there were frequent attempts by labor unions and leftist groups to stage May Day rallies in the square. They were prevented from doing so by the police, resulting in pitched battles between demonstrators and police throughout the district, leaving Beyoğlu shrouded in clouds of tear gas. On May 1, 2009 the authorities finally allowed the demonstrators to enter the square, and for three years May Day rallies here passed without incident. However in 2013 the government forbade the holding of the May Day rally in Taksim on the grounds that ongoing construction in the square posed a safety hazard. The day was marked by violent clashes, as it was again in 2014 when the government not only banned the May Day rally but decreed that henceforth no demonstrations of any kind would be allowed in Taksim Meydanı.

In the winter of 2012 work began on a controversial plan to restructure and pedestrianize Taksim Meydanı, and the people of Beyoğlu were faced yet again with a now traditional landscape of trenches, piles of mud and blocked streets. The plan envisioned routing traffic through tunnels under the square. Only one of these tunnels has been completed, that connecting Tarlabaşı Bulvarı with Cumhuriyet Caddesi. The plan was suspended in the summer of 2013, but since then the municipality has occasionally treated the public to fanciful sketches of what the completed project might look like. On May 6, 2014 the Turkish Council of State voted to cancel the project.

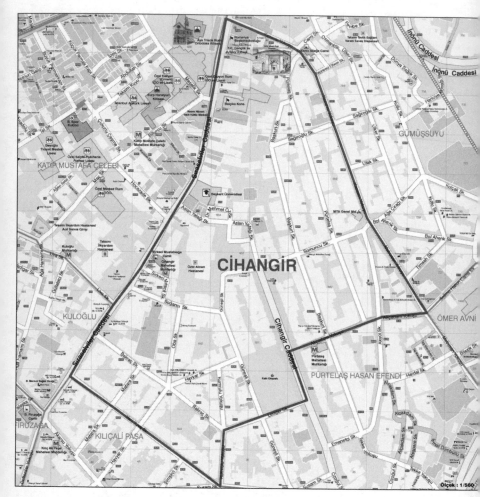

© Beyoğlu Belediyesi Emlak ve İstimlak Müdürlüğü

CHAPTER 8
Beyoğlu Neighborhoods

This chapter will be a series of strolls through various Beyoğlu neighborhoods, beginning with those on the hillside sloping down to the Bosphorus from Taksim Meydanı and the ridge to its north. The avenue that leads out of Taksim Meydanı to the south just off the end of Istiklal Caddesi is Sıraselviler Caddesi, which heads down to the Bosphorus. The towering modern edifice on the south side of Taksim Meydanı is the Marmara Hotel, built in the 1960s. The avenue in front of the hotel is Tak-ı Zafer Caddesi, which one block farther along comes to an intersection, with İnönü Caddesi curving off to the right on its way down to the Bosphorus.

There are four minor Ottoman monuments down the side streets in the neighborhood known as Pürtelaş, bounded by Sıraselviler Caddesi, Tak-ı Zafer Caddesi and İnönü Caddesi. Two of them are on Kazancıbaşı Sokak, which is the first turning to the left from the top of Sıraselviler Caddesi. Along the first block of this street we see the Hafız Ahmed Paşa Çeşmesi, a street-fountain built in 1732. Farther along the street we come to Kazancıbaşı Camii, a mosque founded in the seventeenth century by a janissary officer named Hacı Ali Ağa.

Turning to the right off Kazancıbaşı Sokak on to Pürtelaş Sokak, we come after a few steps to Silahtar [the Sword-Bearer] Mehmed Ağa Çeşmesi, another street-fountain built in 1732.

Continuing along Pürtelaş Sokak and turning left on Somoncu Sokak, at the next intersection we come to Bolahenk Sokak. There we see the Hacı Beşir Ağa Çeşmesi, still another street-fountain built in 1732. The building of three street-fountains in the same year in this neighborhood stems from the presence of the nearby Taksim Maksemi, founded in 1732 by Mahmud I to bring water to Beyoğlu from the reservoirs and aqueducts outside the city. The founder of this particular fountain, Hacı Beşir Ağa, was Chief Black

Eunuch in Topkapı Sarayı during the reign of Mahmud I, one of the most influential men ever to hold that post.

The neighborhood between İnönü Caddesi and the Bosphorus is known variously as Ayaspaşa and Gümüşsuyu. The left side of the avenue was formerly the Muslim section of Grand Champs des Morts, and was only developed after the cemetery was moved in 1938. Much of the area to the right was destroyed in the great fire of 1916. Strolling down İnönü Caddesi, which changes its name to Gümüşsuyu Caddesi, we see on our right the site of the famous and fondly remembered the Park Hotel, and before that of the residence of Baron Alberto Blanc, Italian Ambassador to the Sublime Porte. After the Baron was recalled, the house was taken over by the Italian government and was to be given to the King of Italy to serve as an annex of the Quirenal. However, the Italian government never paid Baron Blanc for the house, which he had built at his own expense. So he approached Sultan Abdülhamid II and explained his difficulty, whereupon the Sultan bought the house and gave it to his Foreign Minister, Ahmet Tevfik Pasha (later to become Grand Vizier). The building (reported to have been a charming three storey neo-renaissance structure) was damaged by fire in 1911, after which it was party rebuilt and another storey was added. In 1930 Tevfik Pasha's son Nuri Okday demolished the family house and built a hotel (a U-shaped, art deco building) which was first called the Hotel Miramare. A year later Nuri went into partnership with Aram Hıdır and the hotel was renamed the Park Hotel.

In its time the Park Hotel bar, which had a broad terrace looking out over the Bosphorus, was the most famous bar in Istanbul. Atatürk was a frequent visitor, and entertained many of his foreign guests here, including King Edward VIII of England and Wally Simpson. The poet Yahya Kemal and journalist, writer and newspaper-owner Nadir Nadi held court here regularly, drinking *rakı* accompanied by olives sprinkled with oregano and cubes of *beyaz peynir* sprinkled with red pepper. Yahya Kemal was so fond of the Park Hotel that he spent the last ten years of his life in a private suite on the second floor. The bar was famous for its gin fizz and for Irish coffee made with real Java coffee that could not be found elsewhere in the city. The bar itself was made of rosewood and oak by a master Italian carpenter. The likes of Mücap Ofluoğlu, Orhan Boran, Bedii Faik, Şevket Rado and Cahide Sonku regularly tangoed at the Park Hotel's *thés dansants*, held in the cavernous art deco dining room. Prime Minister Adnan Menderes (whom Yahya Kemal despised passionately) was also a regular at the Park Hotel, keeping a private suite in which he often held cabinet meetings. The Park Hotel, like the rest of Beyoğlu, suffered from the economic stagnation and political violence of the 1970s, and finally closed in 1979. In 1983 it became the first hotel to be declared a historical monument. Nevertheless, in 1988 the then Mayor of Istanbul Bedrettin Dalan signed a decision allowing a 33-storey hotel on the spot, to be built by Sürmeli chain of hotels. This new construction covered an area much larger than the original hotel, and a number of neighboring buildings were also destroyed. Indeed Sürmeli Company bought an entire street, Ağa Çırağı Sokak from the municipality for 850 million liras.

A number of local residents who had been forcibly evicted filed a lawsuit for damages. They were supported by the subsequent Mayor of Istanbul, Nurettin Süzen, who won an injunction to halt construction and to have a number of storeys demolished. In 1993 the building was bought by Global Holding company, owned by Warren Buffet, for 34.5 million dollars. The rest of the structure was demolished in 2012, and the construction of a new luxury hotel was begun. This hotel, the Park Bosphorus Hotel, opened in November 2013.

A little further along is the monumental structure that houses the German Consulate General and Alman Arkeoloji Derneği [German Archaeological Society]. This was built as the German Embassy in the years 1874-7. Kaiser Wilhelm II stayed here on all three of his visits to Istanbul during the reign of Abdülhamid II (r. 1876-1909). During those visits the Sultan and Kaiser cemented the alliance between Turkey and Germany that eventually brought the Turks into World War I as allies of the Germans and led to the downfall of the Ottoman Empire.

Farther down the avenue we see on our left the former Gümüşsuyu Kışlası, imperial barracks first built in wood by Sultan Abdülmecid. It was rebuilt in its present form in 1861-2 by the Armenian architect Sarkis Balyan for Sultan Abdülaziz. In 1923 it

German Embassy built in the years 1874-1977.

was given over to Istanbul Technical University to be used as its School of Engineering. The building now houses the university's department of mechanical and textile technology and design.

Still farther along Gümüşsuyu Caddesi joins Yeni Dolmabahçe Caddesi, which goes down to the Bosphorus, passing İnönü Stadyumu [İnönü Stadium]. The stadium was built in 1939 and is the home field of the Beşiktaş Football Club.

We now stroll down Sıraselviler Caddesi. The *döner kebab* shops on the right at the beginning of the avenue all date from the early 1970s. The most famous of these is the Kızılkayalar, the first place in Taksim to serve *döner kebab* and the first in Istanbul to serve döner 24 hours a day. Kızılkayalar is also the birthplace of the spicy 'wet hamburger,' which is actually quite revolting but magically becomes delicious after midnight. The terrace above, now occupied by Burger King, was once the famous Eptalofos Kahvesi [Eptalofos Café].

The long yellow building directly across the street was once the home of the famous Maksim Nightclub. This was established in 1918 by an African-American named Frederick Thomas, who fled here with his Russian wife from Moscow, where he had run a popular nightclub called Maxim. Thomas originally opened a night club called Stella in Şişli, next to La Paix Hastanesi, but soon moved here to open Maksim. Maksim, which featured jazz bands and lovely Russian hostesses with whom patrons could dance foxtrot, the shimmy and the Charleston, quickly became very popular. Unfortunately Thomas, a spendthrift and a bon-vivant, died penniless within a few years and Maksim died with him.

It was reopened in 1928 as Yeni Maksim, and featured an Argentinean tango orchestra and an African-American jazz quintet called the Ramblers Five. Yeni Maksim lost its popularity in the late 40s, and is said to have become quite seedy by the end of the 50s. It closed in 1959, to reappear in 1961 after extensive remodeling as Maksim Gazinosu. Over the years, until it closed early in the first decade of this century, Maksim Gazinosu hosted such superstars of Turkish popular music as Zeki Müren, Ajda Pekkan, Bülent Ersoy, Sezen Aksu and İbrahim Tatlıses. One of the occasions on which İbrahim Tatlıses was shot was while he was performing at Maksim. In 2011 Tuna Construction Company began work on a hotel on this site. The original building was to be preserved, but nine floors would be built above it and eight floors would be dug out below. Suits were filed by the Istanbul Chamber of Architects and by the owner of a neighboring hotel to halt the construction. On October 3, 2013 the Istanbul 1st Administrative Court ruled that the project violated article 2863 of the Cultural and Natural Heritage Protection Law and ordered that construction be halted. However, construction not only proceeded but was intensified, and did not stop until January 2014 when one of the complainants threatened to file criminal charges. A previous building on this site housed Greek-French Lycée.

A little way down on the left we pass the Romanian Consulate, formerly the Romanian Embassy. This was originally the home of Muzurus Pasha, who had served as Ottoman Ambassador to London and Paris. He went to great lengths to have the building resemble one of the great homes of the Faubourg St. Germain. He had all of the locks, door-handles, metal doors, railings and window grilles made by a master craftsman in Paris, and all of the furniture made by the famous Parisian carpenter André Charles Boulé. There was an armor-plated room in the basement that contained massive vaults. The Romanian government bought the building with all of its original furniture.

A little further along we pass the site of Kemancı Rock Bar, one of the pioneers of the revival of Beyoğlu's night life in the late 1980s.

Originally on the lower level of Galata Köprüsü, it moved here after the bridge was damaged by fire. In its heyday, Kemancı occupied several floors, but the space has since been divided into several separately owned bars. It was in one of these, Riddim Bar, that a shootout occurred in December 2008, resulting in the deaths of three people. The shooting is rumored to have been the result of a disagreement about money among the original owners.

A few paces along on the left we pass the former embassy, now consulate, of Belgium, built by the architect Kampanakis.

About 300 meters along the avenue passes between the two biggest hospitals in Beyoğlu. The one on the right is Taksim Hastanesi. This was founded in the late 1850s by the newly formed Beyoğlu Municipality as a municipal hospital and was staffed by Franciscan monks and nuns until it was taken over by the Ministry of Health of the new Turkish Republic. The present building dates from 1960. On the left is Alman Hastanesi, which was founded in 1851 by the Charitable Society of the German Evangelical Church and was originally located on Sakız Sokak. It was moved to what is now Tel Sokak in 1853 and to its present location in 1856. The present building dates from 1874.

The side street that leads off from Sıraselviler Caddesi on the north side of Alman Hastanesi is Aslan Yatağı Sokak, 'the Street of the Lion's Bed.' The American poet James Lovett (1924-2005) lived on Aslan Yatağı Sokak in the late 1950s, and one of his poems is about this street. Since the late 1980s it has also been home to Roxy Nightclub.

Aslan Yatağı Sokak curves around to join Cihangir Caddesi, the two streets together with Sıraselviler Caddesi and its extension, Defterdar Yokuşu, forming the boundaries of the neighborhood known as Cihangir.

Cihangir was first settled in the beginning of the sixteenth century. The first settlements were almost exclusively Muslim, constituting an extension of the neighborhood of Fındıklı and mostly confined to the lower slopes. A dervish lodge and a religious primary school are known to have existed near Cihangir Camii from about the middle of the sixteenth century. The upper reaches of Cihangir were not densely settled until Beyoğlu began to expand rapidly in the nineteenth century, and was settled mostly by Greeks,

Tophane and Cihangir from a look at the Galata Tower.

Levantines, Armenians and Jews. While most of the buildings built in Beyoğlu in the latter half of the 19th century were of stone, European in style and in accordance with at least a rudimentary street plan, Cihangir remained a patchwork of wooden mansions and houses in the Ottoman style, interspersed with small farms. This Cihangir was almost entirely wiped out in the fire of 1916, which consumed 1,325 houses in Tophane, Fındıklı, Cihangir and Ayaspaşa. One of the only surviving mansions of this era, on Özoğul Sokak, is Sadık Paşa Konağı, once the home of Michal Czajkowski, an exiled Polish nobleman, who later, after his conversion to Islam, and as Mehmed Sadık Pasha, led a regiment of Ottoman Cossacks into battle in the Balkans during the Crimean War. Czajkowski is also credited with being one of the founders of Adampol, better known as Polonezköy, the Polish village in the outskirts of Istanbul on the Asian side of the Bosphorus.

The 1925 Insurance maps of Jaques Previtch show almost the entire area as *terre incindie*, 'burnt-out land.' That is, almost every building was built after this time, and many of the present streets were laid out during the rebuilding that followed in the late 1920s and early 1930s. Until the 1960s the area was largely Greek and Levantine, and after the Turkish film industry took off in the late

247

1940s, many actors, actresses, scriptwriters and directors from the world of Yeşilçam chose to live here. As with the rest of Beyoğlu, Cihangir suffered decline and decay in the 1970s. Most of the remaining bourgeois fled, to be replaced by migrants from Anatolia, mostly from Sivas and Kastamonu, and crime and prostitution began to increase. Some of the upper areas such as Pürtelaş and Sormagir remained centers of transvestite prostitution until the mid 1990s, when they were driven out by the obsessively determined efforts of the then Beyoğlu police chief Süleyman Ulusoy, known popularly as Hortum Süleyman [Süleyman the Hose] because of his penchant for beating prisoners with a length of rubber hose. Süleyman is reported to have had a particular fixation with transvestites, often interrogating them alone for hours at a time.

Cihangir was the first neighborhood of Beyoğlu to experience gentrification, or regentrification, with a number of famous writers, musicians, directors etc. moving into the lower areas in the early 1990s. It soon became popular with intellectuals, young urban professionals and well-heeled foreigners, and today has the highest rents and property prices in the district.

At its lower end Güneşli Sokak brings us to Cihangir Camii, the mosque from which the street and the neighborhood take their name.

The present mosque, which was built for Abdülhamid II in 1890, is of no interest whatsoever, though in his dedicatory inscription the Sultan boasts that his new edifice is 'bigger and better than the old ones' that it replaced. However, it occupies the site of a mosque built in 1553 by Sinan for Süleyman the Magnificent. The mosque was dedicated to Prince Cihangir, Süleyman's hunchback son, who died in that year of heartbreak, it is said, because of the Sultan's execution of his beloved half-brother, Prince Mustafa. Sinan's mosque was burned down in 1720, as were several other mosques erected successively on the site before the present building. The small mosque garden offers a spectacular view of the Bosphorus and the islands, and is a pleasant place to sit on a hot summer afternoon.

At the first intersection below Taksim Hastanesi on Sıraselviler Caddesi becomes Defterdar Yokuşu, better known as İtalyan Yokuşu. At the far corner to the right at the intersection we see

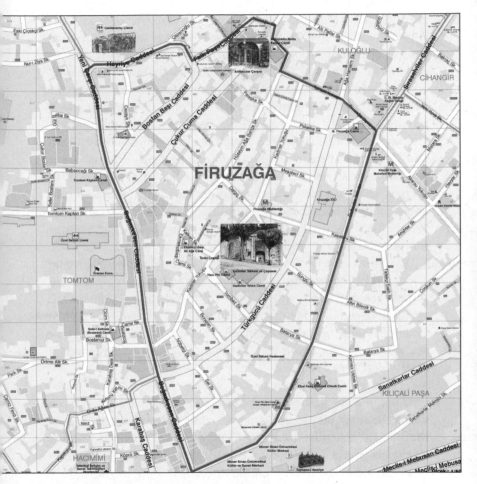

Firuz Ağa Camii, which has given its name to the Firuz Ağa neighborhood to the right of the avenue. This is the oldest mosque in Beyoğlu, founded in 1491 by Firuz Ağa, Chief Treasurer in the reign of Bayezid II (r. 1481-1512). The mosque took on its present form when it was rebuilt in 1823-4, during the reign of Mahmud II (r. 1808-39).

The northernmost of the two side streets to the right at Firuz Ağa Camii is Taktaki Yokuşu, which leads downhill to Çukur Cami Sokak. The latter street and the surrounding neighborhood take their name from Çukurcuma Camii, a mosque built in the mid-sixteenth century by the great architect Sinan for the *Şeyhülislam* Fenerizade Muhittin Mehmet Efendi. The mosque has been totally rebuilt in modern times and now has no architectural interest. Çukurcuma once formed the boundary between a mostly Greek and Levantine neighborhood of late nineteenth-century stone apartment buildings and a mostly Turkish neighborhood of wooden houses. These wooden houses were destroyed in the fire of 1916 and the area remained deserted until the late 1920s. In recent years Çukurcuma has become known for its many overpriced antique shops.

Returning to Firuz Ağa Camii, we continue down Defterdar Caddesi. At the second intersection beyond the mosque Altın Bilezik Sokak leads to the left into Cihangir and Süngü Sokak heads right into the Firuz Ağa neighborhood, crossing Türkgücü Caddesi. On the near right-hand corner of the latter intersection we see a street-fountain built in 1731 by the *Topçubaşı* [Commandant of Artillery] İsmail Ağa.

Farther down the street passes between two hospitals. On the right we see the large İtalyan Hastanesi [Italian Hospital] from which the street takes its alternative name, İtalyan Yokuşu, and on the left is the smaller Cihangir Kliniği [Cihangir Clinic]. On the side street just before Cihangir Kliniği we see the Defterdar Emin Çeşmesi, the oldest street-fountain in Beyoğlu, built in 1687.

At the end of Defterdar Caddesi we come to Boğazkesen Caddesi, which goes uphill from Tophane on the Bosphorus to Galatasaray Meydanı, changing its name Yeni Çarşı Caddesi at its upper end.

We now turn right and start walking uphill along Boğazkesen Caddesi. About halfway up the hill we come to an intersection

250

where Çukurcuma Caddesi leads to the right and Tomtom Kaptan Sokak to the left. The latter street takes its name from Tomtom Kaptan Camii, the old mosque we see on the left. The mosque was founded in the seventeenth century by a mariner named Ahmed Kaptan. The street-fountain near the mosque was built in 1870 by Pirinçci Tahir Efendi.

We walk a short way down Çukurcuma Caddesi and turn right into a cul-de-sac called Dalgıç Çıkmazı. There at No. 2 we find Masumiyet Müzesi [the Museum of Innocence], a museum devoted to created memorabilia from the novel of the same name by the Nobel laureate Orhan Pamuk.

Returning to Boğazkesen Caddesi, we turn right at the next corner on Bostanbaşı Caddesi. Then a short distance along we turn left into Cezayir Sokak, Algiers Street, which we visited on a previous stroll.

At the upper end of Cezayir Sokak we turn left on Hayriye Sokak, and then a few steps farther along we turn right on Yeni Çarşı Caddesi, which we follow up to Galatasaray Meydanı.

Our next stroll will take us through the neighborhood known as Tarlabaşı, which is bordered by Feridiye Caddesi, Tarlabaşı Bulvarı, Ömer Hayyam Caddesi and Dolapdere Caddesi. This area was first settled in the fifteenth century, mostly by Greeks who worked as servants for the wealthy merchants and diplomats of Pera, though there are known to have been a few small Turkish settlements as well. In a letter written while he was living here, the Polish poet and national hero Adam Mickiewicz described it as 'an area of scattered one and two storey houses'. By the middle of the nineteenth century it had become a densely populated and mostly working-class neighborhood.

This neighborhood was completely destroyed by the fire of 1870, and was rebuilt mostly between 1890 and 1910. A survey conducted in 1910 shows Tarlabaşı Caddesi to have been fairly respectable, lined with doctors' offices, jewelers, silversmiths, watchmakers, stationers, pharmacies and music and dance studios. The owners of these establishments were almost entirely Greek, with a sprinkling of Armenians, Levantines and Jews. By the 1960s the avenue was lined almost entirely by shops selling automobile parts. In the 1980s, during the administration of Mayor Bedrettin

Dalan, the avenue was lengthened and widened, and a block-wide swath of buildings through the heart of Beyoğlu was demolished. Since then, when it was renamed Tarlabaşı Bulvarı, it has become distinctly seedy, with stretches lined by disreputable *pavyons* and patrolled by transvestite prostitutes.

From the beginning of the twentieth century until the mid 1960s, Tarlabaşı was almost entirely Greek, with an Armenian neighborhood concentrated in the Sakızağacı neighborhood and a few pockets of Eastern Anatolian Christians. The principal occupations of the inhabitants are listed in a 1910 survey as being sellers of charcoal and firewood, carpenters, furniture sellers, rug merchants and cobblers. Kordela Sokak, now the site of the immense and crowded Sunday produce market, was home to a concentration of Greek theater and movie actors as well as nightclub musicians and singers.

Tarlabaşı was almost completely emptied out by the deportations and forced migration of Greeks in 1964, and many of the buildings were subsequently occupied by squatters, mostly Roma from the nearby and densely populated Roma neighborhood of Kulaksız, later to be joined by migrants from Anatolia.

Since the beginning of the 1990s it has become a largely Kurdish neighborhood, many of the inhabitants themselves the victims of forced migration from villages that were 'cleared' by the Turkish army. There are also pockets of African migrants and Aramaic-speaking Christians from Eastern Anatolia and Northern Iraq. Tarlabaşı is known as an area of extreme poverty and squalor and high crime.

In 2006, a 20,000 square meter area of Tarlabaşı, consisting of 9 blocks and 278 plots was declared the Urban Renewal Area by the Turkish government, at the request of Beyoğlu Mayor Ahmet Misbah Demircan. The clearing of the residents of this area began in 2009, and the forced eviction of the last residents was completed at the beginning of 2012. In the spring of that year the area was cordoned off and demolition began, despite several pending court cases and the continued presence of a number of residents who had refused to leave. On July 20, 2014 the Council of State declared that the project was not in the public interest and ruled in favor of 164 property owners who filed suit against the expropriation of their homes and businesses. Demolition has continued despite the ruling. Meanwhile many of the abandoned buildings within the zone have become home to impoverished Syrian refugees. There are reports that large communities of rats displaced by the demolition have scurried into adjoining neighborhoods.

We begin at Galatasaray Meydanı and walk a few down Hamalbaşı Caddesi to the first corner on the right, where we turn in to Kalyoncu Kulluğu Caddesi. We follow this street, crossing Tarlabaşı Caddesi at the traffic light, and Beyoğlu Central Police Station (frequently the target of molotov cocktails flung by demonstrators with political grievances).

Near the north end of Kalyoncu Kulluğu Caddesi on the right, a block before it reaches Dolapdere Caddesi, we see the Rum Ortodoks Aya Konstantin Kilisesi [the Greek Orthodox church of Ayios Constantinos and Ayia Elena, SS. Constantine and Helen]. This was originally built in 1856-7 and then remodeled in 1897. The church was looted and severely damaged during the 1955 riots.

A short way beyond the church, at the corner of Kalyoncu Kulluğu Caddesi and Serdar Ömer Paşa Sokak we see a small museum. This is devoted to the memory of Adam Mickiewicz (1798-1855), who is renowned as the national poet of Poland as well as of Lithuania and Belarus. At the outbreak of the Crimean War in 1855 he came to Istanbul to organize a Polish force to fight alongside the Turks against Russia. But he died on 22 September 1855 and was buried in a crypt beneath this house. His remains were removed to Paris and then in 1900 they were interred in Krakow's Wawel Cathedral. The house here was converted into a museum on the centennial of his death in 1955.

Retracing our steps along Kalyoncu Kulluğu Caddesi for two blocks, we turn left into Cezayirli Hasanpaşa Sokak. A short way along the street we see a street-fountain built in 1815 by Sultan Mahmud II.

Continuing in the same direction along Zerdali Sokak, we turn right on Karakurum Sokak. At the end of the first block on this street we see another street-fountain endowed by Sultan Mahmud II, this one built in 1830.

Continuing along Karakurum Sokak, on the next block we come to a large church dedicated to the Virgin Mary, in Turkish

Meryem Ana. This church was built in 1962 by the Syriac Orthodox Church. The masses are conducted in Aramaic, the native language of Christ.

Returning to Tarlabaşı Bulvarı, we turn left on Sakızağacı Caddesi. Less than halfway down the left side of the block we come to the former Greek Orthodox church of Ayios Panteleimon, which is now being used by a community of Chaldean Catholics.

After crossing Sakızağacı Caddesi, we turn left into the L-shaped Dernek Sokağı. (At this time, this part of the stroll is not possible as it is within an area under demolition.) The building originally housed Armenian Gregorian church and Anarat Huygutyun Manastırı [Monastery of Anarat Huygutyun], founded in 1843 and now used by various commercial enterprises, including, up until recently, an Irish pub called James Joyce. The monastery is currently under restoration.

There is still another church at the intersection of Sazlıdere Caddesi and Dolapdere Caddesi. This is Rum Ortodoks Evangelistria Kilisesi [the Greek Orthodox church of the Evangelistria], founded in 1893 and still functioning. Within the church grounds there is an *ayazma*, or holy well, dedicated to Panayia Theotokos, the All-Holy Mother of God.

A block to the west of the church, at the corner of Dolapdere Caddesi and Hacı İlbey Sokak, there is a street-fountain built in 1843 by Sultan Abdülmecid. Near the church and the fountain there is a petrol station, which has attached to it one of the last remaining pork butchers in Istanbul.

Beyond Ömer Hayyam Caddesi is an area known as Aynalı Çeşme. There is known to have been a Muslim settlement here as early as the 16th century, and was absorbed into European and Levantine Pera in the 19th century. The Prussian Embassy was located here, though its exact location is not known. On Emin Camii Sokak we can see the massive Alman Evangelik Kilisesi [German Evangelical Church], and next to it Ermeni Protestan Surp Yerrorturyan Kilisesi [Armenian Protestant Church of Surp Yerrorturyan], which is now used by Beyoğlu's Turkish Anglican Congregation. In the 1930s, many Jewish and anti-fascist Germans and Eastern Europeans settled in this area.

Here we come to the end of the last of our strolls through Galata and Pera, today's Beyoğlu.

Afterword

The pace of change in Beyoğlu since we began writing this book in 2010 has been so rapid that we have not been able to keep up with it. If the change continues at this pace, within a few years many of the buildings and places mentioned in the book will not be recognizable as they are described here. Some are already not. The development we have seen is uneven. While many historical buildings that were on the point of collapse have been well restored, many more have been destroyed and replaced by structures that we feel mar the district's face.

The recent structural changes in Beyoğlu are the most extensive since the 1890s, when developers such as Ragıb Pasha built the buildings and arcades that have since become monuments. However, there are important differences between the developers of that time and those of today. Though Ragıb Pasha was by no means above reproach, he and those who were building in Beyoğlu then lived in the district, valued its heritage, and shared a vision of a residential area for the Westernized elite of the city. The majority of those who are building in Beyoğlu today do not live in the district and are concerned more with short-term profit than with the district's integrity or future. The emphasis is on hotels and shopping centers rather than on residences. Many of the apartment buildings that have been restored have been converted into suites, hostels and apart-hotels, or else into multi-storey bars.

However, what has made Galata-Pera-Beyoğlu such a dynamic entity throughout its history is that it has always reflected and imitated the latest trends in the West. In this sense, recent developments in the district certainly reflect the post-capitalist West, and in the broad view are consistent with its character. But if the shopping malls, hotels and hip bars reflect the latest trends in the West, so too does the Occupy Gezi movement that sparked the flame that swept through Turkey in the early summer of 2013. Through most of its history, Beyoğlu, like the West, has been deeply bourgeois and money-hungry and was built on trade and on banking; but it has also always been anarchic, and has always been a refuge for those who seek and fight for freedom.

The future of Beyoğlu is anyone's guess. Our guess is that its unique character and identity will survive in one form or another, if only because an essential element of this character and identity has been a willingness, indeed eagerness, to embrace the new.

Bibliography

Adil, Fikret, *Asmalımescit 74,* İstanbul, 1933

Adil, Fikret, *Gardenbar Geceleri,* İstanbul, 1990

Akın, Nur, *19 Yüzyılın İkinci Yarısında Galata ve Pera,* İstanbul, 1998

Amicis, Edmondo de, *Constantinople,* 2 vol., trans. Maria Horner Lansdale, Philadelphia, 1896

Babinger, F., *Mehmet the Conqueror and his Time,* ed. W. C. Hickman, trans. R. Manheim, Princeton, 1978

Belin, M., *Histoire de la latinité de Constantinople,* Paris, 1894

Çelik, Zeynep, *The Remaking of Istanbul: Portrait of an Ottoman City in the 19th Century,* University of Washington Press, 1986

Deleon, Jak, *Beyoğlu'nda Beyaz Ruslar [The White Russians in Istanbul],* İstanbul, 1990

Dökmeci, Vedia, *Tarihsel Gelişim Sürecinde Beyoğlu,* İstanbul, 1990

Duhani, Said , *Quand Beyoğlu s'appelait Pera,* 1976

Duhani, Said, *Vieilles Gens, Vieilles Demeures,* İstanbul, 1947

Dwight, H. G., *Constantinople, Old and New,* New York, 1915

Eldem, Edhem, *Bankalar Caddesi: Osmanlı'dan Günümüze Voyvoda Caddesi [Voyvoda Street from Ottoman Times to Today],* İstanbul, 2000

Eminoğlu, Münevver ed., *1870-2000: Bir Beyoğlu Fotoromanı [A Beyoğlu Photo-Romance: 1870-2000],* İstanbul, 2000

Esad, Celal, *Eski Galata ve Binaları,* İstanbul, 1911

Evliya Çelebi, *Narrative of Travels in Europe, Asia and Africa,* trans. Joseph von Hammer, Londra, 1834-46

Eyice, Semavi, *Galata and its Tower,* İstanbul, 1969

Freely, John, *Stamboul Sketches,* İstanbul, 1974

Freely, John, Blue Guide Istanbul, 3rd ed., Londra, 1991

Freely, John, *Istanbul, The Imperial City,* Londra, 1996

Gilles, Pierre (Petrus Gyllius), *The Antiquities of Constantinople,* John Ball's translation from *Four Books on the Topography of Constantinople and its Antiquities* (1719), ed. Ronald G. Musto, New York, 1986

Goodwin, Godfrey, *A History of Ottoman Architecture,* Londra, 1071

Grosvenor, E. A., *Constantinople,* 2 vol., Londra, 1895

Gülersoy, Çelik, *Tepebaşı-Bir Meydan savaşı,* İstanbul, 1995

İnalcık, Halil, 'Ottoman Galata, 1453-1543', İstanbul-Paris, 1991, s. 17-116

Hasluck, F.W., 'Dr. Covel's Notes on Galata', Atina, 1904

Hobhouse, John Cam (Baron Broughton), *A Journey Through Albania and the Other Provinces of Turkey in Europe and Asia to Istanbul during the years 1809 and 1810,* Londra, 1813

Johnson, Clarence Richard ed. *Constantinople Today or The Pathfinder Survey Constantinople,* New York, 1922

Koçu, R. E., *Istanbul Ansiklopedisi,* İstanbul, 1958-75

Kuban, Doğan, *An Urban History: Byzantion, Constantinopolis, Istanbul,* İstanbul, 1996

Macfarlane, Charles, *Istanbul in 1828,* Londra, 1829

Millas, Akylas, *Pera, The Crossroads of Constantinople,* 3rd ed., Atina, 2006

Notitia Urbis Constantinopolitanae, Berlin, 1876

Ofluoğlu, Mücap, *Bir Avuç Alkış,* İstanbul, 1996

Özdamar, Ali, *Beyoğlu 1930: Selahattin Giz'in Fotoğraflarıyla 1930'larda Beyoğlu [Beyoglu in the 30s: Through the lens of Selahattin Giz],* İstanbul 1991

Pannuti, Alessandro, 'Italian Levantines among other Non-Muslims: a community's fortune and dissolution despite identity preservation', Meaux, 2008

Pardoe, Julia, *The Beauties of the Bosphorus,* Londra, 1838

Pinto, Bensiyon, *Anlatmasam Olmazdı: Geniş Toplumda Yahudi Olmak [My Life As a Turkish Jew- Memoirs of the President of the Turkish-Jewish Community 1989 - 2004],* İstanbul, 2008

Rasim, Ahmet, *Fuhş-i Atik,* İstanbul 2007

Sauvaget, Jean, *Notes sur le Colonie Genois de Pera,* Paris, 1934

Schneider, A. M. and Nomidis, *Galata, topograohische archaelogischer Plan mit eralauetende Text,* İstanbul, 1944

Scognamillo, Giovanni, *Bir Levanten'in Beyoğlu Anıları,* İstanbul, 1990

Scognamillo, Giovanni, *Beyoğlu'nda Fuhuş ,* İstanbul, 1994

Smith, Albert Richard, *A Month at Constantinople,* Londra, 1850

Sumner-Boyd, Hilary, and John Freely, *Strolling Through Istanbul,* 2nd ed., Londra, 2010

Türker, Orhan, *Galata'dan Karaköy'e: Bir Liman Hikayesi,* İstanbul, 2000

Walsh, Paul, *A Residence in Constantinople,* Londra, 1836

White, Charles, *Three Years in Constantinople,* Londra, 1845

Zat, Vefa, *Eski Istanbul Barları,* 1999

Zarinebaf, Fariba, *Crime and Punishment in Istanbul 1700-1800,* University of California Press, 2011.

Index